ANDALUCÍA
IN FOCUS

A COMPLETE GUIDE

TO THE TOWNS AND COUNTRYSIDE OF ANDALUCÍA

Edilux s.l.

ENGLISH TEXT BY JON TROUT

Published by EDILUX S.L.
Editor: J. Agustín Núñez
Original text: Aurelio Cid Acedo
English translation: Jon Trout
Photographs: Miguel Román and J. Agustín Núñez
Photographic composition: EDILUX S.L.
Layout, design and drawings: Miguel Salvatierra
Printing: Copartgraf s.c.a.
Binding: Hermanos Olmedo s.l.
ISBN: 84-95856-01-8
L.D.: GR-1034/2002
Helpful advice from: Luis Recio

Distribución: Edilux, teléfono y fax: 958 08 2000
E-Mail: ediluxsl@supercable.es

ANDALUCIA

Andalucía, with an area of 87,268 square metres (only slightly smaller than Portugal), accounts for some 17% of mainland Spain and is the largest self-governing region in the country. It has a population of seven million inhabitants. The expression "miniature continent", often used to describe Andalucía, is ideally suited to this regions due to its extraordinary contrasts and immense variety. Grazalema in the west, for example, can claim to be the wettest place in Spain, with an average annual rainfall of over 200 millimetres, whilst the Cabo de Gata at its eastern extreme is the country's driest area with deserts and badland landscapes. The Alpine snows of the Sierra Nevada mountain range are clearly visible from the market gardens of Andalucía's subtropical coast, where fruit such as mangoes, avocado pears and custard apples thrive. The vast rocky solitude of the Sierra Morena, which forms the northern border of Andalucía with the central meseta, is the very antithesis of the watery paradise of the Doñana nature reserve on the Atlantic coast. Even the sea and coastline undergo a dramatic metamorphosis at the Straits of Gibraltar, changing from sunny Mediterranean beaches eastward to a wilder Atlantic coastline to the west, along the length of which the wind has piled up long dunes of golden sand. These physical differences in geography and climate affect the character of the Andalucíans themselves, and it is for this reason that people speak of "the two Andalucías", so different from each other in both physical and human terms.

Nevertheless, nobody would deny the shared sense of identity among the people of Andalucía, in which there is room only for the enrichment that variety brings instead of short-sighted divisions. This unity is intangible rather than physical; it exists in the atmosphere of the region, in the way its inhabitants regard life and in the spiritual heritage bequeathed to them by past cultures and civilisations.

CONTENTS

CONTENTS

CÓRDOBA

GRANADA

MUSLIM GRANADA

CHRISTIAN GRANADA

JAÉN

ALMERÍA

Andalucía

● **Andalucia**

The Romans already considered the south of the Iberian peninsula to be a geographical and political unity, Baetica, which in general lines conformed geographically to the Andalucia of today. The Muslim invaders from Africa called all the conquered lands (at one time most of the Spanish peninsula) "al Andalus", the name which has survived to refer nowadays to the southernmost region of the country, Andalucia.

Above right: Map of Andalucia showing its eight provinces.

Above: the castle at Tabernas in Almería with the Sierra Nevada in the background.

Near right: St. Stephen's doorway in the Great Mosque at Córdoba

Introduction

For centuries foreigners have seen Andalucia as epitomising all things Spanish, even into the XXI century when communications were rapid and reliable. The truth is, however, that the singularity of this region, the character of its people and the depth of their culture are such that they rise above all attempts at generalisation and cliché. The enormous diversity in both the physical features of this land and the personality of its people is best exemplified by the contrast between the fertile valley of its great river, the Guadalquivir, and the ruggedness and austerity of its mountain chains.

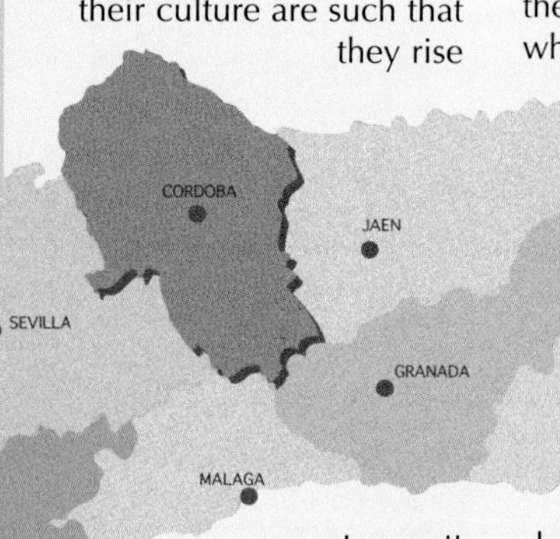

Lower Andalucia is the western area of the region, focused around the driving force of the commercial and political hub of Sevilla on the banks of the River Guadalquivir, the "Great river", which flows into the Gulf of Cadiz on the Atlantic seaboard. Upper Andalucia, the eastern part of the region, straddles the Betic mountain ranges and the valleys between them, fertile plains upon which the area´s main towns stand. The flora and fauna of nearly twenty percent of the countryside is protected in reserves and parks, including Europe's most important nature reserve: Doñana. Thus, large swathes of land remain completely untouched and unspoilt, and safe from reckless development. The richness and depth of its cultural heritage reflects the succession of the many and various peoples who have invaded these lands throughout the ages, settled here and left their buildings and vestiges of their civilisations across the length and breadth of the region. Two major events in its relatively recent history

have left their mark indelibly on Andalucia and its people: the arrival of the Romans, who inherited the earlier civilisations of the Phoenicians and Carthaginians, welded much of Iberia into a single political unit and gave its people

what was eventually to become the Spanish language; and a few centuries later, the invasion of Muslim Arabs and Berbers, who for nearly eight hundred years ruled over some of the most creative periods in the history of Andalucia. The Muslim dynasties in al-Andalus, as most of Spain was then known, preserved the wisdom of the classical philosophers whilst at the same time introducing their own innovations in mathematics and astronomy, and postulating the earliest ideas of an empirical approach to medicine and physics. They also modified and perfected the irrigation systems that the Romans had first introduced into Spanish agriculture. Thus was forged a land and people with impressively deep reserves of strength and culture in their background, a people capable of overcoming later centuries of suffering and decline and facing up to their future with bravery and imagination without losing their own essential identity.

Above: view across the Alhambra and Granada from just above the water garden in the Generalife.
Left: the Colegiate Church-Cathedral at Jerez and the Palace of the Jabalquinto family in Baeza (Jaén).

Above: view of the village of Frigiliana in the eastern Axarquía district of Málaga.
Left: view of the mountains around Ronda, with the village of Benalauría in the foreground.

Andalucía

● **Nature reserves in Andalucia**
The map to the right shows some of the national parks and nature reserves of the region, many of which, due to both their size and the wealth of species of flora and fauna they harbour, represent the most important such reserves in all of Europe. The diversity of their geo-

graphic and climatic conditions is such that they include Alpine environments, where the rare Spanish fir (Abies pinsapo) grows (above), Mediterranean woodlands of cork oaks (Quercus

suber) and desert scrublands, such as those found at the Cabo de Gata in Almería

Protected nature reserves in Andalucia

Andalucia's natural heritage is fortunately beginning to receive as much attention as its monuments and art treasures. Nearly twenty percent of the region is designated in some way a protected area, in the shape of almost ninety nature reserves, parks and areas of special interest.

Nature reserves are widespread throughout Andalucia (see map above) and protect many kinds of ecosystems. Some of the most outstanding are: the Cabo de Gata-Níjar reserve in the east of the region, 34,000 hectares of desert environment, featuring volcanic rocks, sand dunes and salt pans, whilst at the western extreme is the 50,000-hectare Doñana nature reserve of brackish marshes, which shelter a permanent population of rare and endangered flora and fauna and offer rest and sustenance to a host of migratory fowl on their long journeys between Africa and northern climes. Recently damaged by a scandalously negligent accident involving the rupture of a damn holding chemical and heavy-metal waste from a nearby mine, any further destruction of these delicately balanced wetlands would constitute an ecological disaster for Europe as a whole. Occupying the highest point in the Spanish peninsula is the Sierra Nevada national park, which includes within its 170,000 hectares a wide variety of natural environments, from Mediterranean woodland to quite inhospitable Alpine climes, where very rare endemic species are still to be found. Some of the region's mountain valleys contain

quite large inland lakes, such as that at Fuentepiedra at the very heart of Andalucia, where flamingos stop off on their migratory flights. To the north, in the Province of Jaén, the Cazorla, Segura and Villas mountain ranges form the most extensive nature reserve in Spain (24,000 hectares), which is home to 25

endemic species. The slopes of the mountains in Cádiz are thickly forested with cork oaks (Sierra de los Alcornocales) and the rain-soaked hillsides around Grazalema are wooded with Spanish fir. At the heart of the Sierra Morena, on the border with Extremadura, the SIERRA DE ARACENA AND PICOS DE AROCHE national park contains no less than 184,000 hectares of holm oak, cork oak and walnut forests. Also worth mentioning, is the Subbetic mountain range in the Province of Córdoba, with more than 160,000 hectares of protected land.

• **BEACH OF BARBATE AND CONIL** *(above), a typical landscape of dunes and fine sand, which creeps inland amongst the pine trees.*
To the immediate left: views of

Mediterranean bosky landscapes, which in the hillsides of Cádiz provide green pastures for fighting bulls.
On the facing page: the beach at Chipiona (Cádiz), one of the endless, sandy beaches along Andalucia's Atlantic coast.

EXTREMADURA
Parque Natural de la Sierra de Aracena y Picos de Aroche
Parque Natural de la Sierra Norte de Sevilla
Parque Natural Sierra de Hornachuelos
Medina Azahara
Almonaster la Real
Aracena
Alájar
Gruta de las Maravillas
Cazalla de la Sierra
Constantina
Almodóvar del Río
Écija
Carmona
Itálica
SEVILLA
Niebla
HUELVA
Moguer
Palos de la Frontera
Monasterio de la Rábida
Ayamonte
Almonte
El Rocío
Parque Nat. de Doñana
Parque Nacional de Doñana
Matalascañas
Alcalá de Guadaira
Marchena
Puente-Genil
Estepa
Arahal
Osuna
Utrera
COSTA DE LA LUZ DE HUELVA
Vidal & Vidal
Ediciones Turísticas, S.L.
OCEANO
ATLÁNTICO
Acinipo Ronda la Vieja
Zahara de la Sierra
Parque Natural Sierra de Grazalema
Grazalema
Ronda
Ubrique
Parq. Nat. Sierra de las Nieves
Sanlúcar de Barrameda
Jerez de la Frontera
El Puerto de Sta. Mª
CÁDIZ
San Fernando
Parque Natural Bahía de Cádiz
Marbella
Jimena de la Frontera
Estepona
Parque Natural de los Alcornocales
COSTA DE LA LUZ DE CÁDIZ
Parq. Nat. La Breña y Marismas del Barbate
Ruinas de Baelo Claudia
Algeciras
La Línea de la Concepción
Tarifa

CASTILLA-LA MANCHA
Parque Natural Sierra de Despeñaperros
Parque Natural de la Sierra de Andújar
Parque Natural Sierra de Cazorla, Segura y Las Villas
Baños de la Encina
Bailén
Linares
Andújar
Baeza
Úbeda
GUADALQUIVIR
Cazorla
JAÉN
Parque Natural de Sierra Mágina
Parque Natural Sierra de Castril
Orce
Vélez-Blanco
Vélez-Rubio
Baena
Alcalá la Real
Priego de Córdoba
Lucena
Baza
Parque Natural Sierra de Baza
Guadix
Loja
Genil
GRANADA
Tabernas
Parque Nacional de Sierra Nevada
Capileira
Trevélez
Bubión
Lanjarón
Órgiva
ALMERÍA
Vélez-Málaga
Cuevas de Nerja
El Ejido
Nerja
Motril
Adra
Roquetas de Mar
Torremolinos
Benalmádena
COSTA DEL SOL
COSTA TROPICAL
COSTA DE ALMERÍA
MAR MEDITERRÁNEO

MÁLAGA

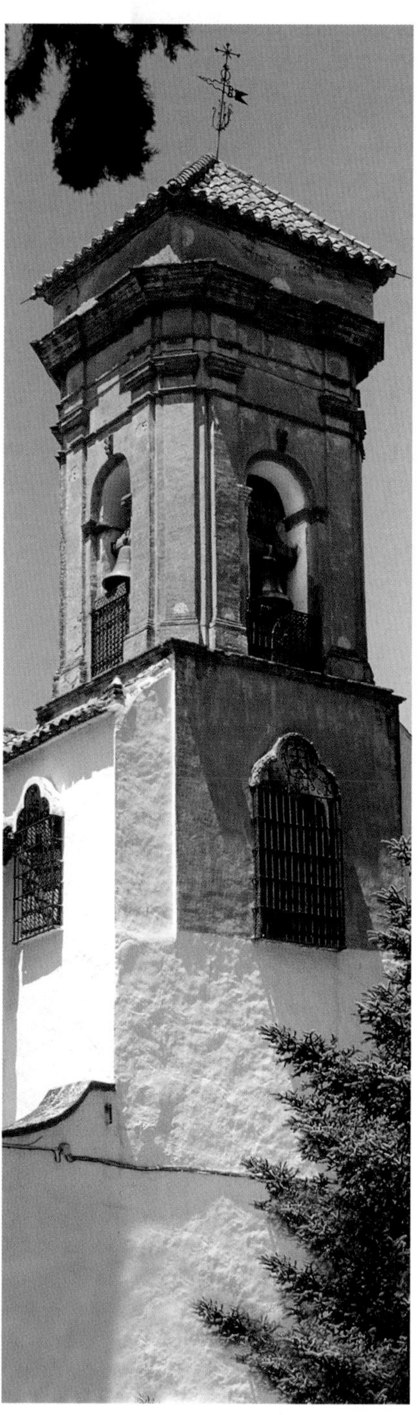

Málaga is known to be a very ancient city, although the exact site of the original settlement has not yet been identified.
In Phoenician, Greek and Roman times it was already a port but the original prehistoric village may well have been located more inland, between the river and the surrounding mountains.
Whatever the truth of the matter, it is easy to understand how Málaga has always been a hub of human activity in the region, It is enough to look at its geographical position to understand the important role the town must have played in Mediterranean trade and commerce in ancient times, and its later strategic importance to the Muslims. Málaga became the capital of an independent taifa kingdom after the disintegration of the caliphate in the XI century and was then absorbed into the Nasrid kingdom of Granada. In the early XV century it found itself at the centre of the internecine skirmishes and civil wars which preceded the ruin of this last bastion of Muslim rule in Spain.
When Málaga finally surrendered to the Christian conquerors in 1487, after the bloodiest battle of that ten-year war, the whole of the western part of the Nasrid kingdom fell with it. Under Christian rule Málaga continued to attract seafarers, traders and merchants, as it had done throughout its history. In the XVI century Genovese merchants founded Spain's first bank here. Three hundred years later the province was very nearly at the forefront of Spain's industrial revolution, which began originally in Málaga, only to be relocated in towns with more readily available supplies of raw materials (and more political clout). During the second half of the XX century Málaga's economy once more took off as it turned itself into the capital of Spain's most profitable industry: tourism. And while the world's boundaries shrink by the day Málaga's cosmopolitan flair will doubtless give it the impetus to go on increasing in importance as a leisure resort in the years to come.

• *Above: view of the city from Gibralfaro (Beacon Hill), from a mid-XIX century engraving. The hill affords a splendid panorama of the city, the port and the bay, with its surrounding mountains. Below: multi-lobed caliphal arches.*

THE ALCAZABA AND GIBRALFARO

The fortified citadel is linked by a defensive wall to Gibralfaro (Beacon Hill), where the Muslims lit a beacon to act as a lighthouse From the original residential area immediately in and around the fortified citadel it winds up the hill to the military watchtower (built on top of an old Phoenician settlement) which dominated the whole of the surrounding terrain, as it still does today.

The citadel was constructed just behind the tiered seating of the Roman theatre, a patent sign of the wealth and importance of the city in those times (right). According to common practice considerable quantities of building materials were pillaged from the Roman theatre for use in later constructions. By the middle of the XX century the Muslim citadel was all but a ruin until it underwent considerable restoration under the guiding hand of Leopoldo Torres Balbás. This architect, expert in the restoration of Moorish architecture, had also recently restored the Alhambra in Granada to some of its original splendour, demonstrating in doing so that drastic action can often be justified if it is combined with a thorough knowledge of the history involved, professional objectivity and respect for the

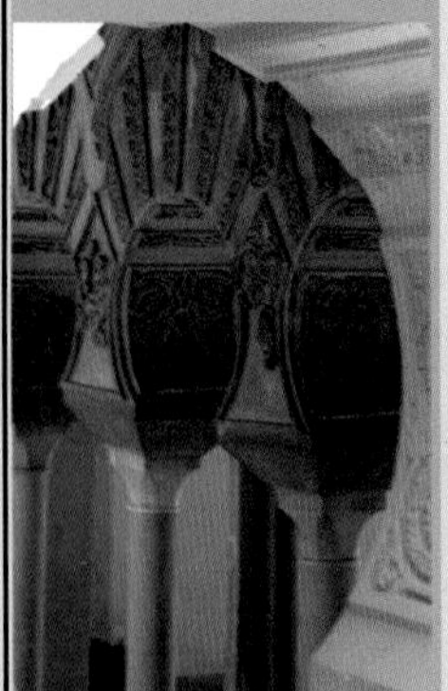

monument itself. The citadel can now be viewed as an important example of mediaeval Spanish Muslim architecture.

Three different levels can be distinguished: the first is the citadel proper with the parade ground in front; the second is the area of the Granadan Guard; and the third comprises the royal palaces, the earliest of which date from the Zirid dynasty at the end of the caliphate in the XI century (opposite page, below), and the latest to the height of the Nasrid dynasty in the XIV century. After the Alhambra they represent the best preserved sequence of mediaeval buildings among the many such palatial complexes which must have graced the Andalucian countryside at the time. The citadel used to house the archaeological museum but this was moved out during the last century and all that remains is the shell forming the cupola of the prayer niche of a mosque (above) and a few restored capitals and vestiges of decoration.

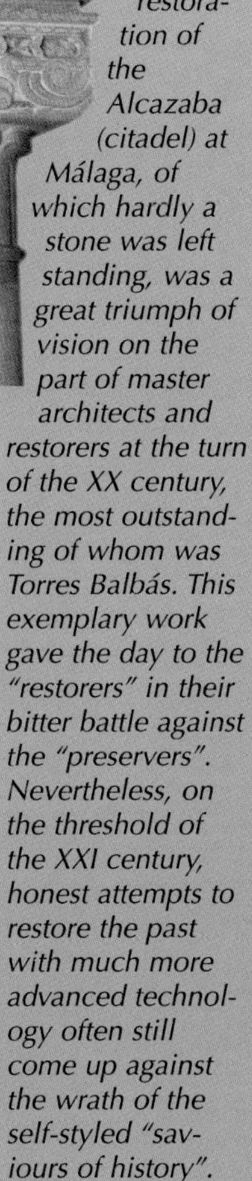

Archaeologists have always recognised that the restoration of the Alcazaba (citadel) at Málaga, of which hardly a stone was left standing, was a great triumph of vision on the part of master architects and restorers at the turn of the XX century, the most outstanding of whom was Torres Balbás. This exemplary work gave the day to the "restorers" in their bitter battle against the "preservers". Nevertheless, on the threshold of the XXI century, honest attempts to restore the past with much more advanced technology often still come up against the wrath of the self-styled "saviours of history".

COLECCIÓN DE ARTE
CONTEMPORÁNEO
FUNDACIÓN LA "CAIXA"

THE METROPOLITAN CATHEDRAL

Just like the city itself, the cathedral is the child of the vicissitudes of its own history. Its foundations were laid over the ruins of the old mosque shortly after the Christian conquest and the church itself was originally designed in the well-established Gothic style. The usual unavoidable delays of the day made its construction drag on until in the middle of the sixteenth century Diego de Siloë, the Renaissance master builder, arrived to work on the sanctuary. His signature is immediately apparent in the high bases to the columns and in the second tier of Corinthian columns, which, although constructed by his apprentices, also have very elongated bases. This imparts to the cathedral a soaring aspect more often associated with the Gothic style, particularly in the apse (above), which remains spacious and airy because it was never cluttered by the choir This was eventually fitted into the central nave, thus diminishing the spaciousness of the interior of the church. Nevertheless, the choir is the cathedral's main architectural treasure, containing as it does some of the very finest stalls, most of them the work of the sculptor Pedro de Mena, whose touch of genius leaves his authorship in no doubt. Unusually, the three naves of the cathedral are the same height, which is reflected in Aldehuela's façade.

• **THE FAÇADE** *(opposite) is wholly Baroque in concept, even though it retains the triumphal triple arch so beloved of the Renaissance, which provides a suitably sobre framework to the Baroque colour of the marble, the fluidity of the columns and finials, and the rhythmic composition that enlivens the second storey with its arched and rose windows, all emphasised by the dual colour of the stone.*

• **CASARES** *(right). Smuggler's way, which starts in Gibraltar and passes through villages such as Gaucín, Benarrabá, Benadalid and Atajate. Flashes of white amongst walnut and chestnut trees, the quintessential green of simplicity. Below: the tower at Arches.*

THE CITY AND THE PROVINCE

Málaga is an old seafaring town, but at the same time modern and cosmopolitan. Apart from its cathedral and the walls and watchtower of Gibralfaro, from the top of which there are magnificent views of the city (facing page, below), Málaga can offer the visitor a veritable botanical garden in the Paseo del Parque (Park Way), which runs between the port and the bright, bustling streets and squares of the town. And above all a marvellous climate. It is the capital of the Costa del Sol, with a population of more than 500,000. It was the birthplace of Picasso and today is home to a museum devoted to his work. Málaga's Intrabetic mountain range, jutting out into the Mediterranean, protects the city and its coastline from the inclemency of the continental weather from the north and at the same time pro-

• **THE COSTA DEL SOL,** *international and cosmopolitan, represents only a small part of the richness and variety that the province of Málaga has to offer and the visitor should not be deterred from exploring the lesser known delights of the mountains just inland. Frigiliana (left) lies in the hills just above Nerja,*

with its impressive limestone caves (above).

vides the wooded ridges where the white villages nestle in the hinterland. To the east of the capital lies the area known as Axarquía, a word deriving from Arabic meaning, quite simply, "east". Blessed with a benign climate, the hillsides of the area are world famous for their sweet wines made from raisins dried in the sun on the very terraces where the grapes are picked from the vine. This eastern end of the Costa del Sol is a rocky coast of cliffs and isolated coves interspersed with villages and small towns such as Vélez Málaga and Nerja, with its impressive karstic limestone caves (below right). Less well-known is the inland mountain area, scattered with simple white villages and farmhouses gleaming amongst the greenery around every bend in the road. Such are the villages of Frigiliana (above), Cómpeta, Arches and Salares, noteworthy for their minarets converted into church towers and

● **Tolox,** *(above and below), close to the Sierra de las Nieves and one of the most beautiful of Málaga's villages, is famous for its thermal baths.*

their narrow, winding streets of whitewashed houses with profusions of flowers cascading from flowerpots on every balcony and terrace. Inland farther still, behind the coastal mountain range, lie the fertile plains of Antequera and Archidona, where archaeological remains bear witness to human habitation from early prehistoric times. In fact, it is only just down the coast at Gibraltar that evidence has been found of the presence of the last surviving Neanderthals, and not far to the east at Orce, in Granada, that traces of the earliest hominids in Europe have been found, dating to more than a million years ago. Farther westward is the mountain range which like a huge amphitheatre looks down on the town of Ronda on the banks of the river Genil. The fastness of these hills has provided shelter in the past for expelled *taifa* barons and latter-day bandits, the folk heroes of Spanish romantic tradition. Abundant rain blows into this countryside from the Atlantic, painting it a myriad shades of greens in Spring. It is also the northern reach of the route of the white villages, which runs south-west from Ronda down through the province of Cádiz Besides the better known white villages there are many more, such as Tolox (above), some no more than hamlets, where the pulse of time still beats much more slowly (left).

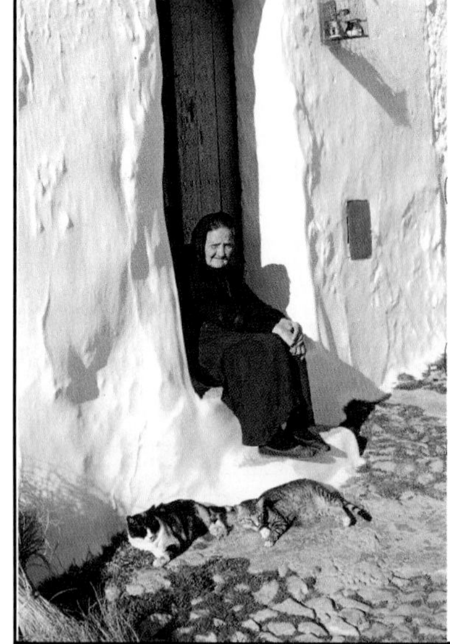

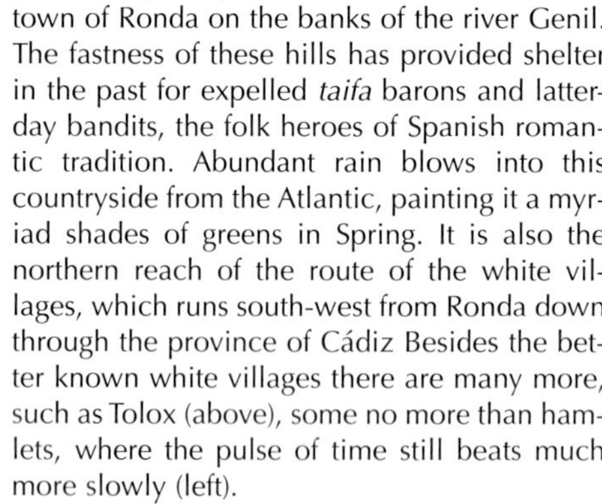

Among the innumerable villages dotted around the Andalucian landscape very few retain the essence of their Arab ancestry as much as those of the mountains of Málaga and Cádiz. They are all built according to simple but practical principles: the houses face southward whenever

possible and have thick walls and small windows to protect them against the heat and the cold alike. They usually have a secluded interior courtyard, which acts as a cool living room in summer. And they are always whitewashed, at least once a year, which decorates, disinfects and holds together the stone-and-mud-built walls. Streetwards the windows are covered with iron grills, reminiscent of the jalousies of their Muslim ancestors, and on every windowsill and balcony flowers, such as scarlet geraniums, blue petunias and mauve fuchsias tumble down over the white walls. In the village squares fountains run with water brought from the nearest spring, essential to villages which until very recently did not have running water in their houses.

A tour through the mountains will also take the visitor to Alpandeire, Faraján, Cartajima, Paruata and, to the west of the river Guadiaro, the caves of la Pileta and el Gato, which have been inhabited since the paleaolithic, and the surrounding villages of Cortes de la Frontera, Benaoján and Montejaque.

• MIJAS, *Both the commanding position and the architecture of Mijas (above and right) are witness to its importance in Muslim times. It also has an interesting square bullring like the first one built in*

Sevilla.
Visitors can take trips around the town by donkey taxi.
From the tranquillity of this vantage point the much busier coasts of Mijas and Fuenjirola can be made out in the distance below.

THE WESTERN COSTA DEL SOL

In the 1960's the Costa del Sol, which had up to that time been a quiet coast of fishing villages, thanks to its benign climate underwent a tourist boom that turned it into the most popular resort on the Mediterranean seaboard. In the province of Málaga alone there are over 100 km of beaches, several modern marinas and the finest range of golf courses in Spain, all of which gives an idea of the social and economic potential involved in a high-quality leisure industry.

But as well as its extensive, sophisticated coastline, the province can also offer the visitor the experience of villages hidden in completely unchanged nooks in the surrounding mountains, their calm atmosphere reflecting a less hurried style of life.

In fact many small housing developments have tried to emulate this same relaxed atmosphere. Benalmádena and Mijas are two examples of such intelligent growth. Despite having had to face up to rapid expansion they have managed to retain a measure of quiet repose. In Benalmádena Costa modern development has led to the creation of a leisure port (right) and submarine park, together with a municipal archaeological museum containing some interesting pre-Columbian artefacts. Fuengirola has been able to preserve its castle of Sohail, which stands at the beginning of a delightful seven-kilometre promenade.

Inland from the coast, the white villages perched on mountain ridges and nestling in dales in the hillsides, so near in terms of distance and yet so different in lifestyle, exemplify a hard-working rural society of modern crops and hardly imaginable landscapes. A tour round los Alhaurines, which the locals call "the countryside", taking in Coín, Monda and Ojén and the Refugio del Juanar, constitutes a fascinating trip into the past of this area. This veritable natural paradise lies only a few kilometres from Marbella and is considered by many to be the intriguing storeroom behind the glitter of the shop out front.

The ancient town of Mirivilia, a mere village until granted a city's charter by the Catholic Monarchs in 1485, is today Marbella, the fun capital of the Costa del Sol. In the XIX century it was about to take the lead in the

• *Building work during the last fifty years along the Costa del Sol has not always respected the natural environment, nor has it been of the highest quality, but sometimes, above all in small developments, it offers a range of the best architectural styles of the period. Above: small estates in Marbella and Torreblanca and the port at Benalmádena (left) .*

● **FUENGIROLA,** *(this page). Despite numerous modern buildings this erstwhile fishing village still maintains a certain local charm. Its magnificent promenade follows the sea front for seven kilometres.*

industrial revolution in Spain with the construction of iron-smelting furnaces but lost its advantage due to political manoeuvring in the north of the country. It was not until the last quarter of the XX century that it started to become the Mediterranean resort of the international jet set. The so-called "Golden Mile" attracts aristocrats, tycoons and world leaders of finance, and stars from all realms of entertainment, whose influence has done wonders to strengthen the local economy.

These high-society personalities have brought with them a train of hangers-on who swarm around the warmth of wealth, situated only a short distance from the tax haven of Gibraltar. Nevertheless, the old town centre still survives, with its narrow streets and squares such as the Plaza de los Naranjos (Orange Tree Square), parts of its old city wall and its XVI century town hall.

A few years ago a motorway was built to ease traffic congestion on the coast road, making driving from town to

• **Steep or stepped streets** *are common in many villages in the region, such as Frigiliana, Mijas and Benaoján. These villages grew up on the hillsides just below mediaeval castles.*

town along this coast an easy affair. At San Pedro de Alcántara, almost on the sea shore, amongst the pines and eucalyptus trees, stand the remains of the only surviving Mozarabic church in Andalucía. Mozarabic art and architecture originated here in Andalucía at the hands of Christians who kept to their religion after the Arab invasion in the VIII century. Many eventually migrated northward where they have left much more of their style than here in the south. Other examples of Mozarabic architecture can also be seen in Bobastro to the north-west of Málaga.

Estepona, is another fishing village to have benefited economically from Marbella's boom and now has a yachting harbour and several golf courses.

• **Puerto Banús,** *(above), a port for the very rich and symbol of a whole way of life. Below: a mass of houses forming a cubist maze, built long before Picasso, but possibly influencing his style.*

• *Left: the beach in Summer at Fuengirola*

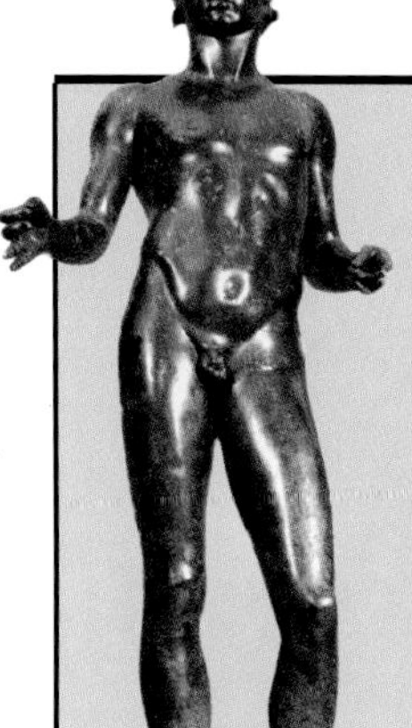

• *Survivors from its Roman days are this famous statue of a young man (an ephebus) (above) and a Venus (below). Both are sculptural marvels from the I century and can be seen in the municipal museum in the Nájera Palace. The caves at la Menga (above), el Romeral and Vera represent an outstandingly important megalithic complex.*

Antequera

Its very name in Latin, Antikaria, meaning "ancient", gives a clear idea that this site had been occupied even then for a very long time. The Romans were probably as impressed as we are today by one of the most important megalithic complexes in the Iberian peninsula, to be found at nearby la Menga (left). Antequera is a smallish town of some 45,000 inhabitants and, lying as it does at the geographical heart of Andalucia, has always been a crossroads for travellers and their traffic. After being wrested from the Nasrid kingdom of Granada in 1410, the town became the centre of border operations throughout the rest of the fifteenth century, thus attracting noble families from Castilla to settle in the town and adorn it with new palaces and churches, most of which survive today. In the neighbourhood of the old citadel are the imposing church of Santa María la Mayor, showing clear aspirations to be a cathedral, the huge Arco de los Gigantes (the Giants' Arch) and the church of San Sebastian, in the high street close by the main square, which is entered through the Nazarene Arch. The town reached its artistic apotheosis during the Baroque period, the Church of the Carmen being an outstanding example of this style. The Portichuelo (right) epitomises the peculiarity of the Baroque in

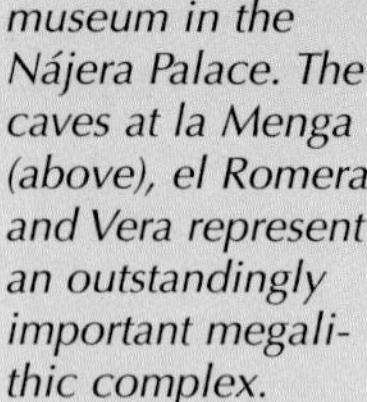

Antequera, which is a dialogue between white lime-wash and red brickwork. This dual colouring extends to the very tiling of the roofs, which can be seen from the watchtower of the fortress. **ARCHIDONA** is another of those Andalucían towns where the fortress is easily confused with the rock upon which it stands: this is the typical medieval symbiosis of rock and castle, a vantage point to dominate the land as far as the horizon beyond. Standing over this craggy ledge today is the church of the Virgen de Gracia, which occupies the building of a X century caliphal mosque (right) built on the site where the Syrians are reputed to have proclaimed Abd ar-Rahman I emir in 756. This is one of the few surviving mosques from that period. There is a splendid view from this point of the XVII century octagonal square (above) in the centre of the town, a splendid example of a Baroque square designed as a public space, a hub of commerce and social life. The countryside surrounding Archidona is an enormous rolling hillside of olive groves.

• **THE OCTAGONAL SQUARE AT ARCHIDONA** *and (below) the mosque.*

Below: Autumn squall over Archidona.

Ronda

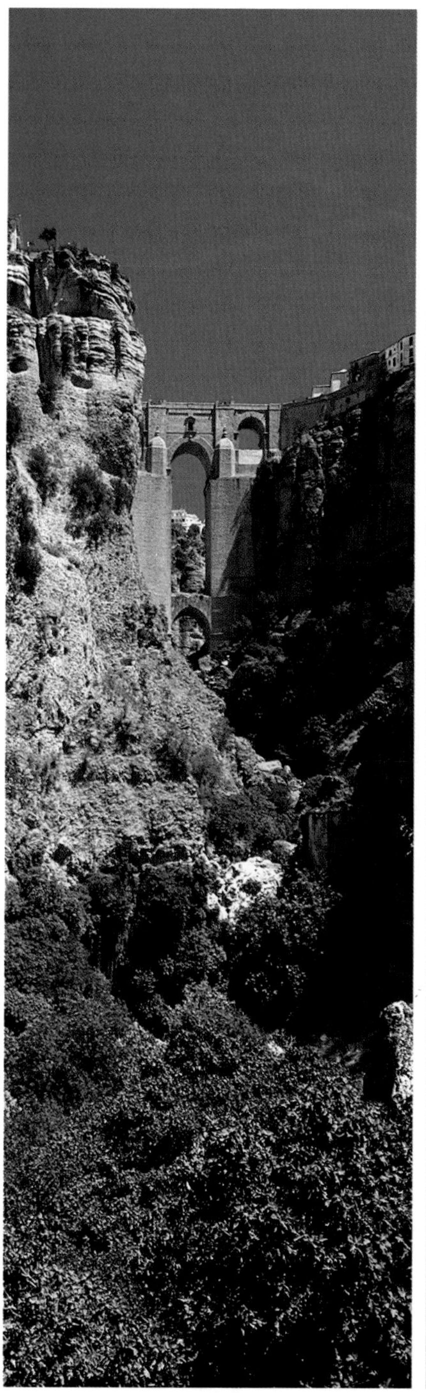

The area around Ronda was already inhabited some 25,000 years ago during the upper palaeolothic when the earliest inhabitants painted on the walls of the el Gato and la Pileta cave systems, the grottoes and galleries of which wind for more than five kilometres through the surrounding limestone hills.

In more recent times the city has always exerted a mysterious magical attraction on travellers. At the end of the XIX century Rainer Maria Rilke wrote, *"I have looked everywhere for the city of my dreams and have finally found it in Ronda."*

Juan Goytisolo exclaimed on seeing Ronda for the first time, *"At last we spied Ronda. It projected from the rugged mountainside as though it were itself a natural extension of the rock and, as the sun fell upon it, it seemed to me to be the most beautiful city in the world."* Ernest Hemmingway enthused, *"The whole city and its surroundings form a perfect romantic setting."* And the passion that Orson Wells still felt for the town long after his visit led him to decide to have his ashes scattered there after his death ... even though these are not the romantic days of the nineteenth century.

Perhaps Miguel de Unamuno was also referring to Ronda when he wrote, *"... ancient village, storehouse of memories, sleeping in the sun, what might lie inside your guardian walls?"*.

• Above: XIX century engraving and right: a view of "the City", which is the name by which the old walled centre of Ronda is known.

Above: mould for making swords (VII century B.C.).

HISTORY OF RONDA

Exceptional archaeological remains testify to the importance of Ronda throughout its history. At the beginning of the XX century stone-age paintings were found on the walls of la Pileta cave (facing page), outstanding among which are a pregnant mare and a curiously shaped fish. They show enormous expressive energy and symbolic power and are without doubt some of the finest such paintings known from the upper-palaeolithic. It is

evident that they were

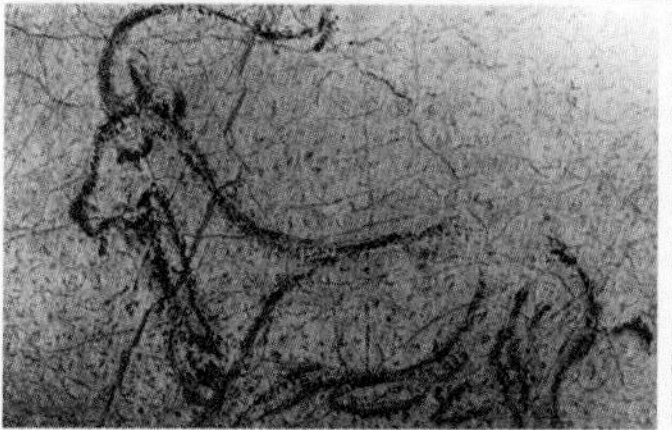

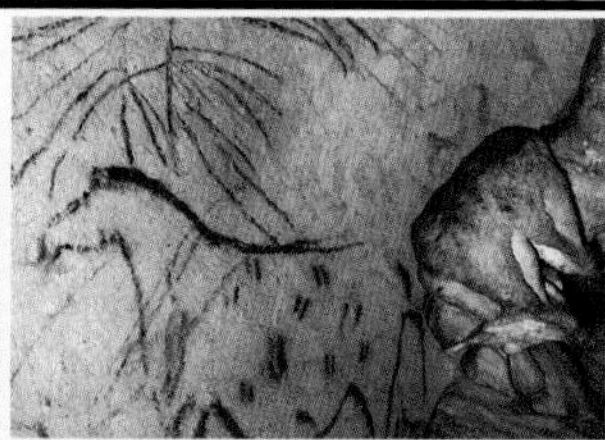

• Left: cave paintings in la Pileta cave, among which are the famed pregnant mare, a somewhat strange fish, bulls, goats and even reindeer.

moulding copper swords in these parts more than 2,700 years ago, and indeed, as historical sources can confirm, for many centuries this was the key area to power in the region. But when we speak of Ronda we must also include the Celtic settlement of Arunda, the Roman Acinipo, also known as Ronda la Vieja, or Old Ronda, a town a few kilometres away from the present-day city, in which a splendid Roman theatre survives with tiered seating carved from the living rock. It is obvious that the stronghold at Ronda was in fact relocated from time to time, probably to satisfy the strategic needs of the moment to control the mountainous amphitheatre, through which tree-lined valleys made for direct paths of invasion up from the Straights of Gibraltar. During the Punic wars a decisive battle is known to have been fought hereabouts between Julius Caesar and Pompey, although its exact site has never been precisely located.

• Left: the ruins of Acinipo, a few kilometres from present-day Ronda. Theatres were the sign of a city's wealth and importance and from what remains of this site it seems to have been one of the most important towns in Roman Baetica.

The Muslims called Ronda Izn-Rand Onda and it was from here in the year 900 that Omar ibn Hassin rode forth to challenge the first Cordoban caliph, the mighty Abd ar-Rahman III, and almost to overthrow the caliphate itself in a struggle between the surviving Visigothic nobility and the new Muslim rulers.

• Below: Roman sculpture on display in the town hall.

Ronda

Ronda' s historic Buildings

The people of the city of Ronda and its surrounding mountains have always been renowned for their independence and very special character, together with their adherence to ancestral traditions in which the most authentic aspects of their Arab ancestry are mixed with the highly Andalucían trait of stoicism and the very immutability of the mountains themselves.

• Above: the walls and gate of Xijara (Alcijara) enclosing " the City", seen from the the Mercadillo district.

(6) Ronda Bullring. The stone-built bullring at Ronda is one of the oldest in Spain and is where the art of bullfighting on foot rather than on horseback originated with Francisco Romero.

(4) The Town Hall is an old militia barracks built in the middle of the XVII century, modified several times since then and finally restored thirty years ago, at which time the splendid Mudéjar coffered ceiling was added.

(8) Mondragón Palace, built in a combination of Mudéjar and Renaissance styles, was lived in by the Catholic Monarchs. It has magnificent courtyards and coffered ceilings. Today it houses the municipal museum.

(9) Arab Baths were found a few decades ago close to the old bridge in what was a neighbourhood of tanners and artisans in Muslim times. Built around 1300, they are some of the best preserved Muslim baths in Spain.

(1) The Church of Santa María

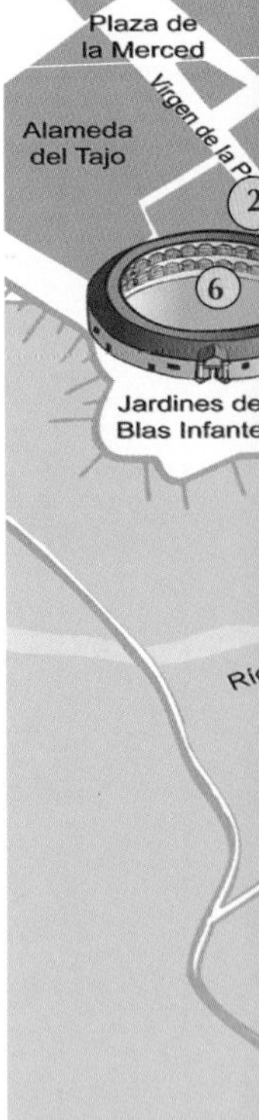

(5) *The Palace of the Marquis de Salvatierra is a fine example of the noble architecture of the XVIII century. Its most outstanding feature are the caryatids with South American features adorning the façade.*

(2) *Statue of Antonio Ordoñez, famous XX century matador, who presides over the bullring together with a monument to Pedro Romero.*

(1) *Corner of the Church of Santa María la Mayor. This collegiate church shows an interesting synthesis of all the styles of architecture that were in vogue during the long years of its construction.*

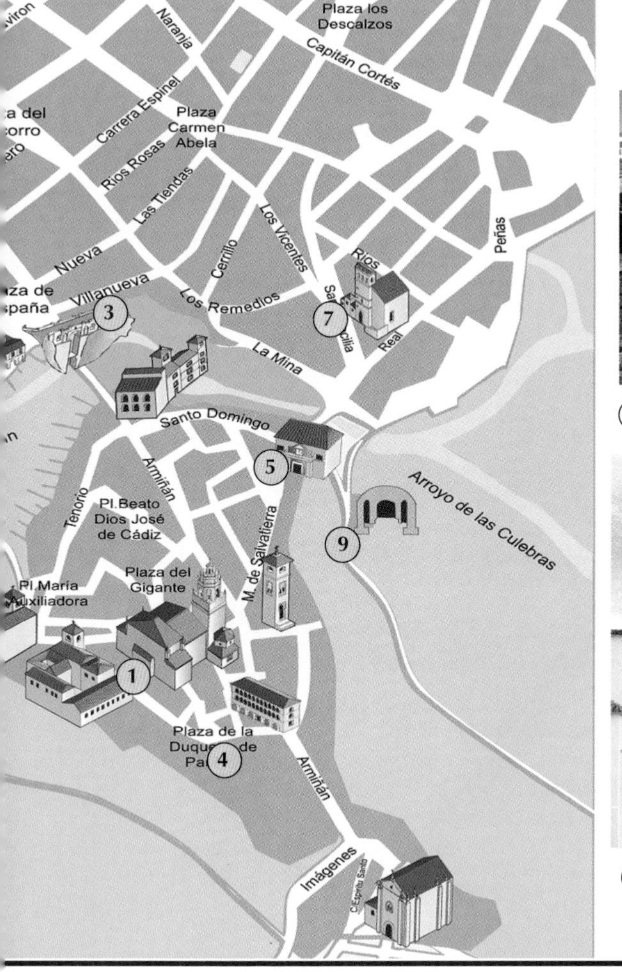

(3) *New Bridge, a gigantic engineering feat of the XVIII century.*

(7) *The Church of Padre Jesus and the spring with eight spouts, in the Mercadillo district.*

• *Above: the Almocabar Gate, built into the old city wall, together with the Church of the Holy Ghost. Right: east wall. Below: the XIV century minaret of St. Sebastian.*

The City

From whichever direction you approach Ronda the town rears up like a white apparition in the midst of a mountainous amphitheatre hewn out of the rock by giants. At a height of 770 metres, the town commands the surrounding plateau, which for centuries was the only way for herds of livestock, caravans, smugglers and armies to journey north from the lower coastal areas.

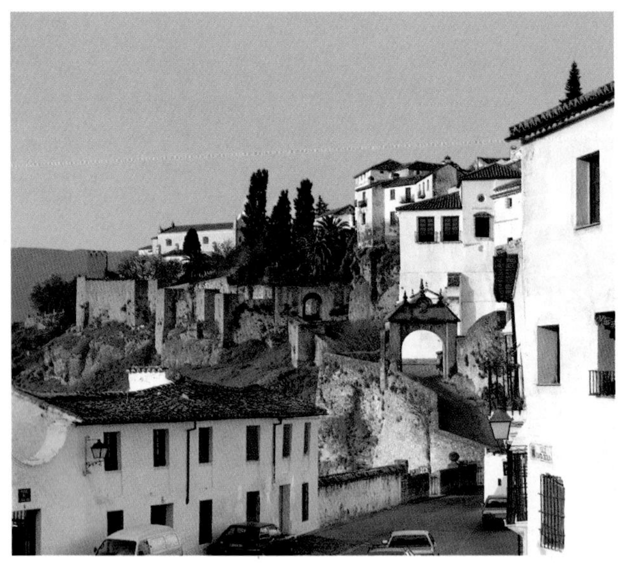

As was usual in these times, the conquerors christianised the Muslim mosque, of which the prayer niche and minaret still remain, and later converted it into the town's main church, Santa María la Mayor, in an unusual combination of Gothic and Renaissance styles. Before the façade is a double tier of balconies over an arcade, which gives a Castillian air to the main square. The Muslims also left the beautiful minaret of San Sebastian (left), some public baths beside the river (XIII to XIV century), the long stairway (360 steps) of La Mina in

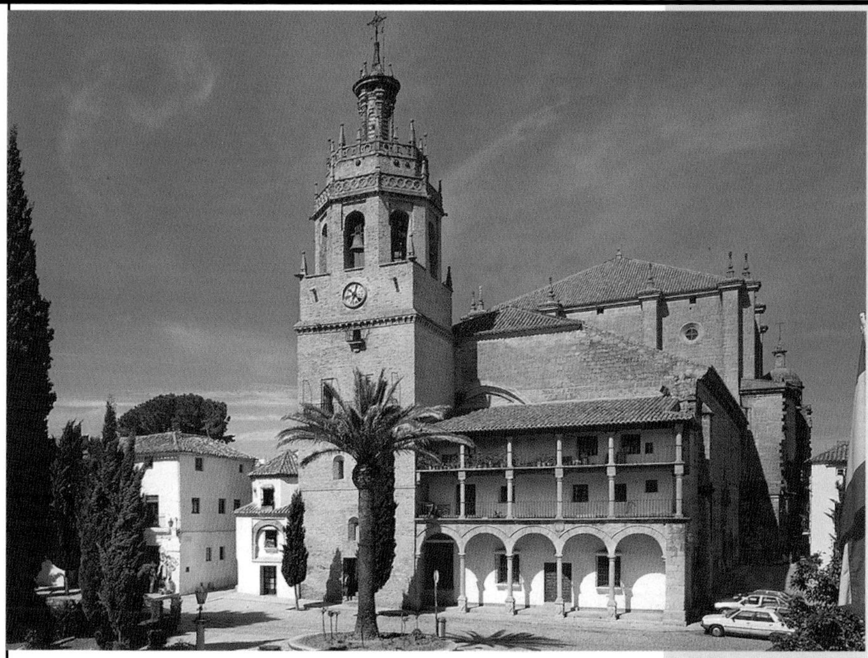

• *Collegiate church Santa María and the Palace of Mondragón*

the Casa del Rey Moro (the Moorish King's Palace) and the Casa del Gigante (the Giant's House), which dates from the same period and is an interesting example of an aristocratic Nasrid mansion, in fact one of the only such private dwellings to have come down to us in such good condition. The Mondragón Palace (right) was originally the abode of emirs but later was adorned with courtyards and Renaissance gardens in the style of the Christian kings who followed them.

The Catholic king Ferdinand was highly pleased with his conquest of Ronda in 1485 and forthwith had the Church of the Holy Ghost (Espíritu Santo) built into the wall next to the Almocábar gate, through which he had made his triumphal entrance into the town. Stretches of the formidable wall still exist. The defences were completed by the impassable gorge of the river Guadalevín and the sheer scarp upon which the city

• *Above: The City Walls viewed from the east,*

including the Xahara gate, clearly Arabic in origin.

stands. But it was in the XVII century and above all during the enlightenment of the XVIII century that Ronda, without turning its back on its Moorish past, adapted to the manners of modern times and transformed itself into the town we know today. Ronda became the most important agricultural and commercial centre of the surrounding area, and its livestock-breeding aristocracy, together with an incipient merchant middle class, began to construct mansions, churches and convents, and also the first stone-built bullring (1784) and the Puente Nuevo (New Bridge) (1753-1793), both designed by the Aragonese architect Martín de Aldehuela. The bullring is grandly impressive in size and design: sixty-six metres in diameter and surrounded by a double arcade of Tuscan columns. The citizens of Ronda already possessed the oldest Royal Equestrian Society in Spain, founded in the XVI century, and now, two hundred years later, they originated and imposed the rules and formal hierarchy upon the tragic dance of death which is fighting the bull on foot rather than on horseback. The Puente Nuevo (New Bridge) spans the gorge almost 100 metres above the river Tajo, passing way above the two earlier bridges to link the City with the

Mercadillo district by the shortest route. Inside it is a room which was originally a high-security prison.

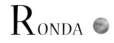

During the War of Independence all through the mountains around Ronda bands of partisans sprang up and invented a new way of fighting the French forces by using "guerrilla" tactics, attacking them by surprise and then vanishing just as quickly into the hills. The original Spanish word, meaning "little wars" or "skirmishes", is now understood worldwide. After the war, with the country in the grip of economic crisis and Andalucía at the mercy of a socio-political structure based on a few landlords who owned vast tracts of land and consolidated their political position by appointing their own sycophants into positions of power, some of the more independently minded partisans stayed in the mountains to become the stuff of romantic legend, the famous smugglers and bandits of the Sierra de Ronda.

• Above: the Arch of Phillip V, built in the XVIII century on the site of an Arab gateway. Below: façade of the palace of the Marquis de Salvatierra.

Amongst the most outstanding modern buildings in the city are: the Arch of Phillip V, which replaced a Arab gateway in the wall, beside which is the Palace of the Marquis de Salvatierra, with an interesting two-tiered portal adorning its façade. Supporting the tympanum that frames the family shield above its typical wrought-iron balcony are some unusual and attractive caryatids with Aztec features (above). A wide entrance hall gives onto an inner patio surrounded by an arcade and this is followed by a rustic garden overlooking the countryside. Spanish firs grow above the line of the garden walls. This tree *(Abies pinsapo)* (left) is a survivor from the Tertiary age and is only to be found around Ronda and Cádiz and some parts of the Ural and Atlas mountains. At the bottom of a steep slope an XVIII century fountain, Fuente de

los Ocho Caños (the fountain with eight spouts) (right), presides over the square of Nuestro Padre de Jesús with its Gothic-Renaissance church, the façade of which is its tower. Not far uphill is the Posada de las Ánimas (Haunted Inn), where Cervantes is said to have lodged. Downhill from the square the road leads to the old bridges and the Arab baths, from the Nasrid period, which are very well preserved due to their having remained undiscovered until the middle of the XX century. Outside the old walls the city extends southwards in what constitutes the third historic "barrio", or neighbourhood, known locally and imaginatively as "el Barrio". It includes the

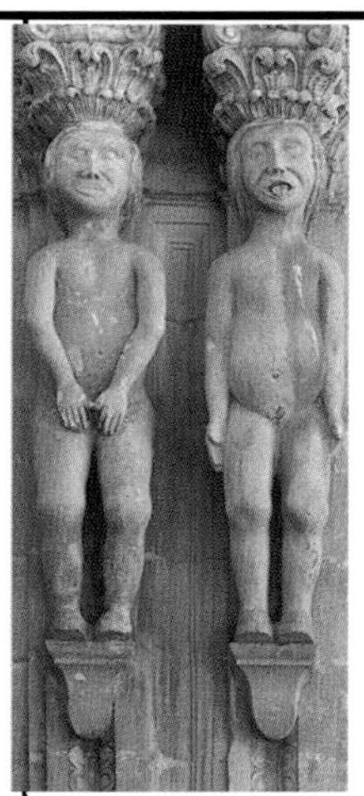

Almocabar Gate and the Church of the Holy Ghost, and above all the traditional district of San Francisco and its church with an Isabelline façade.

Ronda can boast of a considerable number of mansions, many built at the beginning of the XX century, such as the Hotel Reina Victoria, with gardens dedicated to Rainer Maria Rilke, overlooking the surrounding mountains, and the Casa de Don Bosco, built on a superb vantage point over the river Tajo. Gardens are a constant complement to squares and noble houses in Ronda, to the extent, for example, that the gardens of the Palace of the Muslim king Abd al-Maliq were designed by Forrestier. Every corner offers a different view of the city, which is why a local saying has it that "Ronda is full of the best views of Ronda". Particularly attractive are the views from the "parador" (state-run hotel).

• **The Palace of the Marquis of Salvatierra** (*above*) *balcony and caryatids.*

This Muslim palace was rebuilt after the Christian reconquest in the Renaissance style. The courtyard with its arcade and Arab tiles and plasterwork were preserved, together with part of the gardens overlooking the hills beyond.

Left: the Fuente de los Ocho Caños opposite the Church of Our Father Jesus.

On the facing page: view of the mountains from the garden of la Casa de Don Bosco and from the bullring.

• *Above: Castelar de la Frontera, an abandoned mountain village which is gradually recovering its old identity.*

• *Above: The Beach at Tarifa, a surfers' paradise.*

The mountains of Ronda descend to the Straights of Gibraltar (above), thus closing the mountain arc that borders the Guadalquivir basin. It was along here that in years gone by the smugglers' way ran from Gaucín through Jimena de la Frontera to arrive at San Roque in the province of Cádiz. From this eyrie it is often possible to make out the Rock of Gibraltar and the African coast. The area just inland of the straights is called the Campo de Gibraltar. Northward from here the Carbonera range with its oak-wooded slopes (above) has been declared a national park. The only modern plantations allowed here are wind turbines (facing page). Livestock graze the foothills; often fighting bulls!

From the beginning of the 70´s during the last century attempts have been made to industrialise the area in order to make it less economically dependent upon Gibraltar, and a petrochemical plant was built.

But in spite of its enormous

• *Above: the Square at Tarifa in the centre of this the most southerly village in Europe. Its constant winds and Atlantic waves attract surfers from all over the workd.*

size the hoped-for prosperity failed to materialise. Nowadays Algeciras acts as the main port for all traffic in general between Spain and the African continent alongside the port of Gibraltar, whose traffic, however, serves more the strategies and economy of the colony than that of the area of the straights. Hopes for a change in the fortunes of this zone, together with those of North Africa, are still very much in the air.

• *Above: the Rock of Gibraltar, seen from the Spanish military zone. The African coast can be made out in the distance under the clouds.*

CÁDIZ

The province of Cádiz covers an area of 7,385 km^2 and has more than 250 km of coastline. It is essentially a maritime province but can surprise the visitor with its unsuspected variety. In its north-eastern corner the green and forested southern flanks of the Subbettic mountains are dotted with small white villages: such are Arcos de la Frontera, Ubrique, Setenil, Algodonales, Záhara, Olivera and many more; rural paradises away from the beaten track, which still preserve their centuries-old charm. Rain-soaked Grazalema is the highest part of the province, with its woodlands of the now rare Spanish fir *(Abies pinsapo)*. The intense greenery of the forests is thanks to an annual rainfall of 2000 mm, the highest in the whole of Spain. These forests are also home to wild boar, deer, chamois, osprey and many species of eagles, buzzards and vultures. Other towns of equal interest and charm are Medina Sidonia, Jimena de la Frontera, Castellar, and Vejer, a white town perched high up like a stork's nest on its rocky fastness. Many of these towns, like Jeréz itself, are called "de la frontera", or "frontier towns", because this is precisely what they were for centuries during the skirmishes between Castillian Christians and the Muslims of the Nasrid kingdom of Granada. The tourist Route of the Wild Bulls crosses the plain just inland of Gibraltar and goes on to Tarifa via the Janda lagoon, where the Visigoths lost their entire kingdom to invading Berbers in 711 A.D. , an event which was to have profound effects upon the future of Spain.

Cádiz

● **The name Cádiz** *would appear to be Phoenician in origin. These seafarers, coming from modern-day Libya, called it Gadir, meaning "enclosure" or "fortress". This became Gadeira with the Greeks and the Romans referred to the whole area surrounding the tiny archipelago as Gades, from whence came the Gaditan dancing girls who were so popular in Rome. The inhabitants of Cádiz are still known as Gaditans today.*

The History of Cádiz

Cádiz may well be the oldest city in western Europe. Records of a settlement here go back at least 3,000 years to the Iberian Tartessians, who inhabited the south west of the peninsular at that time. Later came the Greeks, then the Phoenicians, who made it their capital in Iberia. The Carthaginians used it as an important trading post until the Romans imposed their rule upon Baetica, as they called the south of the Spanish peninsular. In the modern era it was occupied in turn by invading Visigoths from the north and Berbers from the south, until in 1262 the Castillian king Alfonso X captured it in the name of Christendom and restored to the town the charters and rights it had not enjoyed since Roman times. Throughout its history Cádiz, projecting into the bay like the keel of a ship, has always been a town of seafarers, in constant contact with the peoples of the African continent,

and it was from here that the first adventurers and then merchants opened the way westward to the New World. Cádiz is at one and the same time a Mediterranean and an Atlantic port, its air the essence of the sea and its daylight more brilliant than anywhere else in Spain, all of which have given the city its unmistakable personality.

English naval squadrons have attacked and laid siege to Cádiz from the days of Phillip II, when it was sacked by Drake and burnt to the ground by Essex, to the battle of Trafalgar in 1804. Shortly afterwards the town defied Napoleon's armies for two years until being relieved by the Duke of Wellington, when it established the liberal Parliament of 1812, which was a model for the rest of Europe of the time.

● *In modern times, in 1717, thanks to its deep-water port the city wrested the Commercial Exchange and thus the*

monopoly of commerce with the New World from inland Sevilla with its silted-up river port.

• **An aerial view of Cádiz** *in about 1980, showing why the town is called "a neat little silver cup". The first commercial port was founded in this enclave by the Phoenicians around 3,000 years ago to trade amber, silver and tin. Joined to the mainland by a narrow causeway, it made for an easily defendable trading station. Since then it has been battered by the ebb and flow of history's tide but has persevered stalwartly through to modern times.*

The City of Cádiz

The City of Cádiz is probably the oldest inhabited settlement in the western Mediterranean basin, evidence of which is amply provided by its Phoenician and Greek remains. But despite this the majority of its present-day monuments date only from the XVIII century, when, due to its ideal situation as a deep-sea Atlantic port, it inherited the Centre of Commercial Exchange with the Americas (la Casa de Contratación de las Américas), which had hitherto been housed in Sevilla. During the middle ages Cádiz was scarcely more than a large fishing village but from 1717 onwards it became the main port for the New World and so most of its historic buildings reflect the Gothic and Neoclassical styles of the age, the finest example of which is the Cárcel Real (Royal Prison). The Puerta de Tierra (The Landward Gate) is a magnificent example of a military stronghold, complete with tower, moats and massive walls, built to protect the only landward access to a town constantly under threat of attack. The perpendicular layout of its streets, excellent examples of which survive in the la Viña, Santa María and Pópulo neighbourhoods, clearly reflect a military urban structure.

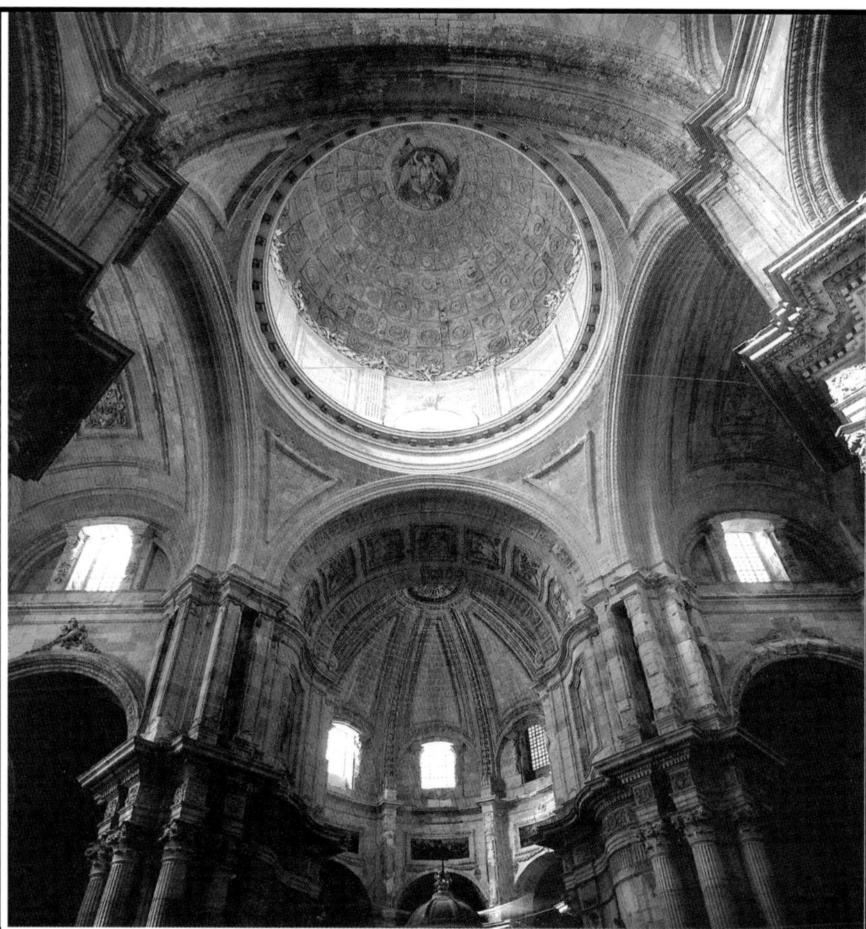

THE CATHEDRAL

Cádiz cathedral is the last of the great Andalucían cathedrals, which, due to the comparative lateness of its construction, wavered between the Baroque and the Neoclassical. Work on it began in 1722, according to the original design by Vicente Acero, but 130 years were to pass before it was finished, owing as always to a lack of funds. Two lateral towers frame an extravagant facade with a concave, semicircular pediment.

Underneath the cathedral in the daringly designed, horizontal low-roofed crypt lie the mortal remains of the musician Manuel de Falla.

• *Within the cathedral (above) Corinthian columns are abutted against huge pillars, drawing and focusing the eye, whilst at the same time accentuating the volume and space of the interior. Below is a view of the cathedral from the Campo del Sur.*

● The collegiate church of the Saviour *at Jerez (above), a cathedral since 1980, with its*

beautiful flying buttresses and wide steps, where every September the festival of the grape harvest is held. Wealthy merchants situated their wine businesses in this area and also built luxurious mansions and town houses with elegant porticoes (above) in the same neighbourhood.
Right: XII century Muslim baths at Alcázar, where there is also a rare example of an Almohad mosque.

The City of Jerez, as might be expected of a town with such a noble history, is full of historic monuments, among which are the XVIII century Collegiate Church of the Saviour (above), with its separate tower, a synthesis of Mudejar influences, the mediaeval Gothic churches of St. Michael (right) and St. James, the latter a fine example of Andalucían flamboyant Gothic, and the castle, with stretches of wall dating back to the XI century. Jerez is also home to the Andalucían Flamenco Centre. And in the world of sport it is the home of Spain's international grand prix motor-racing circuit.
But above all Jerez is renowned for its wine and its horses. A well known tale recounts how a Carthusian monk, after being expelled from his monastery during the confiscation of church property by the french in 1810, lived

alone in the wilds of the province with his two silver-grey horses. A detachment of Napoleon's troops were so impressed with these horses that they confiscated them and bred them for use in the French army. They were in fact two of the few remaining specimens of a strong, agile but obedient and intelligent race of horses which the Carthusian monks have carefully bred from the XIV century.

● **THE HORSES OF JEREZ** *are an Andalucían race deriving from the breeding of Arab and Spanish native stock. They have always been carefully bred, primarily because of their importance for military use and also in the world of agriçulture, but today because of*

their elegance and good temper they are kept and bred for sport and leisure.
The May festival in Jerez, one of the biggest of the year, is devoted to its horses. It includes numerous displays, parades and competitions for the most elaborate harnesses and trappings, dressage and so on. During the rest of the year visitors can also enjoy equestrian displays put on by the Royal Andalucían School of Equestrian Art in Jerez.

• THE WINES OF JEREZ (SHERRY)

The grape harvest is relatively early, in September, after which the grapes are left in the sun. The must is fermented at strictly controlled temperatures before being drawn off, refined and put to mature in casks of American oak.

THE WINE CELLARS

The "miracle" occurs in the wine cellar, when without any rational explanation, each cask decides, as though by its own volition, which type of sherry it is destined to be. The chemical composition of two casks lying side by side may be identical but the trained nose of the vintner will smell out which "*solera*" it belongs to. It may end up being a light, dry, straw-coloured "*fino*", or a more full-bodied "*amontillado*", or else a darker, stronger "*palo cortado*". It may also turn out to be a very different type of fragrant medium-dry wine or even a sweet desert wine.

THE CARTHUSIAN MONASTERY
The Carthusian Monastery of the Defence of the Faith at Jerez was founded in 1463 at a time when this religious order was undergoing an upsurge in popularity throughout Spain.
It has a magnificent Gothic cloister (1478).
At the height of the monastery's fortunes the richly decorative Baroque facade was added (above), contrasting sharply with the austere monastic living quarters and the spacious Cloister of the Dead, surrounded by cypresses, and the smaller close around the church itself. In 1810 its properties were secularised by Napoleon's troops during the War of Independence and then during the disentailment of 1835 it was despoiled, along with most church purtenances at the time.

• **XVII FAÇADE OF THE CARTHUSIAN MONASTERY** *(above). and an old engraving, (below).*

• *From its hilltop, the Castle of Medina Sidonia (above) watches grandly over the pastures below, stretching away to the sea in the far distance. Above: the beach at Tarifa and Sierra Carbonera, lined with modern wind turbines. Right: the ruins of Bolonia (Baelo Claudia), a Roman city whose principal industry 2,000 years ago was that of salting tuna, until it was devastated by an earthquake. Below: the coast at Conil, surrounded by pine trees, and the small bay which shelters pleasure craft from the strong winds that blow along this coast*

Cádiz's immensely varied countryside allows a visitor to follow routes which differ very much in character but at the same time complement each other in providing an understanding of the overall nature of the province and its people. The Wine Route takes in the bay and its ports, the cities of Jerez and Sanlucar and then continues along a coast of never-ending sandy beaches, passing through towns and villages such as Conil, Barbate, Los Caños de Meca, Vejer, Tarifa to arrive at the Straights of Gibraltar, gateway to the Atlantic. Here the constant winds and gigantic waves attract surfers from far and wide, filling the beaches with colour and excitement, and at the same time turn the blades of the modern wind turbines on the Sierra Carbonera.

The Route of the Fighting-Bulls passes through the centre of the province and, although just as interesting, is less well known. From Jerez it takes the road to Medina Sidonia (whose

• **PUERTO DE SANTA MARÍA,** *(left) the baroque facade of the town church, begun in the XV century. The town's most outstanding monument is, however, St. Mark's Castle (below), founded by king Alfonso X The Learned upon the remains of a mosque.*
This fortress is mentioned in the famous mediaeval poetry

cycle Cántigas de Santa María, compiled by King Alfonso and many of them are believed to have been written here.
Left: The church of Santa María at Arcos, built in the XV century although later restored.
Below: the main square in Tarifa.

duke led the ill-fated Armada to England in 1588), then to Paterna, Alcalá de los Gazules and through forests of cork-oaks to Gibraltar. The most charming route is that of the White Villages steeped in the very essence of rural life.

The Route of the White Villages

● **Castellar de la Frontera** *(above) is an abandoned village in the middle of the woods which is only now being brought back to life. The heart of the province, one of the least well known but equally interesting parts of Cádiz, belongs to its fighting-bulls.*
Left: Olvera. Below: View of Arcos de la Frontera.

Above: Jimena de la Frontera in the springtime. Left: Zahara, with the Sierra de Grazalema in the background. Below: Vejer de la Frontera on its hilly promontory. At the bottom of the page: the village of Grazalema amidst the Spanish firs.

The Route of the White Villages follows more than 300 km of winding country roads

● *There are more than a dozen of these white villages, including those nestling within the mountains of Ronda in the Province of Málaga and those that formed the old frontier of the Nasrid kingdom, perched high on mountain ridges and gleaming white against a constantly changing green tapestry of cork and holm oaks and chestnut trees.*

HUELVA

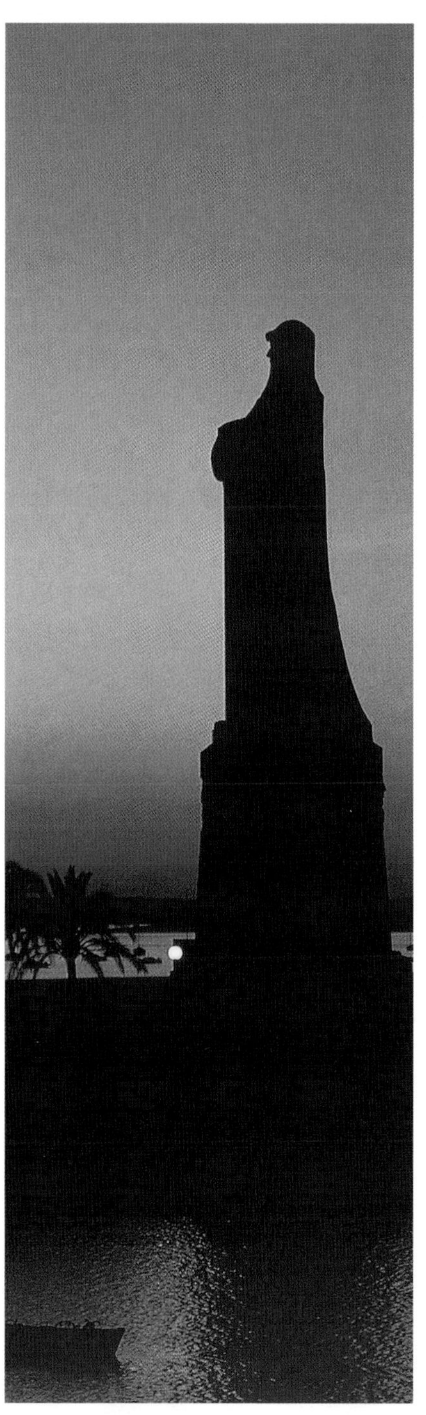

The Sierra Morena forms a rocky spine between the central Spanish plateau and Andalucía, which stretches southwards down to the sea. Huelva is the westernmost province of Andaluca, bordering on Extremadura. It contains the Sierra de Aracena and the Picos de Aroche, a mountainous region covering some 180,000 hectares which was declared a national park in 1989. Like Cádiz it is densely wooded and scattered with gleaming white villages among the oak and chestnut trees. But above all it is home to the Iberian pigs which feed free-range on the acorns of the forest. A combination of the climate and certain peculiarities in the flora and microfauna make the ham produced from these black-hoofed pigs the most succulent in Spain. The best known ham-producing village on these hillsides is Jabugo, but there are many others which cure the hams just as expertly and are well worth the visit: Alájar, shaded by cork oaks and a jewel of local rural architecture; Aroche, still guarded by its medieval walls; Almonaster, famous for its mosque and traditional fandango dancing; Aracena, with its limestone caves; Cortegana, Cumbres Mayores and many more.

The city of Huelva, the most industrial city in Andaluca, lies between the mouths of the rivers Tinto and Odiel and it was here that the earliest civilisations landed on the Iberian peninsular and pushed inland to mine the copper ores which abound in this area. One of the first of these were the Tartessians; their mythical city of Atlantida may not have been far from the floodplains of Huelva.

Niebla is famous for its fortifications, where in 1262 gunpowder was used for the first time in Europe, and also for having supplied Christopher Columbus with many experienced mariners for his voyage to the New World. Also of interest is the church dedicated to Santa María de la Granada, which was converted from a Muslim mosque and still retains the bottom section of the minaret, part of the courtyard (above) and the mihrab, or prayer niche. Two kilometres of red-ochre wall with fifty towers and five gates bear witness to the fact that Niebla was once the capital of one of the independent, warring taifa kingdoms which sprang up after the disintegration of the caliphate in 1031.

● **NIEBLA,** *the Tower of Santa María and its courtyard. Below: The Church of Almonaster la Real, containing many details from the days of the caliphate both in its construction and decoration.*

THE MONASTERY AT LA RÁBIDA The great event in the history of Huelva was the discovery of the New World, that quest for which it provided both caravels and experienced seamen. The small Franciscan convent at la Rábida (an Arabic word meaning "oratory" or "sanctuary") offered lodgings and support to Columbus when he arrived there in 1485. His friend Brother Juan Pérez, erstwhile confessor to Queen Isabel, arranged an audience for him at court, although it was to take him seven years to persuade her majesty to finance his "harebrained" scheme to find land westward over the ocean, a project that had already been turned down by the more prudent Dominican friars in Salamanca.

In the village of Palos de Moguer he met the Pinzón brothers, who recruited the rest of the experienced crew needed for the great adventure.

● THE BEACHES AT PUNTA UMBRÍA *(below), close to the industrial complex of Huelva, thousands of years ago were the cradle of the Turdetan and Tartessian bronze-age cultures. The men of the villages around here have been seafarers from time immemorial and it was from here that Christopher Columbus chose his crews to sail to the New World. The walls around Niebla (below) and a cloister at la Rábida (left).*

THE PILGRIMAGE OF LA VIRGEN DEL ROCÍO AT ALMONTE

THE SIMPECADO

The origins of the pilgrimage to Almonte, like many present-day Christian festivals, are to be found in ancient pagan celebrations of the coming of spring and the reaffirmation of life in this marshland devoted to agriculture and the breeding of cattle.

Pilgrims walking to Almonte.

● **THE PILGRIMAGE OF EL ROCÍO AT ALMONTE** *brings together more than a million people on Whit Monday in a celebration that lasts for several days. For most of the pilgrims its religious significance goes far beyond a mere desire for a yearly re-encounter with nature. Above: Mass held on Whit Sunday. Far left: the Simpecado (a lavishly decorated cart containing an image of the Virgin) and scenes of the pilgrimage on foot. Left: festivities at a stop along the way and crossing the river at Sanlúcar de Barrameda.*

● **THE DOÑANA NATURE RESERVE** *is bordered at the sea by a 30-kilometre-long beach of fine sand, which is blown inland to form characteristic dunes scattered with clumps of marram grass. Pine trees and cork oaks also cling to this sandy environment. Below: Birds roosting in a tree in Doñana.*

THE DOÑANA NATURE RESERVE.

This natural paradise was declared a national park in 1969 and part of the Human Heritage Trust in 1994, which should give some idea of the growing recognition of the importance of this, one of the foremost nature reserves in Europe.

It used to be a wide, shallow bay but sedimentation and man's intervention have turned it into a marshy, flood plane. The reserve itself covers some 50,700 hectares and its surroundings another 54,000 hectares, all of which provide a wetland for 80% of the migratory birds of Europe. The fauna, as in any other ecosystem, form a hierarchical pyramid, at the peak of which in Doñana is the Iberian lynx, although it is nowadays in dire peril of extinction. Another protected species resident in the reserve is the Spanish imperial eagle, scarcely more than a hundred pairs of which remain in the whole peninsula. Much more commonly seen, however, are kites and cranes. The most outstanding among the water fowl are without doubt the pink flamingos, but there are numerous other species of equal interest such as herons, egrets, coots, spoonbills and garganeys, to mention but a few. As far as vegetation is concerned, large cork oaks growing in the middle of the marshes serve as roosts for a multitude of birds, although a

great part of the woodland in the reserve is made up of pine trees, which slow down the incursion of the sand dunes. Finally, forming groundcover, there are a wide variety of bushes and shrubs, including rock roses, heather and marram grass, all of which stabilise the soil and provide shelter for ground-nesting birds. For centuries man's activities were absorbed harmoniously into the natural environment of Doñana but in recent years this fragile balance has been overturned. The preservation of the environment in the

● **THE SIERRA DE ARACENA***(above), also known as the Sierra de Huelva, is scattered with holm-oak and cork-oak woodlands, the last vestiges of the dense forests which covered the whole Iberian peninsula in the not-so-distant past, and nowadays provide both habitat and food for the free-ranging Iberian pigs. Above on the facing page: The town of Aracena. On this page above: the village of Alájar. Left: the estuary of the Rio Tinto*

• Right: The Grotto of Marvels, one of the many underground lakes that give added excitement to the natural beauties of this karstic landscape. Individual caves have been given evocative names to reflect their limestone formations, such as the "the cathedral", "the organ loft".

Doñana Nature reserve is one of the greatest challenges facing us today and in the light of recent natural disasters such as the poisoning of large tracts of land by spillage from mining works while engineers and politicians were looking the other way, it would seem that it is going to be an uphill task.

At the mouth of the river Odiel, not far from Columbus's seafaring villages and close to the chemical-producing industrial estates, there is another nature reserve of more than 7,000 hectares, comprised of sandy marshland which stretches all the way to Punta Umbría and in Spring the whole area surrounding the petrochemical works teems with water fowl, especially spoonbills.

The abundant copper and iron ores and sulphide deposits

HUELV

PUNTA UMBRÍA

Fishing and wine-making are fundamental aspects of life in Huelva.

● *Above: Aracena. Below: anchors left to rust after the fishing disputes with Morocco at the turn of this century.*

of the Andávalo region have been mined since prehistoric times. In the XIX century British companies laid railways and began the systematic exploitation of these mines, thus opening a very important chapter in the history of the area. They built machines and small wagons that could be loaded straight onto ships, the height of technology in those days. The countryside around the mining area, just as the rest of the mountainous parts of the province, is covered with woods of holm and cork oaks, the autochthonous trees of the area, which are capable of surviving forest fires, and produce the acorns to fatten the black-hoofed pigs that produce the most excellent cured ham in Spain, a veritable gift of nature.

● **PEÑA DE ARIAS MONTANO,** *above. Below: sunset over Sanlúcar.*

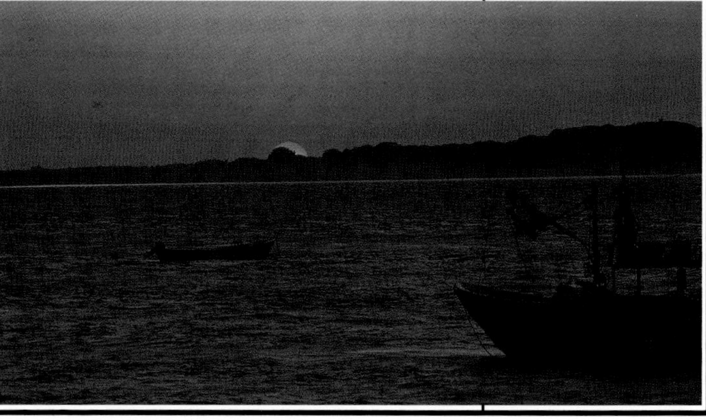

SEVILLA

The earliest references we have to a settlement on the site of present-day Sevilla are of a town called Tartessus, probably built by the Phoenicians as a trading station on the River Guadalquivir around 2,800 B.C. The river has always been Sevilla's lifeblood. Thanks to its easily accessible port and its strategic position dominating the surrounding fertile plains, it first became a centre of the bronze-age Tartessian culture and later a Carthaginian stronghold, the scene of bitter fighting during the Roman occupation of the Spanish peninsula. In 207 B.C. after defeating the Carthaginian army, Scipio Africanus left his wounded veterans in a town he founded and called Itálica, just to the north of the modern Sevilla. This same town was later to be the birthplace of the Roman emperors Trajan and Hadrian. During the Roman civil wars Julius Caesar defeated Gnaeus Pompey in the region and shortly afterwards Sevilla became a Roman *colonia* called Hispalis, the oldest known form of its present-day name. When the Romans withdrew from Spain at the beginning of the V century there came a succession of Germanic invaders, including the Vandals, who stayed here briefly on their way to northern Africa. After the Berber and Arab invasions from Africa the city, its name now mutated to Yxvillia, was second only to Córdoba during the first three centuries of the Arab emirate and then caliphate until it was sacked by Vikings in 844. When the Córdoban caliphate collapsed at the beginning of the XI century Yxvillia became the most important of the numerous *taifa* kingdoms to emerge in the region and the sultan al-Mutamid even aspired to reclaim the caliphate for himself. Nevertheless, finding himself under threat from the Christian king Alfonso VI, in 1090 he asked for help from the Almoravids, a warlike north-African Berber tribe, who came and stayed to impose their rule on the south. They were followed in 1146 by another such tribe, the Almohads, who made Yxvillia their capital. It was they who built the Great Mosque here, with a lofty minaret which stands to this day as the cathedral campanile and one of Sevilla's best known and cherished monuments, the Giralda. Fifty years later the city fell to the Christians, led by Fernando III, and so began the modern age of the city, now known as Sevilla.

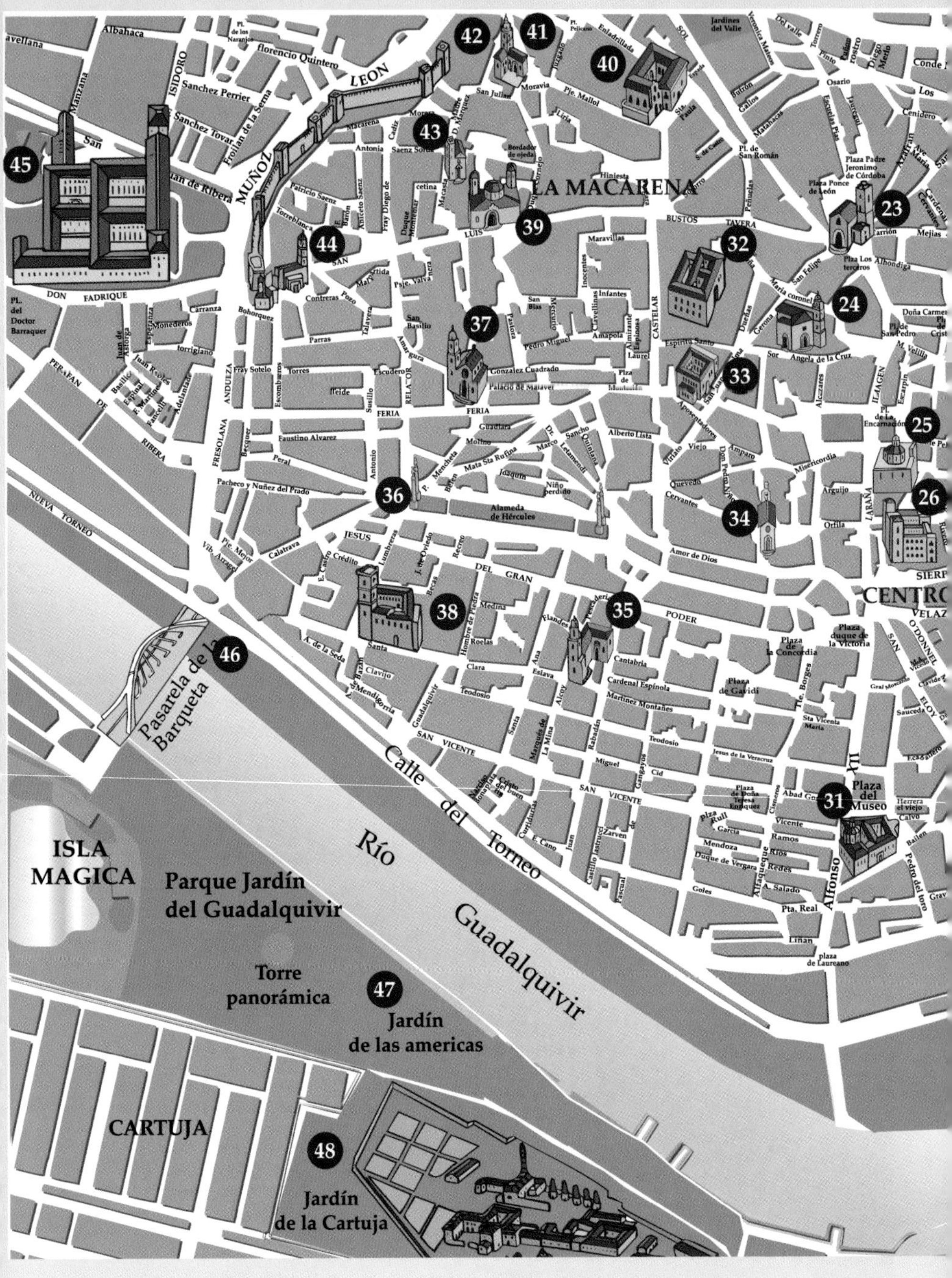

Key to plan

1. *Cathedral and Giralda*
2. *Archbishop's Palace*
3. *Convent of the Incarnation*
4. *Church of the Holy Cross*
5. *Church of St. Mary "la Blanca"*
6. *Hospital of the "Venerables"*
7. *Royal Palaces (Alcázares)*
8. *Archive of the "Indias"*
9. *Charity Hospital*
10. *Theatre of the "Maestranza"*
11. *Bull Ring of the "Maestranza"*
12. *Golden Tower*
13. *Isabel II Bridge*
14. *Church of St. Hyacinth*
15. *Church of St. Ana*
16. *Palace of St. Anthelm*
17. *University*
18. *Exhibition Social Centre*
19. *Plaza de España*
20. *Church of St. Stephen*
21. *Church of St. Idelphonse*
22. *Church of St. Nicholas*
23. *Church of St. Catherine*
24. *Church of St. Peter*

25. *Church of the Annunciation*
26. *Lebrija Palace*
27. *Church of St. Joseph*
28. *Church of Our Saviour*
29. *Town Hall*
30. *Church of St. Mary Magdelaine*
31. *Fine-Arts Museum*
32. *Dueñas Palace*
33. *Convent of the Holy Ghost*
34. *Church of St. Andrew*
35. *Church of St. Lawrence and Jesus the Mighty*
36. *Hercules Boulevard*
37. *Omnium Sanctorum Church*
38. *Convent of St. Claire and the Tower of Don Fadrique*
39. *Church of St. Louis*
40. *Convent of St. Paula*
41. *Church of St. Julian*
42. *Old City Walls*
43. *Church of St. Marina*
44. *Church of St. Giles*
45. *Hospital of the Five Wounds*
46. *"Barqueta" Bridge*
47. *Garden"de las Américas"*
48. *Garden"de la Cartuja"*

• VEIW BY WYNGAERDEN. *The spectacular growth of the city can be seen in this drawing by the Flemish artist Anton van den Wyngaerden from the time of Philip II. Wyngaerden, the least known of the artist-travellers of the 16th century, was however the best graphic reporter of his time, leaving us detailed townscapes of all the principal cities in Spain. This drawing of Sevilla, despite its tendency towards idealisation, is clearly accurate down to the smallest detail.*

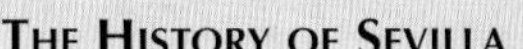

THE HISTORY OF SEVILLA

For more than two thousand years Sevilla has been the gateway to inland Spain. Its port was used by all the early civilisations who came upriver in search of precious metals and trade.

■ ANCIENT SEVILLE, TARTESSUS
A small town was established 2,800 years ago on a gentle rise on the bank of the river at the point where it became more difficult for sea-going boats to navigate upstream. This settlement was the trading centre of the river port used by Mediterranean merchants such as the Phoenicians and the Greeks to ship the mineral wealth of the Sierra Morena mountains back to their homelands. It is from the Greeks in fact that we first hear of the mythical, wealthy kingdom of Tartessus, the reality of which was recently confirmed by the discovery of the fabulous Carambolo treasure horde (right)

■ THE ROMANS. After a protracted struggle the Romans finally pushed the Carthaginians out of Spain to gain complete control over the whole Mediterranean area, and in 207 B.C. the victorious Roman general Scipio Africanus founded a town for his veterans a little to the north of the present-day city, naming it Itálica. Julius Caesar endowed the region and

main town of the area with the status of *colonia* under the name of Hispalis, the original version of its modern name.

■ SEVILLE UNDER THE MUSLIMS

In 711 Sevilla was once again invaded, this time by Muslims. Under the Umayyad emirate the capital was moved to Cordoba but Yxvillia (the Arab mutation of Hispalis) remained influential due to the power of the securely installed Yemenite clans.

A hundred years later in 1031 the caliphate disintegrated and Sevilla, under the Abbadid dynasty, became the most important of the numerous small, independent *taifa* kingdoms that emerged from the resulting social and political instability. A second invasion from North Africa in 1147 brought the Almohads to power. They made Yxvillia their capital and set about rebuilding and encompassing it with a new, longer city wall. It was at this time, in 1221, that the Golden Tower (Torre de Oro) was built. It was under the hundred-year rule of the Almohads that Sevilla became a truly great city, with much of the mediaeval urban structure that has survived to this day.

■ MEDIAEVAL SEVILLA

In 1253, five years after his father Fernando III (the Holy) had conquered Sevilla, his son Alfonso X (the Learned) made his loyal Sevilla a royal city, the city which did not betray him during the civil wars against his own son Sancho, and took up almost permanent residence here. In the XIV century Pedro I, *the Cruel*, took advantage of the damage caused by an earthquake to rebuild completely the royal palaces (Alcázares) in a fusion of Arab and Christian styles which later came to be known as Mudéjar.

•**HERCULES BOULEVARD.** *phot. by J. Laurent. Old chronicles claim that Hercules, one of the most popular heroes of mythology, placed six stone pillars upon the site where Julius Caesar would found the city of Hispalis. Both their statues, sculpted by Diego de Pesquera, were erected in the new Alameda de Hercules (Hercules Boulevard) in the XVI century as a homage to the founders of the city. And there they stand today upon columns and capitals taken from a Roman temple in Mármoles street.*

SEVILLE AND ITS MONUMENTS

Modern-day Sevilla is the accumulated inheritance of all the Mediterranean civilisations which have passed this way and left their impression here; it reflects the history and culture of the whole of Spain and so it is impossible for a visitor to see all of Sevilla in a day.

(9) **PLAZA DE ESPAÑA**
Plza de España.
This is one of the instantly recognisable landmarks of the 1929 Spanish-Americ Exhibition.

(4) **TOWN HALL.** *(Ayuntamiento) Plaza de San Francisco, is a Renaissance building with Plateresque ornamentation, situated between the Plaza de San Francisco and Plaza Nueva and the hub of Sevillian life.*

(10) **FINE ARTS MUSEUM** *(Museo de Bellas Artes), Alfonso XII street. Housed in an old monastery (Monasterio de la Merced), this art gallery is second only to Madrid's* el Prado.

(12) **THE OLD CHARITY HOSPITAL** *(Hospital de La Caridad), Temprado street. The most representative of the many examples of Baroque architecture in Sevilla.*

(11) **THE FORMER TOBACCO FACTORY.** *(Fabrica de Tabaco), built in the XVIII century today houses the University of Sevilla.*

(12) **PILATE'S HOUSE.** *(Casa de Pilatos), Plaza de Pilatos. This sumptuous mansion was built in 1519 by the first Marquis of Tarifa on his return from a journey to Jerusalem. He also introduced the Renaissance style into Sevilla's civil architecture and probably, by his adoption of the procession of the Via Crucis, inspired the Easter processions in the city.*

(2) **ARCHBISHOP'S PALACE,** *built in the XVI century and one of the most outstanding examples of Baroque architecture in Sevilla*

(1) **THE CATHEDRAL**
Plza. Virgen de los Reyes. Sevilla's Gothic Cathedral is the third largest in the world. It was built during the XV century on the site of the former Great Mosque, some elements of which still remain, such as the Courtyard of the Orange Trees and the minaret, nowadays the cathedral campanile, known as the Giralda.

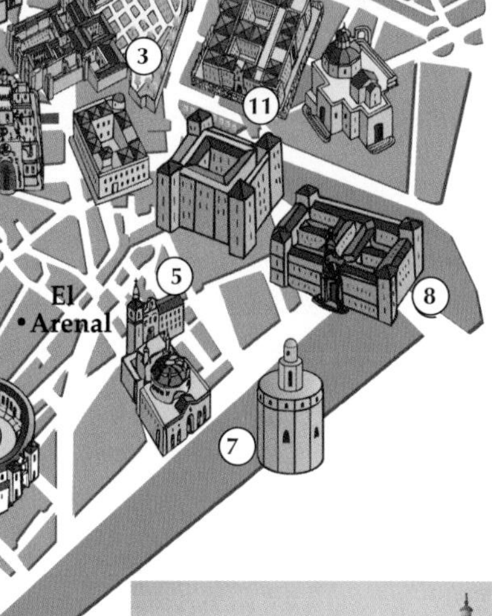

(3) **THE ROYAL PALACES**
Plaza del Triunfo.

(6) **THE MAESTRANZA BULLRING**
one of Sevilla's landmarks.

(8) **THE PALACE OF ST. ANTHELM**
(Palacio de San Telmo).

SEVILLE

• *Above:* **THE CATHEDRAL.**
Below: engraving of the Giralda.

In the early XV century the ecclesiastical authorities decided to build a cathedral on the site of the Moorish mosque, a cathedral of such dimensions that, "When they see it, future generations will think that we are mad". Today, it is the third largest cathedral in the Christian world.

SEVILLA CATHEDRAL

After the reconquest in 1248, the old mosque was consecrated and for 153 years it remained in use as a Christian cathedral. It was common after the reconquest to adapt and consecrate pre-existing mosques in this way until such time as funds were available to build a new church. All that survives of the Great Mosque at Sevilla are the Courtyard of the Orange Trees and the converted minaret, the Giralda.

With its river port close to the sea, Sevilla became during the XIV and XV centuries one of the key mercantile and political centres of the kingdom of Castilla. Such was its economic power that when in 1366 many of its most important buildings were destroyed or severely damaged by an earthquake plans were immediately conceived to build a new cathedral so grand that, "When they see it future generations will think that we are mad". Who the designer was we don't know because all the papers concerning the construction were destroyed by fire, but we do know that building began in 1401 and continued for over a hundred years, guided by the hands of such master builders as Simon of Cologne, Alonso Rodríguez and the prolific Juan Gil de Hontañón. The overall style of the cathedral is late-Gothic: the impressive upward sweep of the rhomboid pillars merging into the ribs of the domes enhances the feeling of space created by the five aisles and complements the

open airy atmosphere thus achieved. The simplicity of line is typically Gothic, indeed almost archaic in its own time, but over the years additions were made, with the result that the Cathedral is the most important artistic complex in Sevilla, representing all its architectural genres and styles. It occupies the entire site of the former mosque except what used to be the outside courtyard. A massive construction, it contains within the main walls five aisles, side chapels, a transept and an apse. Thus there is no specific sense of direction within the church, there being no ambulatory as such, but rather spaces added on, in which chapels and sacristies have been inserted. External flying buttresses support the weight of the upper wall of this severe stone cube, which was built thus to affirm its superiority over the light brickwork of the earlier Muslim structure. The first significant change made to the Cathedral was to the original dome, which collapsed and was re-placed by Hontañón in 1511 with a splendid ribbed cupola. The altar screen in the chancel, the largest in the Christian world, measuring 360 square metres and containing 44 reliefs and over 1000 figures depicting the life of Christ, required more than a hundred years for the first phase alone to be completed. The original style was the Gothic of Dancart, but this later evolved into the

• THE GIRALDA *was originally the minaret of the Great Mosque, built by Ahmed ibn Baso and Ali de Gomera for the caliph Abu Yacub Yusuf around the middle of the XII century. It was crowned with four golden spheres upon a lofty pinnacle to commemorate the battle of Alarcos. In Christian times the top was brought down by an earthquake and replaced by a belfry tower, built by Hernán Ruiz the younger. Above it he erected the 'Giraldillo', the statuesque weather vane that gives the campanile its name.*

Left: the Courtyard of the Orange Trees belonged to the original mosque and was where the faithful washed before prayer.

• **INSIDE THE CATHEDRAL.** *The four aisles, nave and many side chapels are supported by sixty columns. The Renaissance sacristy, designed in 1528, houses the famous Alfonsine astronomical tables.*
Right: detail of one of the side doors.
Below: the tomb of Christopher Columbus, whose remains were finally brought back to Sevilla from Cuba in1899 after Spain lost its American colonies.

Renaissance of Jorge Fernández (1525) and was finally covered in delicate gold-leaf by Alejo Fernández. The main grille was the work of the greatest iron-workers of the age, the two Bartolomés (father and son), from Jaén and Friar Francisco de Salamanca (1518-1529). The latter also made the screen in the Choir, with its 117 stalls and two magnificent organs, built in an uncompromising Baroque style by Duque Cornejo.

In the Royal Chapel, behind the Main Chapel, are the incorrupt remains of king Fernando the Holy, later St Fernando, in a Baroque silver urn, together with those of his son Alfonso X, the Learned, and his wife, Beatrice of Swabia. The Royal Chapel is Renaissance, by Gaínza (1551), although the dome was the work of the Córdoban architect Hernán Ruiz the younger. Presiding over the altarpiece is the XIII century statue of the Virgen de los Reyes (Virgin of the Kings), much revered in Sevilla. She was carved in a French workshop, apparently as a gift to Fernando, the conqueror of Sevilla, from his cousin Louis IX (St. Louis), King of France.

The importance of the Cathedral Chapter is evident in the sumptuous chambers, and especially in the Main Sacristy (1528-1543),

crowned by a cupola designed by Riaño and Gaínza, possibly with some help by Diego de Siloé. Here we can see the magnificent 'Descent from the Cross' by Campagna, San Isidro and San Leandro, by Murillo, one of the most beautiful monstrances created by Arce, and the Alphonsine tryptic. The Gothic-style Sacristy of the Chalices, by Alonso Rodríguez, is presided over by Goya's painting of Santa Justa and Santa Rufina, the patron saints of Sevilla. Also here are pictures by Valdés Leal, Zurbarán's 'Virgin and Child', and 'St. John the Baptist', together with four panels by Alejo Fernández and the famous "Gloria", originally attributed to Tintorreto but now believed to be the work of Juan de Roelas. The Antechamber and Chapter House, by Hernán Ruiz the Younger, have breathtaking domes and floors, but equally impressive are the treasures within the other chapels: the "Virgen de la

• **THE MAIN GRILLE** *is the work of the Bartolomés (father and son) from Jaén and Francisco de Salamanca (1518-29). The stained-glass windows (below) mark the beginning of a golden age in Spanish glass-work.*

• *Left: a wooden Cristo de la Clemencia measuring nearly 2m, carved by Martínez Montañes.*

• *Detail of the altar.*
• *On the facing page and overleaf are views of the Cathedral.*

Antigua" chapel, the sailor's haven, the monument to Cardinal Mendoza by Domenico A. Fancelli; "The Baptismal Chapel and the Vision of St Anthony' by Murillo, which was once stolen but later recovered. The Capilla de Scalas has 'The Virgin of Granada' from the workshop of the Della

• **STAINED-GLASS WINDOW** *by Enrique Alemán, who seems to have modelled the figure on Charles V.*

Robbia family. Alonso Cano painted a demure-faced Virgin of Bethlehem for the same chapel, an unusual subject for this painter. The Capilla de San Pedro contains canvases by Zurbarán, painted expressly for the chapel.
Other treasures of the Cathedral include the Chapter and Columbian Library, with 90,000 volumes, dating from the donations of Alfonso X and including the Book of Hours belonging to Queen Isabel the Catholic and the 20,000 volumes donated by Fernando Colón (the son of Christopher Columbus), with texts and documents bequeathed to him from his father.

THE CATHEDRAL OF SEVILLE

Both the Cathedral itself and its contents constitute an anthology of the many styles and works of art which have contributed to its construction over the centuries. It was begun in the XV century in the late Gothic style upon the foundations of the Great Mosque, some parts of which, such as the Courtyard of the Orange Trees and the Giralda, still remain. The sacristy and royal chapel date from the XVI century. Evolving from the Renaissance came the exuberant Baroque of other parts of the building. The Cathedral contains a collection of valuable paintings and sculptures dating from the XV century which are of considerable importance in the history of European art.

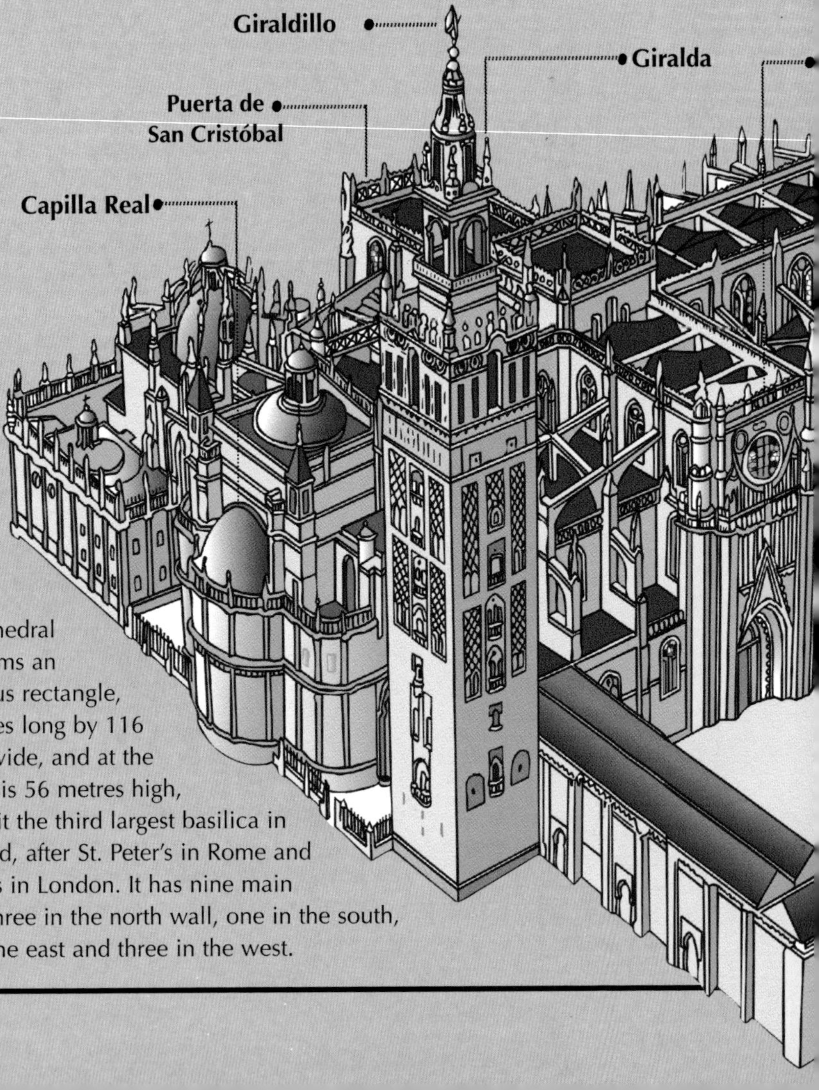

The Cathedral itself forms an enormous rectangle, 76 metres long by 116 metres wide, and at the transept is 56 metres high, making it the third largest basilica in the world, after St. Peter's in Rome and St. Paul's in London. It has nine main doors, three in the north wall, one in the south, two in the east and three in the west.

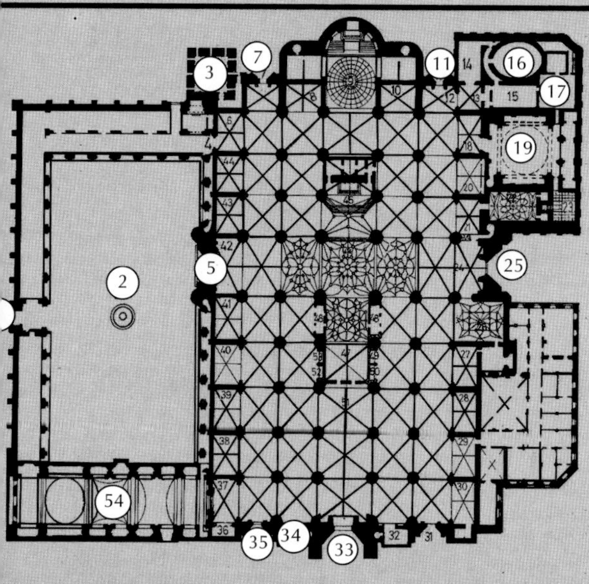

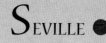

KEY TO PLAN

1.- Puerta del Perdón
2.- Patio de los Naranjos
3.- Giralda
4.- Puerta del Lagarto
5.- Puerta de la Concepción
6.- Capilla del Pilar
7.- Puerta de los Palos
8.- Capilla de San Pedro
9.- Capilla Real
10.- Capilla de la Concepción Grande
11.- Puerta de las Campanillas
12.- Altar de las Santas Justa y Rufina
13.- Capilla del Mariscal
14.- Sala de ornamentos
15.- Antecabildo
16.- Sala Capitular
17.- Patio del Mariscal
18.- Tránsito a la sacristía Mayor
19.- Sacristía Mayor
20.- Capilla de San Andrés
21.- Capilla los Dolores
22.- Sacristía de los Cálices
23.- Patio de los Óleos
24.- Monumento a Colón
25.- Puerta de San Cristóbal
26.- Capilla de la Antigua
27.- Capilla de Hermenegildo
28.- Capilla de San José
29.- Capilla de Santa Ana
30.- Capilla de San Laureano
31.- Puerta de San Miguel
32.- Capilla de San Isidoro
33.- Puerta de la Asunción
34.- Capilla de San Leandro
35.- Puerta del Bautismo
36.- Capilla de los Jacomes
37.- Portada del Sagrario
38.- Capilla de San Antonio
39.- Capilla de Scalas
40.- Capilla de Santiago
41.- Capilla de San Francisco
42.- Crucero Brazo Norte
43.- Capilla de las doncellas
44.- Capilla de los evangelistas
45.- Capilla Mayor
46.- Crucero
47.- Coro
48.- Pórtico del coro
49.- Capilla de la Concepción chica
50.- Capilla de la Encarnación
51.- Encarnación
52.- Capilla de La Estrella
53.- Capilla de San Gregorio
54.- Iglesia del Sagrario

• The original Muslim minaret *was 70 metres high but with Christian additions is now 94 metres. The tower has no staircase but a gently sloping ramp which finishes just below the belfry. It is said that the Castillian king Fernando III rode to the top of the minaret on horseback on the day he entered Sevilla in triumph. The climb is well worth it for the superb views.*

The Giralda

The Giralda in Sevilla is the most slender and graceful of the three surviving Almohad minarets; the others are the Kutubiyya in Marrakesh and the Hasan Tower in Rabat. It is also one of the very few buildings of Islamic Spain left unscathed by Christian intervention as it was left practically untouched, although given new symbolism as the cathedral campanile. The minaret was begun in 1184 by the architect Ibn Basso with a base of stone blocks, some of which were taken from an earlier Roman construction. After a pause of four years work restarted under Ali al-Gomari, this time in brick, and ten years later he finished it off with the *yamur* ,or pinnacle, with four great spheres.

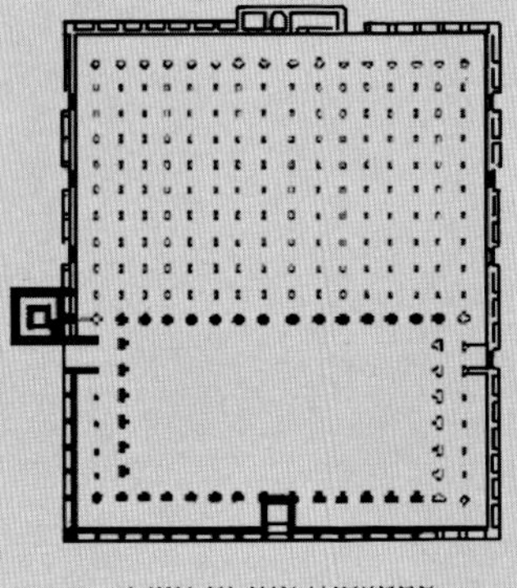

The central body of the tower is made up of chambers with Almohad vaulting placed one on top of the other, around which winds the ramp, narrowing as it ascends. The 1356 earthquake, which damaged the Alcázar (constructed during the reign of Pedro I), also brought down the pinnacle of the Mosque, which was duly replaced in 1400 by a bell-tower. In 1558 Hernán Ruiz the younger, at the height of the Renaissance and during construction of the cathedral, was inspired to add five separate, ascending elements to the extant body of the campanile. The first and largest is known as Campanas (the bells), followed by Reloj (the clock), Estrellas (the stars), Redondo (the round one) and, highest of all, Penacho (the summit). Topping it all, as did the *yamur* before it, is the Giraldillo, the winged statue, symbolising the triumph of the Christian faith.

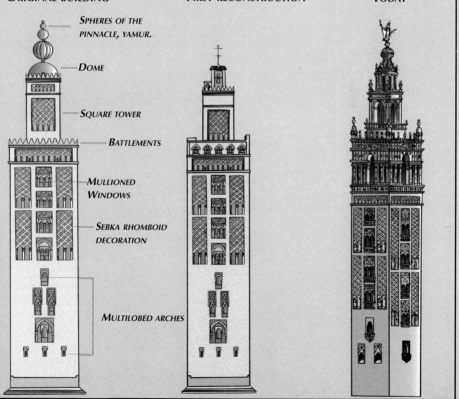

ORIGINAL BUILDING

SPHERES OF THE PINNACLE, YAMUR.

DOME

SQUARE TOWER

BATTLEMENTS

MULLIONED WINDOWS

SEBKA RHOMBOID DECORATION

MULTILOBED ARCHES

FIRST RECONSTRUCTION

TODAY

•FAÇADE OF THE PALACE OF DON PEDRO. *This palace, of Abbadid origin, was rebuilt for king Pedro by craftsmen from Granada and Toledo, accustomed to adapting the remains of old Almohad palaces to the new taste for the Mudéjar style. This style incorporates Islamic designs, decorations and techniques into essentially Christian-style buildings; multilobed arches abound, bricks are laid in rhomboid patterns (sebka), wood is used as a decorative element and walls are adorned with inscriptions in Arabic*

cursive script. Granadan architects copied this type of façade from the Mexuar of the Alhambra (see above).

•ENGRAVING OF THE ROYAL CITADELS

THE ROYAL CITADELS *(Reales Alcázares)*

The Royal Citadels date back to the X century caliphal palace-fortress. The palace complex has been adapted and remodelled according to the needs and tastes of succeeding monarchs up to the present day.

Archaeological excavations have revealed that in Roman times an important commercial and military settlement existed at this point on the banks of the River Guadalquivir. It was from the XI century, however, during the Abbadid dynasty, that the area became the centre of an influential *taifa* kingdom, following the caliphal tradition. Invasions by the Almoravids in 1086 followed by the Almohads in 1146 introduced features that are typical of Sevilla today, such as pools, arches and courtyards containing fountains, trees and flowers. This

• **THE COURTYARD OF THE MAIDENS** *(Patio de las Doncellas) was the centre of palace life, as can*

be seen by its proportions and decoration. The ground floor (XIV century) is in the Mudéjar style, with multi-lobed arches, paired columns and a tiled dado. Above it is a XVI century arcaded gallery with balustrades, which is nevertheless in perfect harmony with the very different architectural style below.

On these pages are several views of the patio.

Almohad style spread throughout the Moorish lands of al-Andalus as far as the Alhambra Palace in Granada, where it is still admired seven hundred years on.

After Sevilla fell to Ferdinand III in 1248, his son, Alfonso X had a Gothic palace constructed, and it was during this period in Sevilla and also in Toledo that the uniquely Spanish architectural style known as Mudéjar developed. It represented the complete synthesis of two cultures, in which Almohad decorative styles were incorporated into Gothic Christian art. The summit of understanding between the two cultures was attained during the reign of Pedro I of Castilla, who placed personal and political relationships above religious beliefs. Ten years after the earthquake of 1356 he had the Muslim Alcázar reconstructed as a royal palace. Renaissance tastes became prevalent in Spain during

• The Courtyard of the Dolls (Patio de las Muñecas) (150° view). A small intimate patio with a delicate air and intricate decoration clearly influenced by the Nasrid style. The upper floors (right) are a XIX century restoration.

•XIX century engraving of a moorish patio.

the reign of the emperor Charles V and their influence is particularly evident in the Courtyard of the Dolls (Patio de las Muñecas) (above), with its columns, coats of arms and other decorative elements. The Hall of the Ambassadors (Salón de Embajadores), together with the neighbouring Courtyard of the Maidens (Patio de las Doncellas), formed the heart of the palace, around which the royal chambers were grouped. Its dimensions and layout follow quite closely those of the earlier Abbadid palace, with splendid triple horse-shoe arches inspired by those at Medina az-Zahara near Córdoba. Nevertheless, the more elaborately worked ornamentation and the brilliance of its colouring is typical of the Mudejar innovations of king Pedro I, and shows clear influence of the Granadan Nasrid style. The Muslim palace already contained many intricately carved capitals plundered from the palatine city of Cordoba by al-Mutamid for his

• **The Courtyard of the Dolls** *(left), Hall of the Ambassadors (centre) and a romantic composition (above).*

beloved Rumaikiya, as Abderramán III is reputed to have done before him for his concubine Zahara in Córdoba. King Pedro I, moreover, probably had the palace remodelled for his lover María de Padilla. The Courtyard of the Dolls also lies within the heart of the palace chambers, but is set somewhat apart and has a more intimate atmosphere. Its elegant proportions have retained their charm despite innovations such as later additions to its height. The columns of various hues (left) hardly seem capable of bearing their capitals, which increases the overall impression of fragility. The delicate rhomboid stucco-work, dating from Almohad times, contributes still more to the air of transparency and grace. The wooden lacework above the doorways and lining the ceilings is an outstanding feature of the Alcázar. The designs of

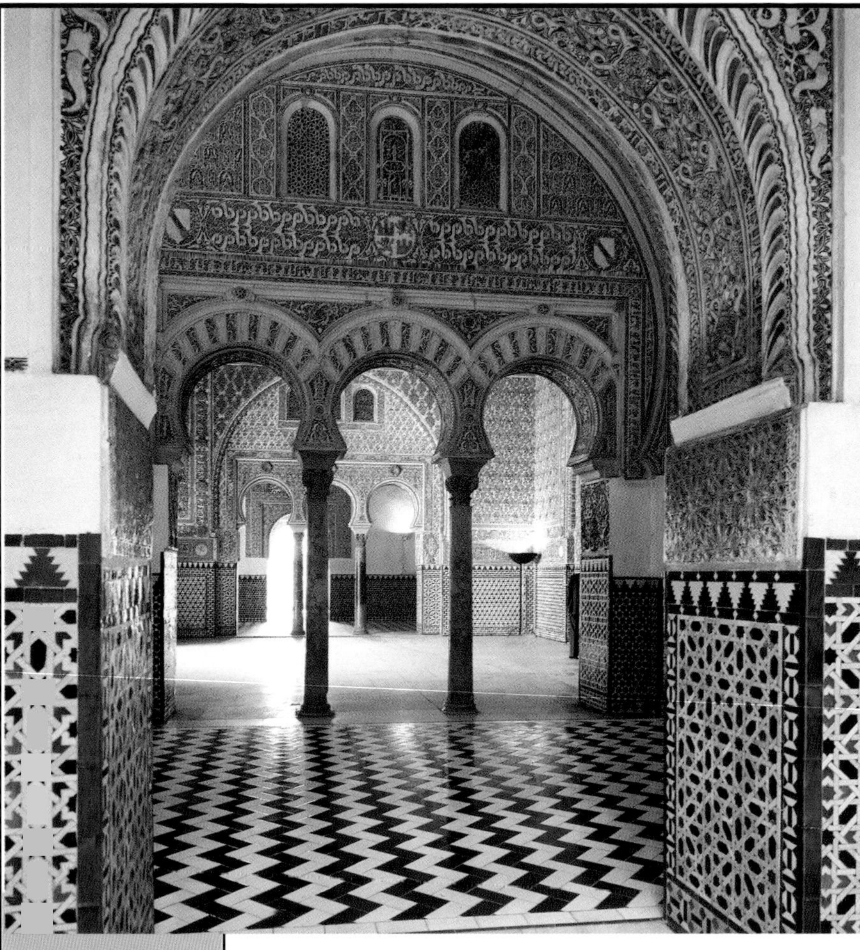

• **HALL OF THE AMBASSADORS.** (*above and previous pages*).

• *Right: a tapestry-map of Charles V's Tunisian war. (Spain appears as though viewed from central Europe, i.e. upside down.)*

• *Opposite: wooden ceilings in the palace, dating mainly from the time of the Catholic Monarchs.*

this type of work, usually carried out by Moorish carpenters, were predominantly geometric in accordance with Islamic law and thus readily adaptable to different ideologies. For this reason they are often found adorning Castilian churches and palaces. Furthermore the content and composition of such designs were susceptible to almost unlimited development. The gardens of each succeeding culture form an essential aspect of the palace complex and indeed gardens were always considered to be interrelated with the buildings around them and created as part of the architectural whole.

THE ROYAL PALACES

One of the most remarkable things about the Royal Palaces is that they reflect the entire modern history of the city. Building and alteration work took place over ten centuries and so the buildings comprise the essence of each moment of that history as it was lived and of each artistic influence, native or foreign, worthy enough to leave its mark. The Alcázares, or royal citadels, are thus a synthesis of architectural and decorative art from the caliphate onwards.

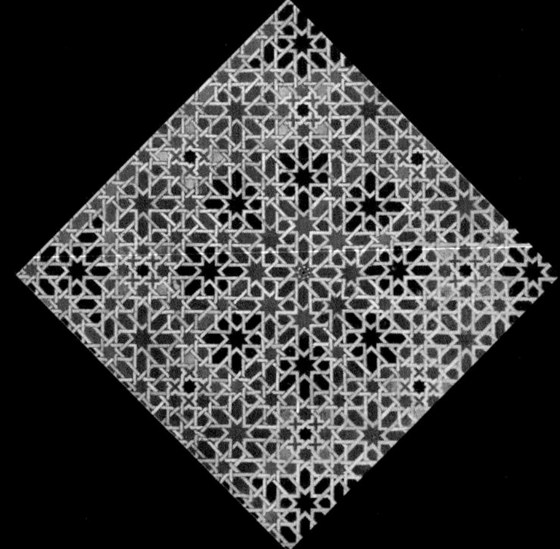

• GEOMETRIC DESIGN

In Islamic art a repetitive geometric rhythm is one way of expressing the unity of God and mosaic decoration is an especially suitable medium for this reiteration.

Almost all of these mosaics were made by Muslim craftsmen working for Christians, and although some were brought here from the Alhambra in the XVI century we should not forget that there was an important cultural and commercial interchange between Granada and Sevilla as early as the XIV century. The demand for Granadan potters was especially great and many set up workshops in the Triana district of Sevilla, some of which remain to this day.

• **THE PALACE GARDENS** *have undergone many changes over the centuries and little remains of the originals but they are still impressive in their size and variety of styles, from discrete Mannerist corners to Romantic arbours.*

• **CHARLES V PAVILION** *and view of the gardens. The emperor Charles' wedding to princess Isabel of Portugal in 1526 in the rich city of Sevilla clearly demonstrated his interest in the city. For this event he remodelled the Alcázar and ordered this Mudéjar-Renaissance pavilion to be built by Juan Hernández.*

• *This XVI century tiling in the Courtyard of the Maidens is a good example of the evolution of ceramic mosaics which for centuries have decorated the wainscoting of Sevillian houses.*

• *The Santa Cruz district was the mediaeval Jewish neighbourhood and still retains its maze of narrow streets and alleyways. The houses, following the Muslim tradition, are centred around a closed patio filled with plants and flowers, which in later centuries would be opened up with windows protected by wrought-iron grilles.*

• **YARD OF WASHINGTON IRVING'S HOUSE.** *This is in the Callejón del Agua (Water Lane), named after the aqueduct which passed through here carrying water from the village of Carmona to the Alcázar.*

• *Right:* **PLAZA DE ALFARO** *the setting for the opera 'Figaro'.*

THE SANTA CRUZ DISTRICT

Although it was reconstructed in the early twentieth century, this quarter still expresses the very essence of Sevilla. It was here, around the Alcázar, that Ferdinand III and Alfonso X gave the Jews a home after their expulsion from Moorish territory. The Jews were well treated by Pedro I during the XIV century, but suffered severe persecution

in 1391 and were finally expelled a century later, when their synagogues were converted into Christian churches. This district of Sevilla, which retains its secular structure, reflects the urban development of the city both in Muslim and Christian times. The Moors ignored the rigid geometry of Roman architecture and

their whitewashed houses crowded together in the *jaima* around the mosques, their daily meeting places, in a labyrinth of streets and blind alleys. These were very narrow, to provide protection against the harsh summer sun, while the houses were constructed around yards containing a fountain or well and abounding with vegetation. The Christian reconquest brought with it the introduction of squares and open public spaces. The Santa Cruz quarter is a mixture of these elements: the inner

•**Plaza de la Santa Cruz** *is the most typically Sevillian of squares, with its wrought-iron balconies and small lanterns hanging from the Cruz de la Cerrajería, the central cross, which is a masterpiece of XVII century Baroque ironwork. The painter Murillo was buried here.*

courtyard, previously a private space, is now open to view, but discreetly, through barred windows and doorways. A fresh surprise awaits the visitor around every corner.

The Hospital de los Venerables

This former shelter for destitute priests was built in the late XVII century in the Baroque style with a simple rectilinear courtyard and an exuberant chapel that constitutes one of the finest examples of Andalucían Baroque, containing paintings by Valdés Leal. Murillo also painted works for this foundation, and his house-museum stands nearby. Today it is the headquarters of the Focus Foundation.

Another delightful area is that formed by the callejón del Agua and calle de la Pimienta, while the most well known of all is the tree-lined Plaza de Doña Elvira, near to the former Corral de Comedias, where open-air music is often staged. The white and yellow-ocher houses contrast with the vivid colours of the ceramics in the workshops, which are so characteristic of the Triana district of Sevilla. Also worth seeing are the Plaza de Alfaro, the setting for the opera

•**Don Juan,** *the famous Sevillian libertine, was originally invented by Tirso de Molina, although his fictional character may well have been based on don Miguel Maraña, founder of the Charity Hospital. Later authors and composers inspired by the subject include Molière, Mozart, Dumas, Byron and Zorilla. There is a statue of don Juan in the Plaza de Refinadores.*

• *Below:* **THE FAÇADE OF PILATE'S HOUSE** *(Casa de Pilatos), a sumptuous palace built by Don Fadrique Enríquez de Ribera on his return from a pilgrimage to Jerusalem in 1519, with its classical triumphal arch is reminiscent of that of a Roman villa.*

"The Marriage of Figaro", and the Plaza de la Santa Cruz, with its magnificent XVII century wrought-iron cross. In the Plaza de los Refinadores stands the proud statue of the seducer, don Juan, a native of Sevilla, who achieved world fame in the works of Molière and Mozart, among others.

PILATE'S HOUSE (La Casa de Pilatos)

The Renaissance arrived in Spain in the early XVI century, imported by enlightened noblemen such as Tendilla and Mendoza, who were to have an enormous influence on contemporary architecture. In Sevilla, don Fadrique Enríquez, Marquis of Tarifa, enamoured of the splendour of Italian classicism, commissioned this palace, which was to become the inspiration and guide for so many other distinguished mansions in the city after 1533. The façade of the building, with its classical arches, is reminiscent of a Roman villa. The name of the palace refers to the house of Pontius Pilate in Jerusalem, where its owner had been on pilgrimage. The effects of this pilgrimage on don Fadrique served as the inspiration for the Holy Week processions in his native Sevilla. The central courtyard is pure Italian classicism: two large

sculptures, the Greek goddesses Ceres and Minerva, preside over the corners;

busts of emperors line the walls, and in the centre is a Genovese marble fountain beneath a statue of Janus, the Roman god whose two faces gaze backwards towards the old and forwards to the new. The first floor features a Gothic balustrade and Renaissance arches, whilst the Mudéjar influence is represented by socles, stuccoed panelling and arches above plain columns. This juxtaposition and mixing of styles in a harmonious blending of elements and materials produces a wonderful sense of balance, the essence of

• **THE CENTRAL COURTYARD** *of the palace, containing a mixture of decorative elements, Renaissance forms and classical sculptures. Right: an engraving of the same courtyard.*

• *The Casa de Pilatos is home to an extraordinary wealth of art treasures.*

what has come to be known as the Sevillian style. One further attraction, quite as interesting as the palace itself and its surroundings, is the extraordinary archaeological collection displayed in this courtyard and in the two gardens known as el Grande and el Chico.

The descendants of the Enríquez de Ribera family, who later intermarried with the Medinaceli family, completed this unique collection with works of classical art and the priceless private archive of the ducal family.

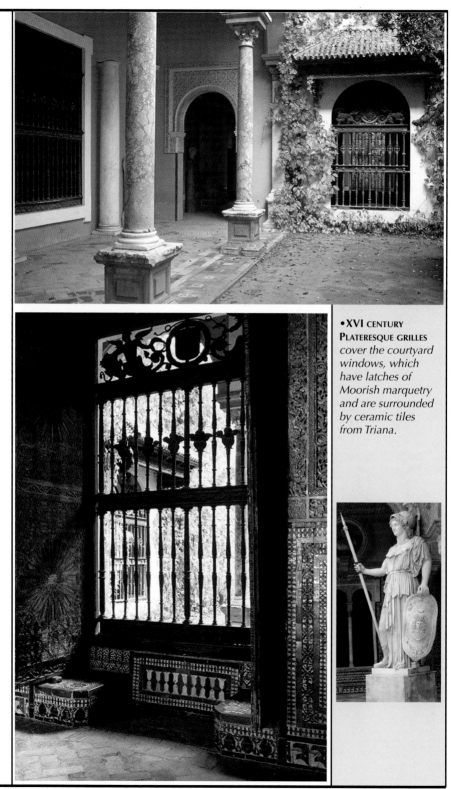

•XVI CENTURY PLATERESQUE GRILLES *cover the courtyard windows, which have latches of Moorish marquetry and are surrounded by ceramic tiles from Triana.*

THE TOWN HALL (Ayuntamiento)

The present-day town hall was built to honour the wedding in 1526 of Charles V to his cousin Isabel of Portugal. The city council decided to move into the Lonja, or merchantile exchange, in the Plaza de San Francisco and construct a new town hall worthy of the royal event and of a city which, after the discovery of America in 1492, was being rebuilt as the financial capital of the empire. Diego de Riaño, who had already worked on the cathedral, supervised the work on the town hall for seven years, during which he built the south and east façades in the purest Renaissance style.

The chapter house upstairs is the repository of the municipal archives, which contain a wealth of important documents concerning the history of Sevilla from the time of the Catholic Monarchs onwards.
The council also owns a valuable collection of XIX century paintings obtained when church property was disentailed in 1835. It includes works by Velázquez, Zurbarán, Valdés Leal and Murillo.

•**A VIEW OF THE TOWN HALL**
This engraving from 1738 shows the cathedral chapter during the feast of Corpus Christi in procession across the Plaza de San Francisco with the town hall in the background.
Below: the arms of Sevilla and the rebus of Alfonso X, 'no-madeja-do' [She (Sevilla) did not betray me].

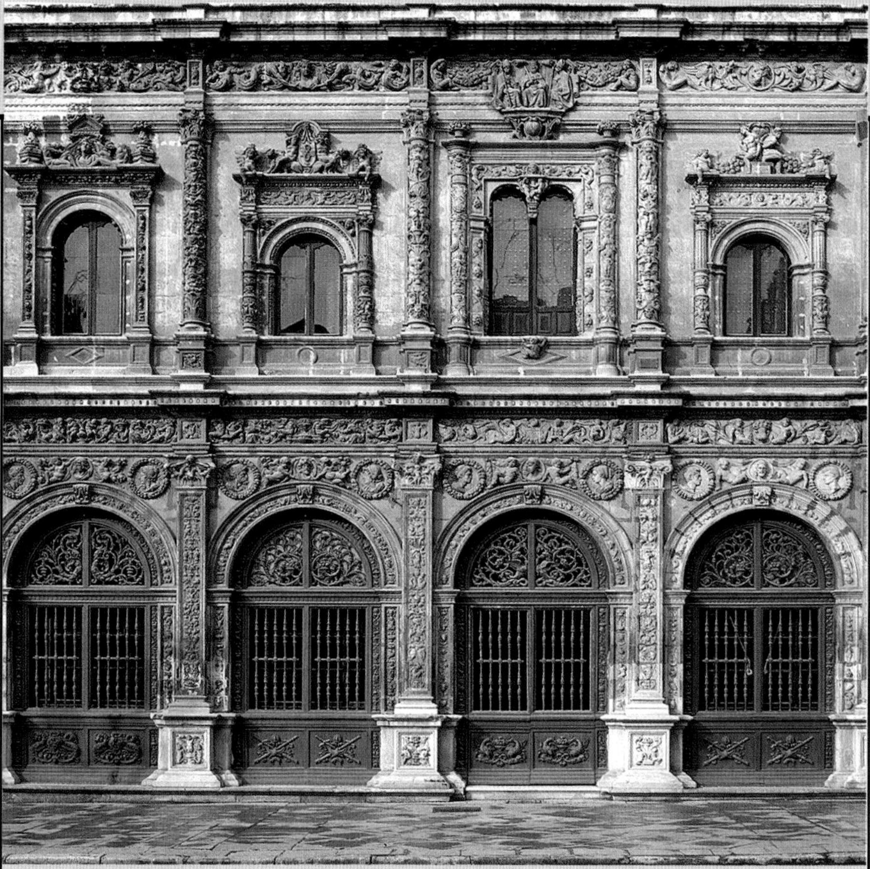

• The east façade giving onto the Plaza de San Francisco. *was built by Diego de Riaño in the first decades of the XVI century when the Renaissance, highly embellished with Plateresque ornamentation, became firmly rooted in Spain. The medallions depict both mythical and historical personages, prominent among whom are Hercules and Julius Caesar, the legendary founders of the city.*

As can be seen from the upper window on the right, the building was never completed. and during the XIX century many difficulties had to be overcome to finish off the other façade giving onto Plaza Nueva.

• The medallions *not only represent classical gods and heroes traditionally associated with the early history of Sevilla, but also details alluding to the recent wedding of Charles V, which serve to emphasise the grandeur of the historic moment.*

• **THE GOLDEN TOWER** *was built as an outpost defensive tower at the end of a spur of the city wall which joined the Alcázar and the city to its water supply.*

THE GOLDEN TOWER *(Torre del Oro)*

Standing on the banks of the Guadalquivir in the Arenal district, is together with the Giralda one of Sevilla's best known symbols.

Built in 1220-1221, the name Golden Tower derives from the gleaming golden ceramic tiles with which it was originally faced, and not from any American gold bullion which it may have housed. In fact, although the treasure ships from the New World unloaded at these docks, the bullion was stored in the nearby Casa de la Moneda (the Royal Mint).Today the Golden Tower houses a small maritime museum.

Photograph taken by J. Laurent in1868.

XVIII century engraving of stevedores unloading at the dockside (from Laborde).

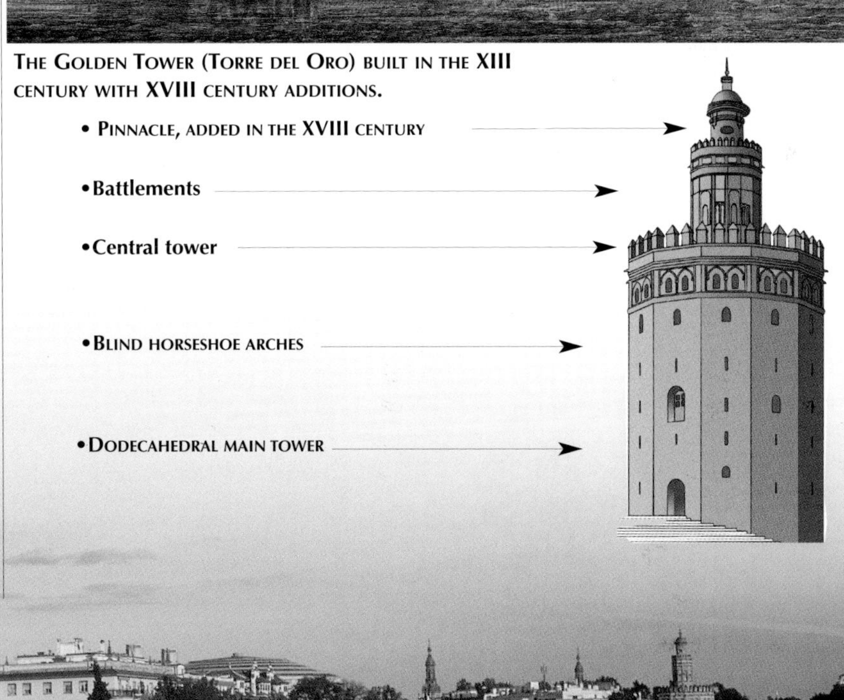

THE GOLDEN TOWER (TORRE DEL ORO) BUILT IN THE XIII CENTURY WITH XVIII CENTURY ADDITIONS.

The Baroque doorway contrasts with the rest of the Neoclassical façade.

THE FINE-ARTS MUSEUM

(Museo de Bellas Artes) is housed in the former Convento de la Merced (Convent of Mercy), a XVII century Baroque building, which is itself a reconstruction of an even older edifice. The museum was set up in 1835 to house the works of art that came into the state's hands upon the disentailment of church property. As an art gallery it is second only to the Prado in Madrid. The collection of Baroque paintings of the Sevillian school is outstanding and it also contains sculptures and collections of ceramics as well as decorative architectural pieces.

'The Virgin of the Caves by Francisco de Zurbarán (XVII century). Room V is the old church.

As in the original convent, a grand staircase provides a frame for the central area, which is divided into three courtyards and the main cloister. On display in the vestibule is a collection of tiles rescued from the convent. Room I contains Gothic paintings by Bartolomé Bermejo and in the Renaissance Room there are works by Gerard David, Torrigiano (left), Lucas Cranach and El Greco, among others. The altarpiece is on show in Room III and in Room IV canvases by Alonso Cano, Vázquez and Pacheco.

Door of la Calahorra castle

'Santiago El Mayor' by José de Ribera, (XVI century).

The erstwhile convent church (Room V) now houses the best of the Sevillian Baroque school, including Roelas' "Martyrdom of St. Andrew", Zurbarán's "Apotheosis of St. Thomas" and canvases by Herrera the elder and Murillo, with the pictures he painted for the Capuchin convent, which has since been pulled down. On the second floor, Room VI contains more Spanish and Sevillian-school Baroque paintings, including a 'St. Paul' by Ribera, and works by the Granadan Alonso Cano. Room VII is devoted to Murillo and his disciples, Room VIII to Valdés Leal and Room X to 17 canvases by Zurbarán, including the famous ones he painted of the monks of the Carthusian monastery, where Martínez Montañés also worked. Room XII contains more of the Sevillian school and Room XIII the Romantics. "The Expiration of Christ" (1575) should not be missed.

El Greco's portrait of his son, Jorge Manuel.

«La Dolorosa». by Murillo, (XVII century).

'Portrait of Don Cristóbal Súarez' de Ribera by Diego Velazquez (1620).

"Canon Duaro" by Francisco de Goya.

• **THE INNER COURTYARD** *is divided into two identical patios, each with a central fountain containing motifs alluding to compassion and charity. They are surrounded and interconnected by galleries of Tuscan arches, which support the upper floor. The walls are decorated with pictures in Dutch tiling.*

THE CHARITY HOSPITAL *(Hospital de la Caridad)*

This Charity Hospital already existed in the XV century but it was not until 1647 that the Charity Brotherhood, then under the spiritual direction of don Miguel de Mañara, re-established it and gave it new impulse. The brotherhood built the Baroque church, with a single nave, and decorated it with pictures and sculptures exemplifying the religious virtues, above all charity, the guiding rule of the order. The artists chosen to furnish the church included Valdés Leal, who left us two exemplary paintings, 'In ictu oculi' and "Finis gloriae mundi', which allude to vanity, death and bodily corruption, and Murillo, who painted six masterpieces of subjects more agreeable to the eye. Most of these were looted by the French marshal Soult in 1810, although some few remain, including "St. John of God with a sick man" and "St. Elizabeth of Hungary curing ringworm". Among the

greatest masterpieces of Baroque sculpture to be found here is Pedro Roldán's Tableau of the Entombment (right), set in a black-and-gold altarpiece, by Valdés Leal. This retable (left) reveals the full repertory of Baroque art and is representative of many other similar ones in Sevilla; a small temple flanked by spiral, fluted (Salomonic) columns which support the entablature. The whole is based upon a play of salient and retreating shapes, shifting geometrical facets and complicated changes in rhythm and movement, all intended to exalt the symbols contained in the tableau within.

• **THE FAÇADE** *is also constructed in the form of a retable (above) with XVIII century tiling. There are two Baroque courtyards inside the building, designed by Falconete, with polygonal fountain basins at the centre and Italianate figures alluding once more to pity and charity.*

• *Left: the entombment by Pedro Roldan*

• Right: the main façade of the bullring of the Real Maestranza. Above: the Prince´s box, dating from the beginning of the XX century; on the facing page: the social headquarters of the Real Maestranza de Caballería

• ENGRAVING OF THE BULLRING *and below: a XIX century drawing of the façade by Richard Ford.*

THE BULLRING OF LA MAESTRANZA

Another emblem of Sevilla is the bullring of the Real Maestranza de Caballería (Royal Equestrian Society), which dates back to the XVIII century. The Noble Brotherhood of San Hermeregildo in Sevilla supported the old tradition of fighting the bull on horseback and Philip V, the first Bourbon king, who was also devoted to this art, duly conferred upon the brotherhood the title of "Royal Equestrian Society". In 1707 the society began to construct a square, wooden enclosure for bullfighting in the popular and somewhat scurrilous Arenal district of the city. The plans and building techniques were constantly being altered until by 1761 part of it, now in stone, was finished to the design of Vicente San Martín. Twenty years later the splendid Prince's box, designed by the Portuguese Cayetano de

Acosta, was finished, and named in honour of the king's son. The bullring used today was not completely finished until 1881. Inside is a museum with exhibits ranging from the beginning of bullfighting to the present day. Among these are bronzes by Benlliure and a drawing by Picasso.

• **THE MAIN FAÇADE OF THE PALACE OF ST. ANTHELM.**, *formerly the seat of the Marine University, it now houses the Andalucían Regional Government.*

MARÍA LUISA PARK

At the end of the XIX century the historic heart of Sevilla around the Jerez Gate (Puerta de Jerez) was subject to substantial urban reform. Part of the garden of the Palace of St. Anthelm (San Telmo) was donated to the city to become María Luisa Park and the Alfonso XIII Hotel was built near the old tobacco factory

PALACE OF ST. ANTHELM

This attractive Baroque building, now the seat of the Andalucían Regional Government, was founded by the Marine University as a residential seminary for naval orphans, and thus its name, St. Anthelm being the patron saint of sailors. In 1788 it was converted into a College of Nautical Studies for the training of pilots and master navigators. Subsequently it became the property of the Duke and Duchess of Montpensier, who made it their residence in 1848, when the palace was one of the landmarks of romantic Sevilla. In addition to the facade by Figueroa, other noteworthy features include the staircase and an elegant columned reception hall.

• **DETAIL OF THE FAÇADE OF THE PALACE, DESIGNED BY FIGUEROA.**

THE OLD TOBACCO FACTORY.

Nowadays the administrative centre of the University of Sevilla, this was one of the largest and most well-known buildings in Spain during the XVIII century and among the

most innovative in pre-industrial Europe. In its day the tobacco factory was considered to be a revolutionary structure, due to such new concepts as its modular layout, drainage, underground network of piping to control humidity within the factory, and a complex system of ventilation. Tobacco curing and production was a lucrative state monopoly in which up to 3,000 women were employed, including the Carmen made famous by Bizet in his opera.

•**Façade of the old Tobacco factory,** *now the seat of the university.*

María Luisa Park

Much of the charm of Sevilla resides in its attractive parks and gardens in the very heart of the city, lending a delicate perfume to the streets in the spring and a coolness to the air in summer. The Alcázar and the Murillo gardens were generously enlarged by Princess María Luisa Fernanda in 1893, when she donated half of her own gardens from St. Anthelm's Palace. This much-needed new space in the city was thus incorporated into the park that bears her name. In the spirit of the times the gardens, laid out by the French designer Forestier, are romantically bucolic, intended to inspire feelings of nostalgia for bygone days of pastoral innocence. They were opened in 1914, and special care was given to the selection of plants and flowers and to the ever-present water in pools, fountains and springs. The park is also in itself an important botanical garden with a superb wealth and diversity of species; it extends over 38 hectares and contains around 1000 palm trees and more than 3000 trees of other species.

•*Above: a photograph by J. Laurent (XIX century) of the Hercules Boulevard*

•**Coat of Arms of the Tobacco factory.**

• **Plaza de España.**
Above: a 180° panoramic photograph.
Taking advantage of the free hand given to him in the design of the project, the architect decided upon a new concept for a colonnaded public space, a peaceful environment in which the emphasis would be on relaxation and communion with nature in contrast to the hustle and bustle of city life which it replaced. This modern approach is nowadays accepted as essential to any healthy urban development.

The Spanish-American Exhibition of 1929

The original idea for the Exhibition arose from the notion of hosting a cultural event of international scope at a time when commercial fairs were in decline, and also of course as an attractive way of encouraging tourism. With this in mind, the architect Aníbal González designed a series of buildings and pavilions to be constructed within María Luisa Park, thus creating the monumental twin spaces of the Plaza de España and the Plaza de América, surrounded by lush greenery. These developments came to be landmarks within the revitalised city of Sevilla. The semi-circular Plaza de España is in the north western area of the park. It has a porticoed gallery and is flanked by two towers 80 metres high. Bordering the square is a canal crossed by Venetian-style footbridges with balustrades adorned with ceramics from the Triana district. The base of the semicircle is lined with benches decorated with panels of painted tiles, each illustrating an episode in the history of a Spanish province. This square was the focal point

of the Exhibition and was designed as a Palladian-style villa. The combination of woodwork, brick and ceramics offered new creative possibilities and reinterpreted the shapes and spaces of the Mudejar architectural style that inspired it. Marble was used as a complementary material to vary the rhythm and to highlight differences in textures, whilst stone was also incorporated as a nod towards the Renaissance.

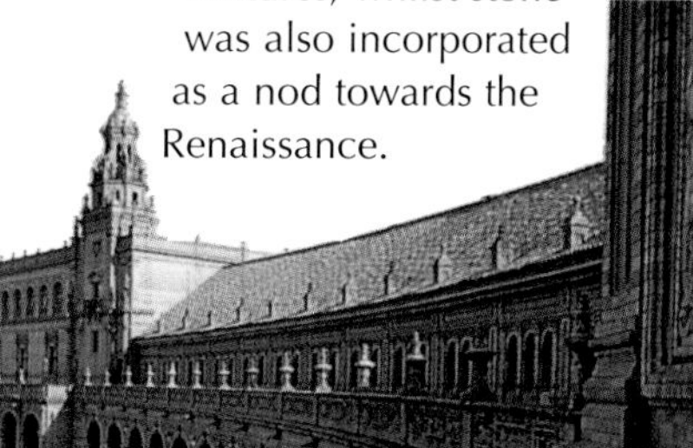

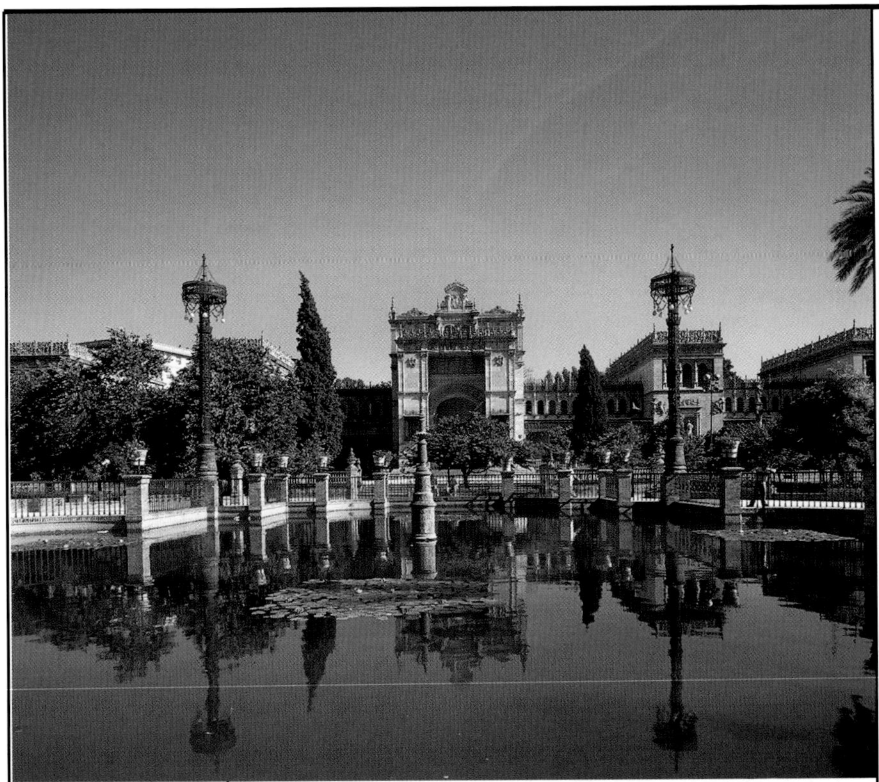

• **The Archaeological Museum** *was founded in 1946 in the neo-Renaissance Pavilion of the Spanish-American Exhibition. It contains an extensive collection of objects from different ages and cultures of the Guadalquivir valley, from the palaeolithic to the XVI century. The most striking single exhibit is the famous Carambolo treasure, a hoard of gold jewellery dating from 650 B.C. The wealth of artefacts from Italica bears witness to the importance and cultural advancement of this Roman town, especially under the emperors Trajan and Hadrian, who incidentally were born there.*

■ **Plaza de América,** at the southern end of María Luisa Park, was designed by Aníbal González as the Spanish-American Exhibition's ceremonial square. It includes a synthesis of all the styles which have gone into Sevillian architecture over the centuries, from Mudejar to Neo-Classic, Gothic-Plateresque to Renaissance and Baroque. This wealth of styles began a new trend which came to be known as "historicist art" or "traditional regionalism". The square is focused around three pavilions: the Mudéjar Pavilion, the Royal Pavilion and the Renaissance Pavillion, the latter of which today houses the Archaeological Museum.

The Royal Pavilion is built of brick and glazed ceramics in the flamboyant Gothic style, known in Spain as Isabelline, a style that was employed in countless churches and monasteries during the late-XIV and XV centuries.

• *The Museum of Traditional Art and Folk Customs was originally the Mudéjar Pavilion and from 1972 the Ethnographic Museum. Although some of the exhibits are older, most date from the XIX and XX centuries, with a great variety of traditional costumes, utensils and tools of all sorts, agricultural implements, jewels, lamps, silver- and glassware and woodwork. There is also an ample collection of the local Triana ceramic ware. Some of the museum's rooms are reserved for temporary exhibitions.*

THE MUDÉJAR PAVILION draws its inspiration from mediaeval Islamic architecture in a subtle synthesis of Caliphal, Nasrid and Mudéjar styles. Nowadays it houses the Museum of Traditional Art and Folk Customs.

THE RENAISSANCE PAVILION houses the Archaeological and Fine-Arts Museums.

• SEMANA SANTA (EASTER) IN SEVILLA. *This is the high-point of the year and the Sevillians work tirelessly for months to decorate the heavy floats borne by volunteers who might have to shoulder up to 50 kilos each for between four to twelve hours..*

The colourful and attractive processions represent hours of selfless effort and organisation, reflecting the penitential spirituality which is the true reason behind what might seem to visitors to be no more than a showy folk festival

FIESTAS AND POPULAR TRADITIONS.

According to long-respected tradition Sevilla's greatest festivals are held in the Spring, almost without cease, as though fulfilling an insatiable desire to live every moment of the season to the utmost. Thus, Holy Week is followed by the April Fair and then by the pilgrimage to the Virgen del Rocío at Almonte in the Doñana national park some kilometres to the south - although attended by brotherhoods from all over Spain, this pilgrimage is very close to the hearts of the Sevillians. Then comes the festival of the May Crosses, which, no sooner over, is overtaken by Corpus Christi.

Semana Santa.

Although Holy Week celebrations have in general been related to former pagan rites of spring, the precise origin of this popular event here in Sevilla, a public manifestation of Christian faith, is more recent. In fact, it dates from the Council of Trent, when the Church encouraged the explicit demonstration of religious feeling, the exaltation of the Eucharist and the dramatised spiritual instruction implicit in the processions. In the sixteenth century, one of Sevilla's

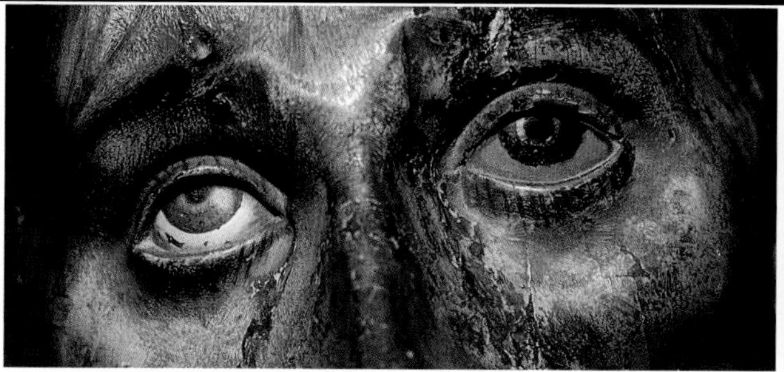

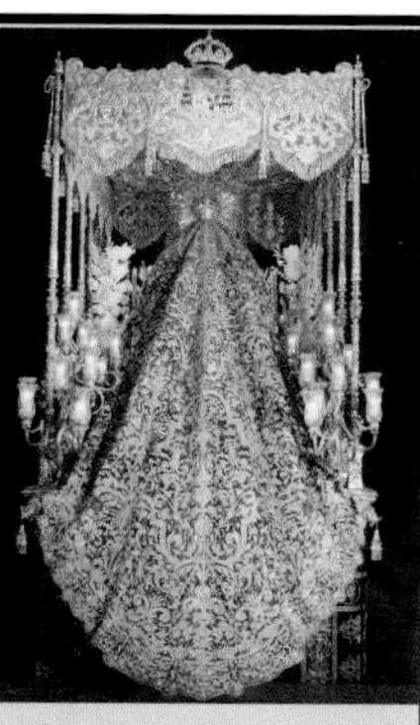

richest knights, don Fadrique de Ribera, on his return from a pilgrimage to Jerusalem decided to re-enact the procession of the Via Crucis he had witnessed there. During the seventeenth century this religious procession was imitated by guilds of artisans and professionals, each bearing the image with which they identified themselves. More than 50 such brotherhoods came into being and during Holy Week they participate in over 100 processions, all following an

established itinerary. The colour and vivacity of some of these processions, including short eulogies to the Virgin sung "spontaneously" to her by devotees in the crowd, contrast starkly to the sombre sobriety of the penitential brotherhoods, which file past in silence, their spirit of sacrifice offering a timely reminder of the depth of religious feeling that lies beneath this otherwise festive occasion.

• **IMAGES OF HOLY WEEK.** *Above: an intricately embroidered silk shawl; above left: The Expiration of Christ; left: one of the Holy Week floats; and below: the 'Cachorro' float leaving the church.*

The exit of the floats from their respective parish churches and their eventual return are the highlights of the processions. The "foreman" directing the float has to give instructions with military precision to guide the bearers shuffling blindly beneath them.
Holy Week in Sevilla is redolent of the scent of incense and melting wax, of jasmine and orange blossom on the night air, and the sound of "saetas", darts of anguished song dedicated spontaneously to the Virgin along the route.

•THE APRIL FAIR (LA FERIA) *Entrance to the fairground is through a monumental gate especially designed and erected anew every year. Inside the enclosure more than 1000 small* casetas *line the avenues of a temporary village, with lights and garlands.*

•LAS CASETAS
The caseta, *as its name implies, is a small house or marquee, normally of canvas, which becomes a home from home for Sevillians during the spring fair. Most are privately owned by groups of associates, although others are set up by large organisations or corporate bodies and are open to the public.*

THE APRIL FAIR

The April Fair is traditionally held a couple of weeks after Easter Sunday. The modern-day fair goes back to the mid-nineteenth century, although its roots lie in the annual cattle markets of

the middle ages, which were commonplace to most towns in southern Andalucía. These commercial occasions were also an excuse for more general revelry and when, with the

rise of commerce and industry, country ways became less important so the revelry ousted the livestock trading. During recent times the fair has seen a boom, with more than 1000 casetas set up in the fairground, known as the Barrio de los Remedios. And here for a whole week

Sevillians eat, drink, talk and enjoy the music and dancing, in fact, live. The

• **THE APRIL FAIR AT THE BEGINNING OF THE XX CENTURY.** *These pictures show the origin of the Feria as a livestock fair, but even today there are horse parades and shows.*

• **THE GYPSY OR FLAMENCO DRESS,** *exuberantly decked out with flounces and frills, is Sevillian in origin, though its popularity has spread to other areas and other fairs. Over time it has been developed and adapted and every year changes according to fashion, but always provides spring in Sevilla with grace, colour and movement.*

casetas are a colourful spectacle in themselves, decorated down to the most exquisite detail, where the townspeople themselves dress in all their traditional finery. The wide avenues of the fairground are a thoroughfare for some of the most elegant, superbly trained horses in Europe, either ridden or harnessed to traditional carriages.

The *casetas* are the rendezvous for parties that go on every night until dawn, when their owners go home to snatch a couple of hours' sleep before returning to the fray. Visitors should bear in mind though that Sevilla is in many ways a very closed society, and should consider it an honour to be invited to a private *caseta.*

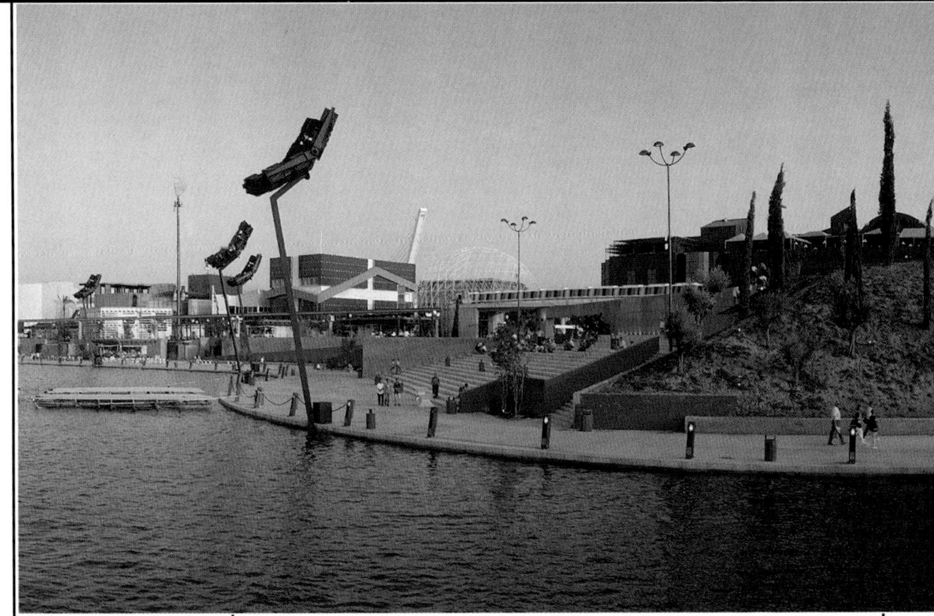

• **EXPO 92**

"Cartuja Island", a flat area of land caught between two branches of the River Guadalquivir, was an ideal site for the International Exhibition of 1992. Eight new bridges were built to connect it with the city.

CARTUJA ISLAND

It was hoped that this strategic area of Sevilla would benefit from Expo 92 both in its infrastructure and technological development but in fact neither of the exhibitions held in Sevilla during the XX century completely lived up to the expectations for future development that had been so grandiloquently aired by the politicians of the day.

THE UNIVERSAL EXHIBITION OF 1992 (EXPO 92)

Nevertheless, some improvements to the city were bound to be made. The pavilions from the Spanish-American Exhibition of 1929 were turned into embassies, institutes, museums and cultural centres. As far as Expo 92 is concerned, some of the "intelligent" buildings constructed on Cartuja Island have had their lives extended in two ways: a science and technology park has been set up with the

co-operation of the University of Sevilla and the private industrial sector to act as an incubator for scientific research; and in the services sector a successful theme park (La Isla Mágica) has been opened, which has also managed to take advantage of some of the buildings around which Expo was centred. The aim of this is to satisfy the increasing demand for multimedia and interactive events, incorporating state-of-the-art technology. One such application is the "Puerta Triana Cultural Space", which seeks to combine culture and entertainment, something which Sevilla has always been supremely good at.

• **THE CARTHUSIAN MONASTRY OF SANTA MARÍA DE LAS CUEVAS** *was founded in 1400, although the church was not built until some fifty years later. It was amplified in the XVI century. The original monastic elements, Gothic, Mudéjar and Baroque, were restored as part of the Expo programme. Christopher Columbus stayed at the monastery when visiting Sevilla and after his death in Valladolid in 1506 his body was brought here for burial before being exhumed and taken off again to Santo Domingo in 1542. It is now a museum, exhibitions centre and the headquarters of the Andalucían Centre for Contemporary Art.*

< ITALICA

After his victory in the second Punic War in 206 B.C. Publius Cornelius Scipio, "Africanus", founded Itálica, the first Roman city built in Spain, for his retired veterans In time the city became one of the most important in the Roman empire, especially after 53 A.D. when the emperor Trajan was born there. He was later to choose another Itálica "old boy", Hadrian, to succeed him as emperor. Hadrian bestowed the honour of *colonia romana* on the area and richly endowed the city with many of the buildings that survive in ruins today. The emperor Theodosius' connections with Itálica are not so clear but he also took an active interest in glorifying the city.

THE HOUSE OF BIRDS
A magnificent tesselated floor showing 32 different species of birds, in a house in Itálica.

•**TRAJAN** *was the first emperor to promote the fortunes of his native Itálica and his successor Hadrian, like Augustus a great builder, made it a colony and richly endowed it with all sorts of monuments.*

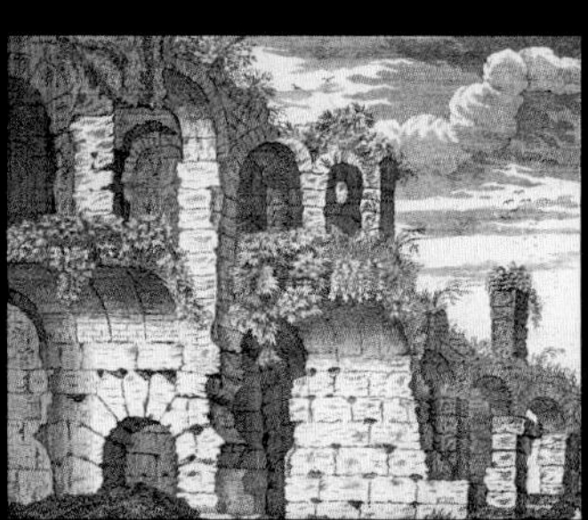

For centuries, but especially in the Romantic age of the XIX century, Itálica has been an inspiration to poets and other writers for the beauty of its ruins. It is salutary, however, to read the graphic accounts of its despoliation during the same century.

• **The amphitheatre at Itálica** *was one of the largest in the Roman world, with a capacity for 25,000 people. It is elliptical, its axes measuring 160m by 137m, and gives us a clear idea of the size of the population at that time. Many of the statues which adorned it are now in museums.*

• **The Mosaics (above: Neptune)**

The importance of this town is also reflected in the streets, which are all of 15 metres wide, compared to the 10 metres of the streets at Pompeii, and their magnificent mosaics which, though sorely plundered over the centuries, remain eloquent reminders of Itálica's past grandeur.

Carmona by D. Roberts

THE PROVINCE OF SEVILLA includes an enormous variety of ecosystems and geographical features. The Sierra Morena mountain range in the north, its lower slopes covered with cork and holm oaks, represents the kind of terrain that for centuries was typical of most of Spain. Very different is the rich river basin of the Guadalquivir, on the banks of which lie Sevilla itself and other important towns in the province. To the south the country becomes hilly again, rising to the Subbetic mountain chain, containing the famous "white villages" of the Provinces of Málaga and Cádiz. And finally, to the south west, the Guadalquivir winds its way to the sea, through the flat wetlands and marshes of the Doñana national park and nature reserve.

•**THE HERMITAGE OF CUATRO VITAS, BOLLULLOS DE LA MUTACIÓN.** *The Guadalquivir flows sluggishly seaward through this cattle-raising area at the edge of the marshes. Numerous farmhouses (cortijos) such as this one at Cuatro Vitas (above) line the traditional route taken by the pilgrims to el Rocío, where curiously this XIII century Almohad minaret was used as a chapel tower for the old hermitage.*

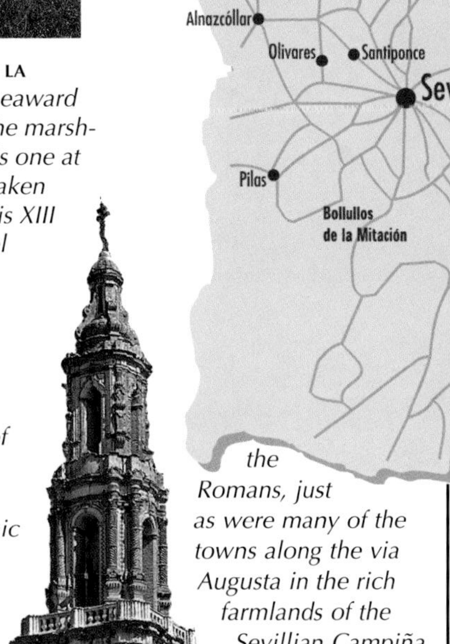

•**UTRERA,** *the church of Sta. María de la Mesa, with a Gothic interior and Renaissance façade.*

The church of San Gil at Écija is a XV century Gothic building but has a Baroque tower, like so many others in this "city of towers". Écija was founded by the Romans, just as were many of the towns along the via Augusta in the rich farmlands of the Sevillian Campiña,. The Muslim defences seen today were built upon the remains of the original Roman wall.

• *The church of St. John the Baptist at Écija is Baroque, as are almost all the church towers in Écija. It is constructed entirely of brick and tile-work cleverly combined in intertwining designs and forms, resulting in an almost Rococo exuberance.*

• **THE CÓRDOBA GATE AT CARMONA,** *although set into the reconstructed Roman city wall, through which the via Augusta passed, dates only from the end of the XVII century. The gate itself, of grandiose and martial mien, is more Neoclassical than Baroque.*

• **THE CHURCH OF SAN PEDRO AT CARMONA.** *The intention of the builders of this church was to pay homage to the Giralda rather than to imitate it and thus they called it "la Giraldilla". It was begun in the XV century and the tower was eventually added in the XVII century. It comprises all the architectural forms and elements which would give rise in the XX century to the neo-Mudéjar style.*

Badonlasa
Estepa
La Puebla de Cazalla
Osuna
Villanueva de San Juan
Montellano
Pruna

• **CARMONA COUNTRYSIDE**
This picture clearly shows the important role played by agriculture in the fertile campiña lowlands from Roman to Muslim times. From the heights of the castle of King Pedro I (now a parador) wheat fields stretch to the farthest horizon.

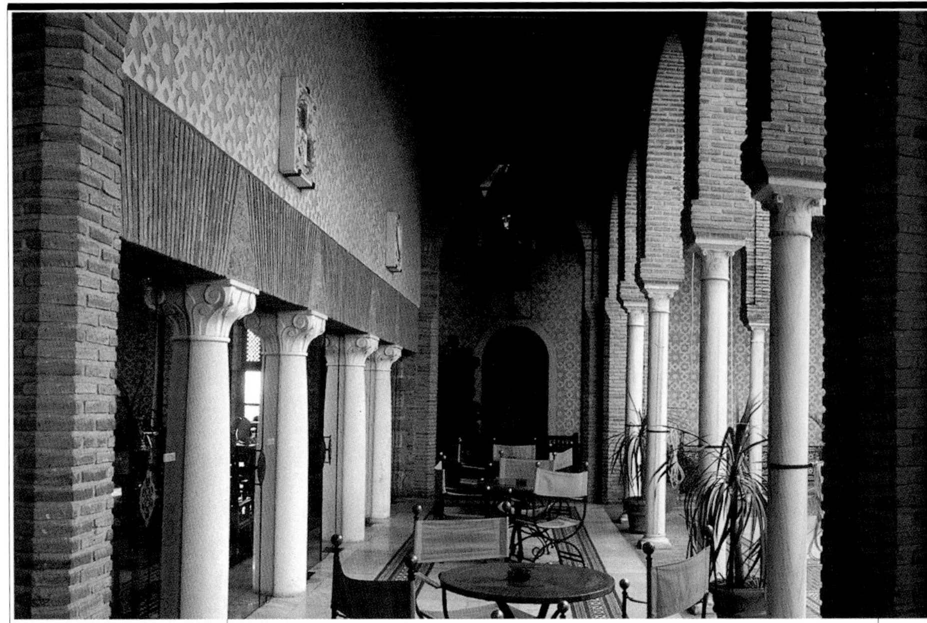

• THE PARADOR

i **TOURIST OFFICE**
• OFICINA DE TURISMO
Puerta de Sevilla s/n
telf..95 595 36 26

G **MUSEUM**

• ROMAN NECROPILIS AT CARMONA
Avda de Jorge Bonsor, 9.
Telf. 95 414 08 11

FIESTAS

• *PILGRIMAGE OF THE VIRGEN DE GRACIA IN SEPTEMBER.*
September.

■ CARMONA

Carmona is an ancient town, probably Tartessian in origin, although its present name derives from the Carthaginians, who called it "Kar-Hammon", or "Town of Hammon", in honour of their sun god. The Romans knew it as "Carmo Romana"; and we can still see the amphitheatre and the remains of what was the necropolis for over 600 years, where there are almost 800 tombs, of which only 250 have been excavated. Some of these are in fact entire villas buried in the ground. Also visible are parts of the wall around the town, including the impressive Sevilla Gate, altered somewhat by the Arabs when they refortified the town. It was a significant stronghold, occupying as it did a key position high above the wheat fields of surrounding countryside, just 40 km from Italica

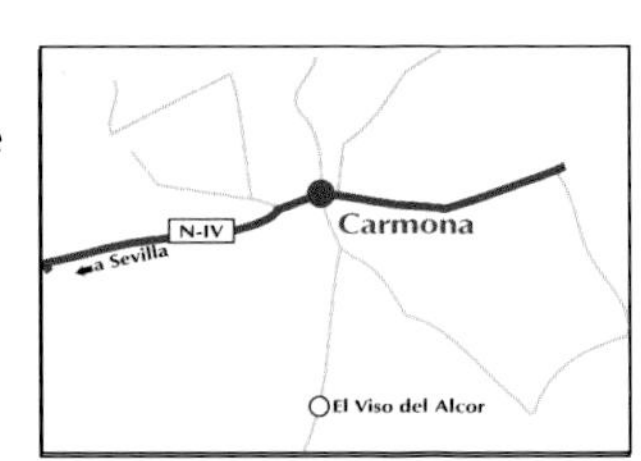

and bordering the calzada, the Roman road along which armies marched and merchants transported much of the wealth of the province. In about 1350, a hundred years after the Christian reconquest, King Pedro I had a palace constructed for his lovers (with dungeons for his enemies) over the former Almohad fortress, known locally as "the High Place". The splendid modern parador (above) was built on the ruins of this palace. The old town centre bears witness to the importance of the town's history with its many noble mansions, churches and convents.

• **THE CHURCH OF SAN PEDRO**. *Below left: the main square, Carmona.*

• **THE FAÇADE** *of a Baroque hermitage in Carmona*

• *Above:* **ALCALÁ DE GUADAIRA.**
Alcalá de Guadaira means "The Fortress on the Hill" and, as its name would suggest, the town has a magnificent Almohad castle with eight crenellated towers. Beneath the castle are the foundations of a Roman fort and astride the river a Roman bridge with seven spans, repaired at the end of the XVIII century. Also to be seen are remains of Roman and Moorish flour mills, which supplied Sevilla long before Alcalá became famous for its own bread.

■ Écija.

The modern motorway from Sevilla to Córdoba follows the old Roman road. Along it just to the east of Sevilla, lying in a small depression on the banks of the River Genil, at its highest navigable reach, is Écija, the Roman "Astygi". Of its Muslim fortress, built on the remains of a Visigothic Christian basilica, only two gates and four towers have survived.

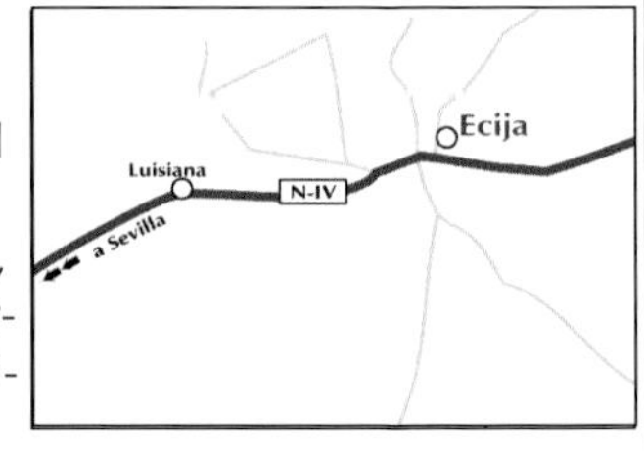

The earthquake that destroyed Lisbon in 1755 caused considerable damage to the town, but relative economic prosperity at the time allowed the citizens to undertake urgent repairs. Indeed, advantage was taken of the disaster to build grand new squares such as the Plaza de España. This is popularly known as "el Salón", a name sometimes given in Andalucía to public areas which serve as places to greet friends and acquaintances during the afternoon stroll at the

weekend. Mansions and churches were restored, but above all the eleven towers, which had suffered badly. These were all rebuilt in a late Baroque style with local peculiarities based on an ingenious combination of colours and materials, chiefly brickwork and ceramic tiling, giving the 'city of towers' its very singular aspect. It is almost possible to refer to an Écija style, which influenced builders way beyond the immediate region. Of the four palaces in the town, two, the Peñaflor, with its long façade (nowadays a *parador*), and the Vadehermoso, are the best examples of this mixture of styles and influences.

•PLAZA DE ESPAÑA (EL SALÓN). ÉCIJA THE CHURCH OF ST. JOHN.

i **TOURIST OFFICE**
Plza. de España. 1. telf. 95 590 29 33-19

•PALACIO DE PEÑAFLOR
Emilio Castelar. 26. telf. 95 483 02 73

•THE FRYING PAN OF ANDALUSIA

Sevillians love nicknames and Écija is popularly known as 'the frying pan of Andalucía', a graphic description of the scorching temperatures during August (which don't go down at night).

•**VIEW OF ESTEPA** *and, right: la Torre de la Victoria, almost 40 metres high, built in 1760, but with no church to accompany it.*

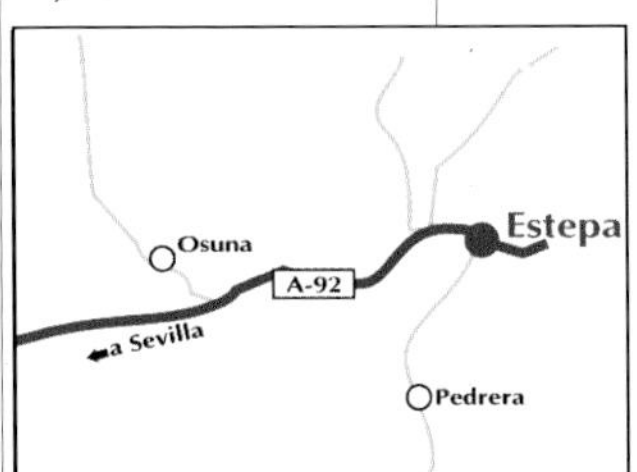

G **MUSEUM**

•**ARCHEOLÓGICAL MUSEUM PADRE MARTÍN RECIO.**
C/Ancha, 14. Telf. 95 591 40 88. Gratuito.

i **TOURIST OFFICE**
•**OFICINA DE TURISMO**
Casa de la Cultura. 22. telf. 95 591 27 71

< **FIESTAS**

- *Pilgrimage in May*
- *Octava Virgen de los Remedios*

■ ESTEPA

This village lying on the slopes of the San Cristóbal ridge is famous for its *mantecados*, or shortbread pastries. The Roman historian Titus Livy reported that in 207 B.C. the inhabitants of "Ostipo" chose to die rather than surrender to the besieging Romans. From the "Balcony of Andalucía" at the top of the ridge a visitor can enjoy wonderful views of the undulating countryside. There are also ruins of the mediaeval walls and the castle keep overlooking the village. Outstanding sights in the village include the Victory Tower (right), with its five brick storeys erected on a stone base, the church of the Assumption and the church of Carmen with a lovely Baroque entrance of stone and black tiles.

■ OSUNA

Osuna also stands on a hill overlooking the wide plain

and is too of Iberian origin. The Romans called it "Urso", but probably not because of the bears that inhabited the area during those days. Then came the Muslims, followed by the Christian reconquest in the XIII century in a similar pattern to the history of all these large villages in the Andalucían countryside, reflecting the constant ebb and flow of political intrigue and conquest.

Osuna was one of the frontier towns between the worlds of Islam and Christendom. The town was controlled by the Order of the Knights of Calatrava, led by the Girón family, who were the driving force behind its growth and renewed prosperity. In 1562, after the foundation of the University in 1548, Pedro Téllez Girón was honoured by King Philip II with the title of Duke of Osuna. The town soon became an important intellectual and artistic centre with new churches and aristocratic palaces and mansions.

• MONASTERY OF LA MERCED OR CONVENT DE LA ENCARNACIÓN

Córdoba

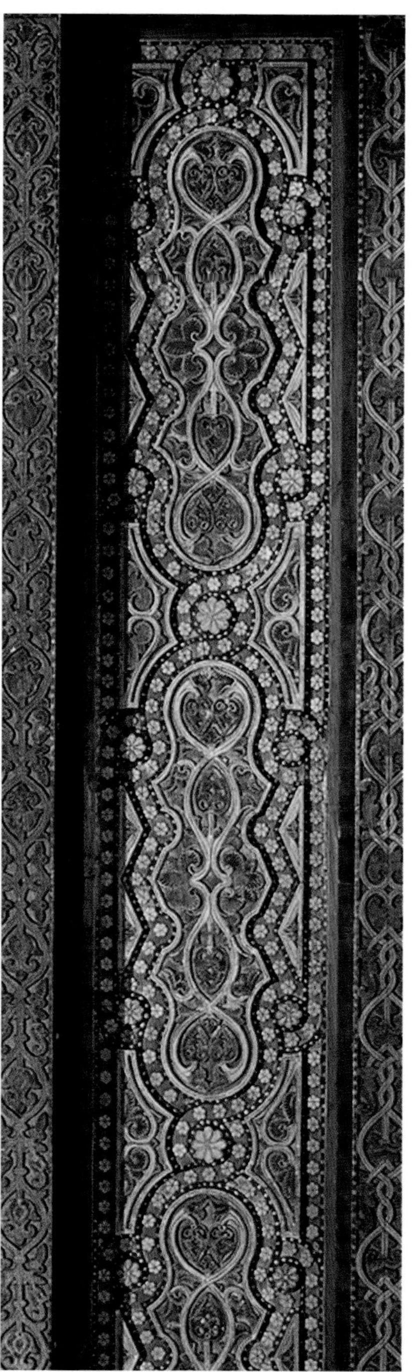

The city of Córdoba lies on the north bank of the river Guadalquivir, nestling in the foothills of the Sierra Morena. To the south the province of Córdoba opens into wide fields of wheat and distant olive groves. It is one of those cities whose privileged position has always made it the centre of events that have moulded human history and culture. Muñoz Molina writes in his book *Córdoba de las Omeyas,* which offers possibly the most refreshing and objective view of the city, *"Córdoba is not a decadent town, one of those haughty cities languishing in its own past, in which life becomes stifled (...) it maintains its own elegant poise, made of the web of dreams and the substance of time itself ...; there are places here which seem to contain the entire essence of the universe hidden and untouched. Córdoba only gives a glimpse of her true beauty to those who stroll unhurriedly, to those who have time to appreciate in every street a wall enclosing an ancient convent or the columns that once embellished the façade of a noble palace, or perhaps a courtyard giving off the freshness of a cool well in the burning heat of a summer's day".*

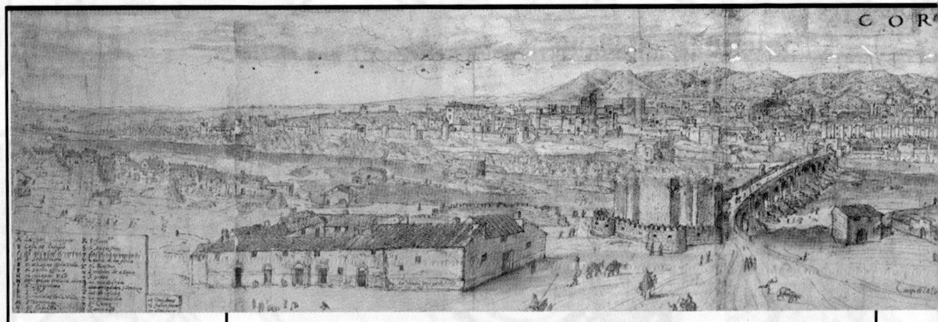

• **A VIEW OF CÓRDOBA** *drawn by Anton van den Wyngaerde in 1568*

• **LITHOGRAPH OF THE BRIDGE GATE** *(1836).*

• **SENECA.** *Lucius Annaeus Seneca (4 – 65 A.D.) was born into an aristocratic Córdoban family and became one of the foremost philosophers of Roman times.*

THE HISTORY OF CORDOBA

The Romans first arrived in Corduba, as it was known at that time, in 206 B.C. and made it an official colony in 169 B.C. Patrician Roman families soon settled there and in 152 B.C. it became the capital of Baetica, or Lower Hispania. In 45 B.C. more than 20,000 of its inhabitants were slain by Julius Caesar for supporting the sons of Pompey in the Roman civil war but the city managed to maintain its power in the region until the emperor Diocletian moved the capital to Hispalis (modern-day Sevilla) during the third century A.D. One illustrious son of Córdoba was Nero's tutor, Seneca, the stoic philosopher, whose ideas embodied the spirit of the Andalucían people and whose attitudes became quintessential to popular belief. Other famous sons of the city were the poet Lucan and the early Christian bishop Hosius. Córdoba was virtually destroyed when barbarian tribes invaded from northern Europe in the V century, but recovered slowly until in 711 Arabs from North Africa ousted a weakened Visigothic monarchy and five years later made Córdoba the capital of al-Andalus. This was the beginning of a new period of splendour, particularly from 756 onwards when Abd ar-Rahman I, the last survivor of the Umayyad dynasty from Damascus, the rest of whom had been slain by the rival Abbasid family, founded a new dynasty and independent emirate here. The new emir set up in Córdoba a strong, centralised state, based not upon the old desert tribal regimes, where each new ruler was elected by vote amongst the elders, but rather upon a power base of trade and commerce, thus paving the way for the succession of his own descendants to the throne, the most important of whom was to be Abd ar-Rahman III. At the beginning of the X century Abd ar-Rahman III managed to stifle the endemic spirit of revolt among the local populace and in

• **THE TEMPLE OF CLAUDIUS MARCELLUS.** *The columns now standing in front of the town hall were reconstructed from a Roman temple.*

•Historical documents
There are many extant documents that testify to the scientific and artistic legacy which al-Andalus left to the western world. Among the many scholarly disciplines that Arab culture introduced to Europe were cartography and surgery

•Madinat az-Zahra *According to legend Abd ar-Rahman III built this royal city some eight kilometres from Córdoba for his favourite, Azahara. (936-1010)*

929 took to himself the title of caliph and extended his power throughout the Iberian peninsula and much of North Africa. With the new caliphate, independent of Baghdad, Córdoba's period of greatest splendour began and lasted for more than 100 years. The caliph renovated and added considerably to the Great Mosque, founded by his forbear Abd ar-Rahman I in 784 and extended by Abd ar-Rahman II in 833. At vast expense he also began to build Madinat az-Zahra, the richest and most luxurious royal city the western

•A forest of columns *in the Great Mosque.*

• A manuscript *from the library that existed in Córdoba during the caliphate of al-Hakan II.*

• The caliph Abd ar-Rahman III *consolidated the prosperity and prestige of the caliphate which he himself founded. Left: two likenesses of the caliph, both made after his death.*

• **AVERROËS** *(born Córdoba1126, died Marrakech 1198), renowned for his treatises upon medicine, mathematics and astronomy, but above all for his philosophical works.*

• **MAIMONIDES** *(born Córdoba 1135, died Egypt 1204), a great Jewish scholar, philosopher and physician. At the age of twenty-three he was forced to flee with his family to Fez to escape religious persecution at the hands of the fanatical Almohads in al-Andalus.*

world had ever seen. When Abd ar-Rahman III died in 961 his son al-Hakan II continued with the work on these great building projects. At this time Córdoba probably equalled Constantinople and Baghdad in wealth and power; it was famous for its libraries and scholars and is said to have contained at its height 3,000 mosques and 100,000 shops. Al-Hakan's throne was usurped by the general Abu Amir Muhammad al-Mansur, who completed the construction of the Great Mosque and other public works, but by appointing a series of mediocre generals to positions of high office by 1013 had led the caliphate into ruin and by 1031 into complete demise, when its territories disintegrated into a series of petty kingdoms known as *taifas.*

Intellectual apogee.

The decline of the caliphate was accompanied by an upsurge in learning and intellectual enquiry with the appearance of such renowned and influential figures as the poet ibn Hazam (994 - 1064), the philosopher and jurist Averroës (1126 - 1198) and the Jewish theologian and physician Moses ben Maimon, otherwise known as Maimonides (1135 - 1204), who wrote, among many influential works, the Mishne Torah, a learned commentary on the Jewish code of law. Among the most important *taifa* kingdoms was Sevilla. This kingdom eventually absorbed Córdoba into its realm and its ruler al-Mutamid was about to restore the caliphate when once again intrigue, internal feuding and constant harassment from the Christian kingdoms to the north ruined his plans. He asked for help from the Almoravids, a fanatical north-African desert tribe, who promptly invaded the peninsula in about 1085, setting back the Christian advance on the south by some two centuries.

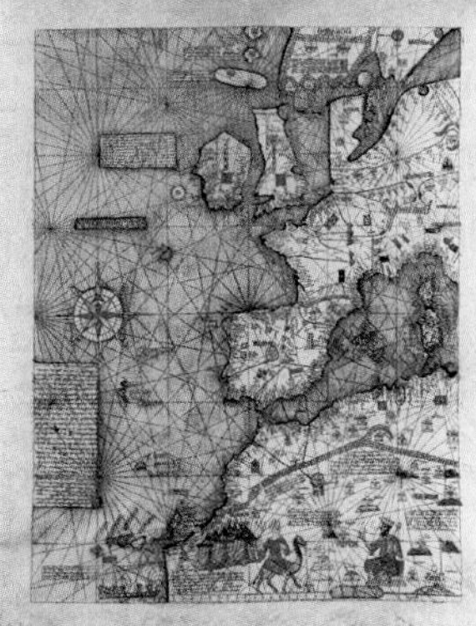

•**HISTORICAL DOCUMENTS**
There are many extant documents that testify to the scientific and artistic legacy which al-Andalus left to the western world. Among the many scholarly disciplines that Arab culture introduced to Europe were cartography and surgery

•**MANUSCRIPT COPIES** *of the Koran from the Almoravid period, above.*

• **THE ALBOLAFIA MILL,** *really a water wheel, is situated just down-river from the Roman bridge. It dates from the XII century and is typical of the hydraulic ingenuity of Andalucían Muslims. These great wheels were rotated by the current generated in deliberately constructed mill races, or weirs, and lifted the water with their paddles carrying earthenware containers, from whence it was collected both for drinking and irrigation. Such systems were used widely throughout the Muslim world during the middle ages and are still to be found in use to this day. Here at Albolafia the water wheel is just one of a chain of four mills situated on a line of small islands between weirs stretching across the whole river. Today the area is a nature reserve just in front of the Great Mosque and is home to many interesting species of birds and animals.*

• **THE SCIENTIFIC LEGACY OF AL-ANDALUS,** *gleaned during the middle ages from the learning of the classical world, was fundamental to the rebirth of learning in the west after the dark ages. Averroës, for example, introduced Aristotle's philosophical ideas to the Christian world and his metaphysical thought, which he brought to Rome and Toledo, served as the basis for philosophical perspectives that have survived to this day.*

•**THE MINARET OF ABD AR-RAHMAN III,** *part of which still survives in the tower of Córdoba Cathedral*

Córdoba

The city

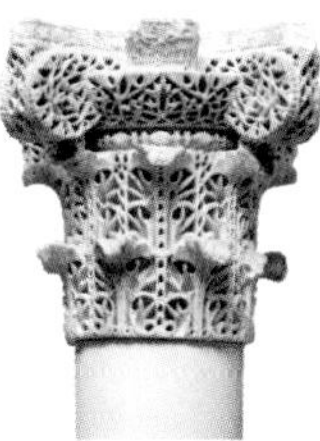

Honeycomb capital.

According to both archaeological remains and extant chronicles, Córdoba's walls at the beginning of the XI century stretched for 22 kilometres, which means that the city was more extensive in the middle ages than it is today, at the beginning of the XXI century. The present-day historical city centre occupies no more than a few hectares on the banks of the river, much too small an area for what was in the X century the most powerful and prestigious city in the western world.

① The Synagogue.

Calle Judíos 10, 957 20 29 28.

This is one of only three mediaeval synagogues remaining in Spain. It was built in the heart of the Jewish quarter at the beginning of the XIV century. Its architecture is in the Mudéjar style and its stucco walls are covered in Hebrew inscriptions.

③ The citadel (Alcázar) of the Christian Monarchs.

Calle de las Caballerizas Reales, s/n 957 42 01 51.

In 1328 King Alfonso XI ordered this fortress to be built close to the Great Mosque upon the remains of previous Roman and Arab structures, including a Muslim bath-house. It was to be called the citadel of the Christian Kings to distinguish it from the nearby castle which had been used by the Muslim caliphs. The Catholic Monarchs, Ferdinand and Isabel, lodged here at times during the long years of the Christian reconquest. It was later used by the Inquisition and then until 1951 as a prison. Nowadays its gardens and fountains lend it a much more agreeable aspect.

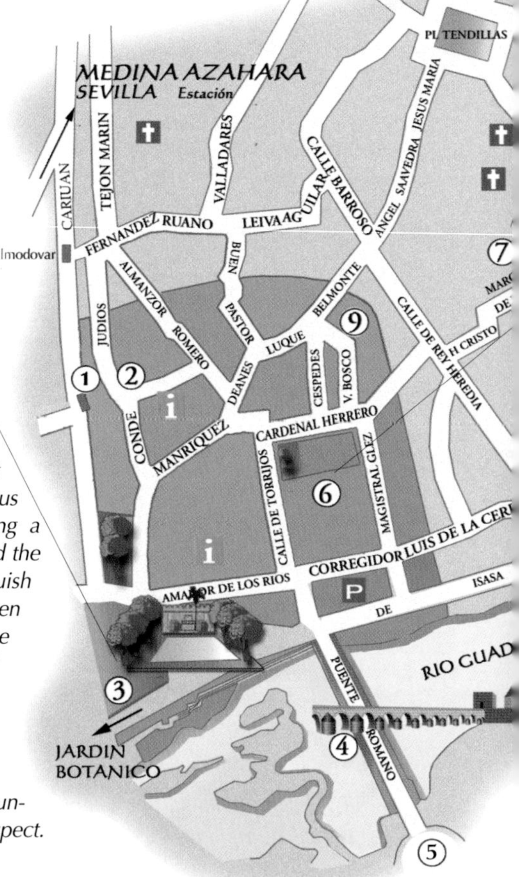

⑧ The Julio Romero de Torres Museum

Plaza del Potro 1, 957 49 19 09.

This museum is dedicated to the work of the famous Córdoban painter, who managed to capture on his canvas the soul of Córdoba's womanhood of his day.

② The Taurine Museum.

Plaza de Maimónides s/n, 957 20 10 56.

This is Córdoba's most visited museum. It contains exhibits representing all aspects of the bullfight together with memorabilia of the great names of the bullring in Córdoba, such as Lagartijo and Manolete.

⑦ THE ARCHAEOLOGICAL MUSEUM.

Plaza de Jerónimo Páez, 7 957 47 40 11.

This museum is worth a visit not only for its exhibits but also for the Renaissance mansion which houses them. It has important local archaeological finds on show from the Roman, Visigothic and Muslim periods.

⑥ THE GREAT MOSQUE

The Great Mosque at Córdoba is one of the world's architectural wonders, the most striking example of Islamic art in the West and also one of lasting importance because of its technical and aesthetic innovations and its influence on the history of western art and architecture.

Palacio de Viana
E DE ALFONSO XIII
CALLE DE SAN PABLO
CAPITULARES
DE MORALES MARIA
CORDOBA
DIARIO
DE LOS RIOS
MAESE LUIS TORNILLO
GUTIERREZ
PAJA
CARLOS RUBIO
CALLE DE SAN FERNANDO
SAN FRANCISCO
DON RODRIGO
8
CALLE LINEROS
LUCANO
CONSOLACION
GRANADA
PASEO DE LA RIVERA

⑨ BLOSSOM LANE

This narrow street, with its brilliantly contrasting geraniums hanging down against whitewashed walls, and the cathedral tower in the background, is perhaps the most representative of many such streets to be found in the old quarter of the city.

④ ROMAN BRIDGE

The Roman Bridge still rests upon its original Roman foundations, although having been the scene of numerous skirmishes and battles, and the victim of daily wear and tear, its superstructure has had to be rebuilt several times during its lifetime.

⑧ FINE-ARTS MUSEUM.

PLAZA DEL POTRO, 1.957 47 33 45.

This museum is devoted mainly to artists of the Sevillian school, with paintings by Murillo, Zurburán and Valdés Leal, among others.

⑤ THE CALAHORRA TOWER

Standing on the south side of the river this tower was the key fortress guarding the mediaeval bridge. Today it houses the Museum of the Three Religions (Muslim, Jewish and Christian) and is designed to show Córdoba's prominence in learning and culture during the X century.

1. Mosque/Cathedral.
2. Conference and Exhibition Center.
3. Palace of the Christian Monarchs.
4. Triumph of St. Raphael (statue)
5. Bridge Gate.
6. Roman Bridge and Calahorra Tower.
7. Arab Water Wheels.
8. Old City Walls.
9. Blossom Lane.
10. Bull-fight Museum and Souk.
11. Old Sinagogue.
12. Chapel of St. Bartholomew.
13. Almodóvar Gate.
14. House of "las Ceas" or "el Indiano".
15. Church of the Holy Trinity.
16. Seat of Military Government.
17. Church of St. Nicholas "de la Villa".
18. Church of St. Hypolitus.
19. Conservatory
20. Compañia Church.
21. Church of St. Victoria.
22. Archaeological Museum.
23. Portillo Arch.

24. *House of the Marquises of Carpio*
25. *Church of St. Francis.*
26. *Museums of Fine-arts and Julio Romero de Torres.*
27. *Inn of the Colt.*
28. *Plaza de la Corredera.*
29. *Church of St. Peter.*
30. *Church of Santiago.*
31. *Town Hall.*
32. *Church of St. Paul.*
33. *Church of the Villalones.*
34. *Church of St. Andrew.*
35. *Church of St. Mary Magdelaine.*
36. *Circle of Friendship.*
37. *Church of Santa Marta.*
38. *Plaza de los Dolores.*
39. *Church of Santa Marina.*
40. *Palace of the Marquises of Viana.*
41. *Church of St. Augustine.*
42. *Church of St. Raphael.*
43. *Church of St. Lawrence.*
44. *Convent of the Trinitarians.*

• The Great Mosque at Córdoba. *Right: a view of the prayer hall. The twin colours, based upon the combination of brick and stone voussoirs, alternating red and white, creates an illusion of space with no defined axis, static whilst at the same time dynamic, opening in all directions at once. Only 856 of the original 1,013 columns remain, the others having been demolished during Christian reforms.*

• Above: the minaret of the mosque at Kairuan (Tunis); below: a view of the mosque at al-Aksa in Jerusalem.

Earlier architectural examples.

After the first mosque at Medina the next to be built were those at Kufa (638) and Amru (642), which already had brick-built columns. Shortly after this the Umayyads, the true initiators of Islamic architecture, raised the Dome of the Rock in Jerusalem. But the mosques which began the architectural tradition in the early years of the VIII century and shaped the direction of later Islamic art were the Great Mosque at Damascus in Syria (also known as the Umayyad Mosque), built in 707 (above: the courtyard of the Great Mosque at Damascus) and al-Aqsa in Jerusalem, built in 710 (below). In all of these mosques the debt to pre-Islamic Christian basilicas is clearly visible, with their naves lined by arches supporting an upper solid stretch of wall upon which a second tier of smaller, more graceful arches is set to let in the light. This structural sequence can be seen quite commonly in classical architecture. The decoration of the walls also clearly falls within this classical tradition, with Roman-Byzantine mosaics depicting other structures and gardens. This was soon to disappear, however, and give way in the great-mosque at Córdoba to what we recognise as typically Islamic designs, based upon the repetition of geometric elements and highly stylised vegetal designs framed by religious inscriptions. The influence of Syrian architectural design spread through north Africa via Qariuan in Tunis and thence to Spain and Córdoba, where eighty years later it would be given a fresh impulse, which improved on many features of the original mosques upon which it was modelled. Unlike the earlier mosques, such as that in Damascus, where the dominating theme of the architecture was strictly aligned, solidly defined and imposingly high, the Great Mosque at Córdoba relies on a new concept of space, horizon-

tal rather than imposingly vertical, static whilst at the same time dynamic, open in all directions. Another anomaly often pointed out is the orientation (qiblah) of the prayer niche (mihrab), which instead of facing Mecca (N112° from Córdoba) is orientated N150°, Various explanations have been put forward for this curiosity, some more curious than the curiosity itself, but the most likely is the entirely pragmatic one that the Muslims had already been using part of the old Church of St. Vincent for some time and when it was converted entirely into a mosque they saw no reason to start knocking down the whole structure to realign it with Mecca. Nevertheless, there have been suggestions that Abd ar-Rahman I orientated his mihrab towards where he first set foot in Spain and in fact N150° from Córdoba aligns directly with the small coastal village of Almuñecar, where legend has it that he landed on Spanish soil.

• **Mosaics.** *In the Umayyad mosque (above) the mosaics clearly follow the late-Roman-Byzantine tradition.*

The hues are predominantly golden upon green-and-blue backgrounds (left: mosaics from the mihrab *at Córdoba.*

• **The prayer hall** *of of the Great Mosque at Damascus, where an impression of height and illumination is achieved by arraying a second tier of lighter arches above the bulk of the columns of the lower arcade.*

• *Above: Engraving of the Great Mosque at Córdoba and the Roman Bridge.*

• *Above: a romantic engraving of the inside of the mosque. Below: wide-angled view from the tower.*

The building of the Mosque

The following commentary is to be found in contemporary Arab chronicles:

When the number of Muslims grew in al-Andalus and Córdoba was flourishing, and Arab princes settled there with their armies, the mosque became too small and they had to attach galleries to the walls, which caused a great nuisance to the people, who suffered a great deal because of the cramped space...

When the Arabs first conquered Córdoba they bought from the Christians half the Church of St. Vincent to use for their Friday prayers and thus the church was shared between Muslims and Christians. The rapid increase in the size of the Muslim population, however, soon rendered this arrangement unworkable and so in 784 Abd ar-Rahman bought the other half of the basilica to erect a mosque on the site. He paid the Christians well for their property and allowed them to build new churches in other parts of the town.

Work on the mosque went apace as the Muslim masons took advantage of building materials already present in the basilica and plundered a lot more, such as columns with their bases and capitals and even shafts of timber, from the surrounding ruins of Roman and Visigothic mansions. The rulers who had

ordered the construction participated very closely in the building work and specialists on the subject have often speculated on whether Abd ar-Rahman had architects brought from Syria or whether he himself designed the mosque. Whatever the truth of the matter, the underlying Syrian influence is quite obvious, but on top of this, local ingenuity contributed new creative architectural and decorative ideas that were to make the design of the mosque at Córdoba a model to be followed by others for centuries to come. The mosque was open for prayer in 785, just a year after work began, although it was not finished by the time Abd ar-Rahman died in 788. It was left to his son Hishan I to put the finishing touches to the square minaret in the courtyard, which was completed in 793.

•Left: the Great Mosque at Damascus. Abd ar-Rahman I was highly influenced by the architectural traditions of the Near East, where he had spent much of his youth. Below: a Turkish miniature celebrating the call to prayer by the first muezzin, who by all accounts was a negro called Bilal.

• **The imposition** *of one row of arches upon another had its architectural precedents in Spain. The Roman aqueduct at Mérida, for example, combines superimposed masonry arches in which brick alternates with stone, just as in the voussoirs of the mosque in Córdoba.*

• **The VI century Church of San Juan de Baños** *is one of several Visigothic constructions in the Iberian peninsula that used the horse-shoe arch long before the arrival of the Arabs in the Spanish peninsula*

• **The structure of the horse-shoe arch,** *is based on the superimposition of arches the individual vertices of which shift in alignment as they descend in the vertical plane of the arch itself.*

The concept of the mosque (in Arabic *mezquita,* meaning "a place to prostrate oneself") originated at the house of the prophet Muhammad when he and his followers met for Friday prayer. It was an open yard in which some palm trunks supported a thatch of woven branches to protect the worshippers from the heat of the sun. There was no tradition of permanent

The Aqueduct of the Miracles at Mérida

architecture among desert dwellers; it was the Umayyads who, under the influence of Greco-Roman tradition, raised the Dome of the Rock in Jerusalem in 687 and the Great Mosque in Damascus in 707. In Córdoba the need for a much wider space than that provided by a high basilica-like structure made a virtue of necessity and thus inspired brilliantly innovative architectural ideas.

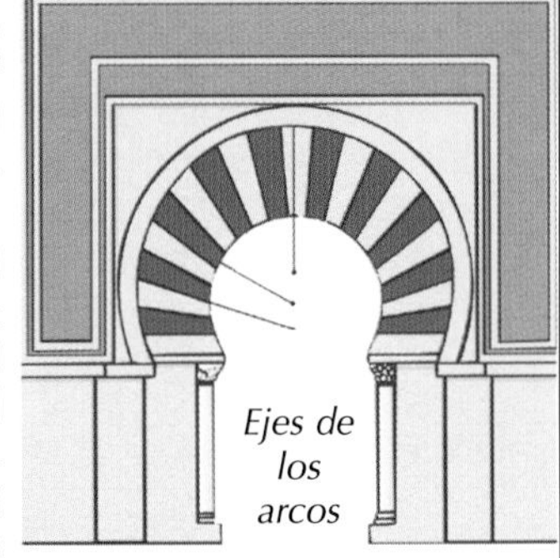

The materials used to build many mosques in Spain at this time were plundered from nearby Roman and Visigothic ruins. In Córdoba the columns found round and about were not so tall as those used in Syrian mosques and could not provide the height required and so the creative genius of the unknown architect, probably inspired by the Roman Aqueduct of the Miracles at Mérida (see above), decided to create first of all

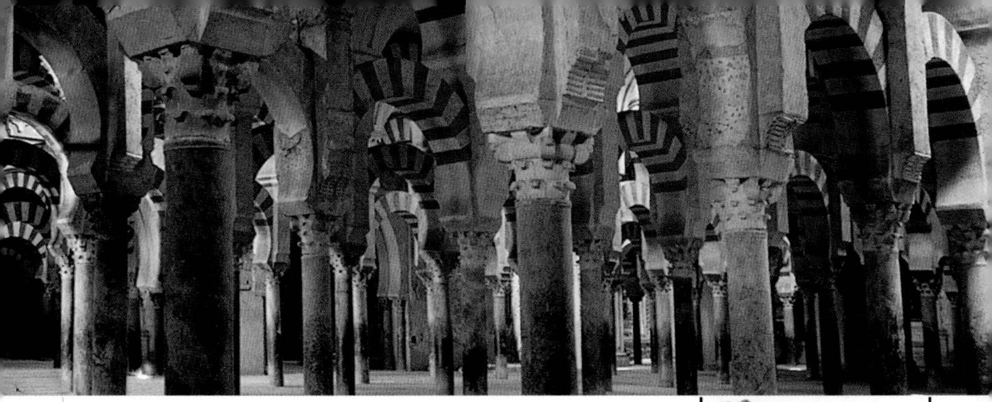

a horizontal line of imposts from which he "hung" the columns of various sizes, making them all the same height by adding extra sections beneath them to build up their bases or else sinking them into the ground if they were too tall. That is say, he evened out their irregularities from below rather than above. Upon the columns he placed the also plundered capitals and above these heavy cymas, or abacuses, in the shape of inverted tree trunks so as

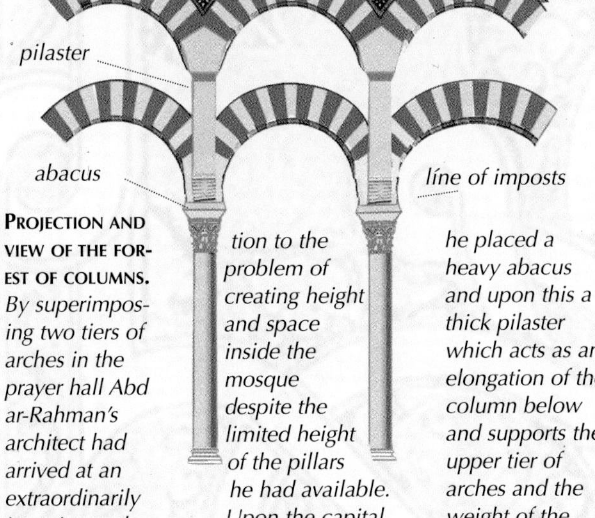

PROJECTION AND VIEW OF THE FOREST OF COLUMNS. *By superimposing two tiers of arches in the prayer hall Abd ar-Rahman's architect had arrived at an extraordinarily ingenious solution to the problem of creating height and space inside the mosque despite the limited height of the pillars he had available. Upon the capital of each column he placed a heavy abacus and upon this a thick pilaster which acts as an elongation of the column below and supports the upper tier of arches and the weight of the roof.*

to gain volume while ascending. On top sit even wider pilasters, their salient shafts adorned with newly crafted mouldings designed in Córdoba. Finally, on top of the pilasters he installed the springings for the upper tier of semicircular arches, which were also wider than the pilasters themselves, all of which supported the roof. But this elegant structure, wider at the top than at the bottom, was intrinsically unstable and in danger of collapse and so the architect came up with the ingenious solution that makes the Córdoba mosque so special: he fitted in a lower tier of horse-shoe arches resting upon the abacuses and abutting crosswise with the width of the pilasters supporting the upper arches, thus acting as tie beams to brace the whole structure firmly together. In this way he was able to leave the arches completely open and give the mosque a sensation of space and light.

• **A REMINDER OF HOMELANDS.** *The forest of columns within the mosque must have reminded Arab worshippers of a grove of date palms, because for them the date palm was the quintessential symbol of their distant homeland, just like the mosaic that adorns the reliquary in the Umayyad mosque, which symbolises the fact that paradise is to be found in Damascus (see the illustration below).*

• **Space in the mosque.**

Henri Stierlin remarks that, *"Never before had such wide internal spaces been conceived of by such simple means as columns supporting relatively small arches. Neither the hypostyle rooms in the Pharaonic temples at Karnak and Luxor nor Roman basilicas, nor Constantinian churches could compare with these delicate spaces so full of air and light. Probably only the largest of the Roman and Byzantine cisterns had given rise to schemes such as this."*

Another innovation compared to the Umayyad Mosque at Damascus is that the aisles run towards the *qiblah* rather than parallel to it. The central aisle, which leads to the *mihrab,* is wider, in the style of a church nave, and gives the impression of an overall convergence towards the *mihrab* but without disrupting the uniformity of the overall space of the mosque.

Left: part of the first extension to the mosque ordered by Abd ar-Rahman II in 833, when eleven more naves were added running in the direction of the qiblah. *Building materials pillaged from other sites were again used in the construction, although seventeen of the new capitals were carved by Córdoban stonemasons. The columns stand without bases and are all smooth except for two, which have vertical fluting, and one with a spiral design.*

THE EXTENSION OF THE MOSQUE.

Although the Great Mosque was built over a period of more than 200 years, during which time modifications were constantly being made to it, the original basic structure was only ever added to, never radically altered, perhaps to some degree in respect to its designer, but above all because it already comprised all the elements and technical and aesthetic discoveries common to perfect works of art. Hishan I (788-796) finished off the work begun by his father Abd ar-Rahman I by building the first minaret. Forty years later Abd ar-Rahman II (822-852) made the first extension to the prayer hall (833), adding eight new aisles, half of which are now lost beneath the Christian cathedral. During this building phase, which took fifteen years to complete, old columns were also used from other ruined buildings. These were set directly into the floor without bases but any missing capitals (seventeen in all) were replaced by new ones carved in Córdoban workshops. A hundred years after that, in 951, the caliph Abd ar-Rahman III built a new minaret 48 metres high, of which only 22 metres survive today, incorporated into the cathedral tower. The influence of this minaret is to be seen reflected in all the new minarets built thereafter throughout the western Islamic world. On widening the courtyard Abd ar-Rahman had also to restructure it entirely, extending it 60 metres farther to the north. He also surrounded its three hitherto open sides with the *riwat*, a six-metre-wide arcaded gallery in which pillars alternate with columns. But it was his son, al-Hakam II, the pious, learned prince, who had been supervising the work on the royal city of Madinat az-Zahra on his father's behalf, who decided on the very day he ascended to the throne that the mosque had once more become too small to satisfy the demands of his ever growing population and set out to extend it again. He demolished the *qiblah* wall and moved it 12 aisles farther to the south, as far in fact as the river would allow, thus making the prayer hall 104 metres long. He erected the maqsura, a screen to form a sanctuary before the *mihrab*, and converted the *mihrab* itself into the most refined example of the whole mosque. The final extension to the mosque was made twenty-four years later by the usurper general Abu Amir Muhammad al-Mansur, who widened it eastwards by eight naves.

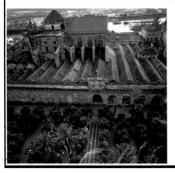

THE DIFFERENT BUILDING PHASES OF THE MOSQUE

1. THE ORIGINAL CONSTRUCTION UNDERTAKEN BY ABD AR-RAHMAN I IN 785.
2. THE EXTENSION ADDED BY ABD AR-RAHMAN II IN 833.
3. ADDITIONS MADE BY ABD AR-RAHMAN III IN 945.
4. THE MAQSURA AND NEW MIHRAB BUILT BY AL-HAKAN II IN 961.
5. FINAL EXTENSIONS ADDED BY AL-MANSUR IN 987.
   A) THE COURT OF THE ORANGE TREES.
   B) THE MINARET.

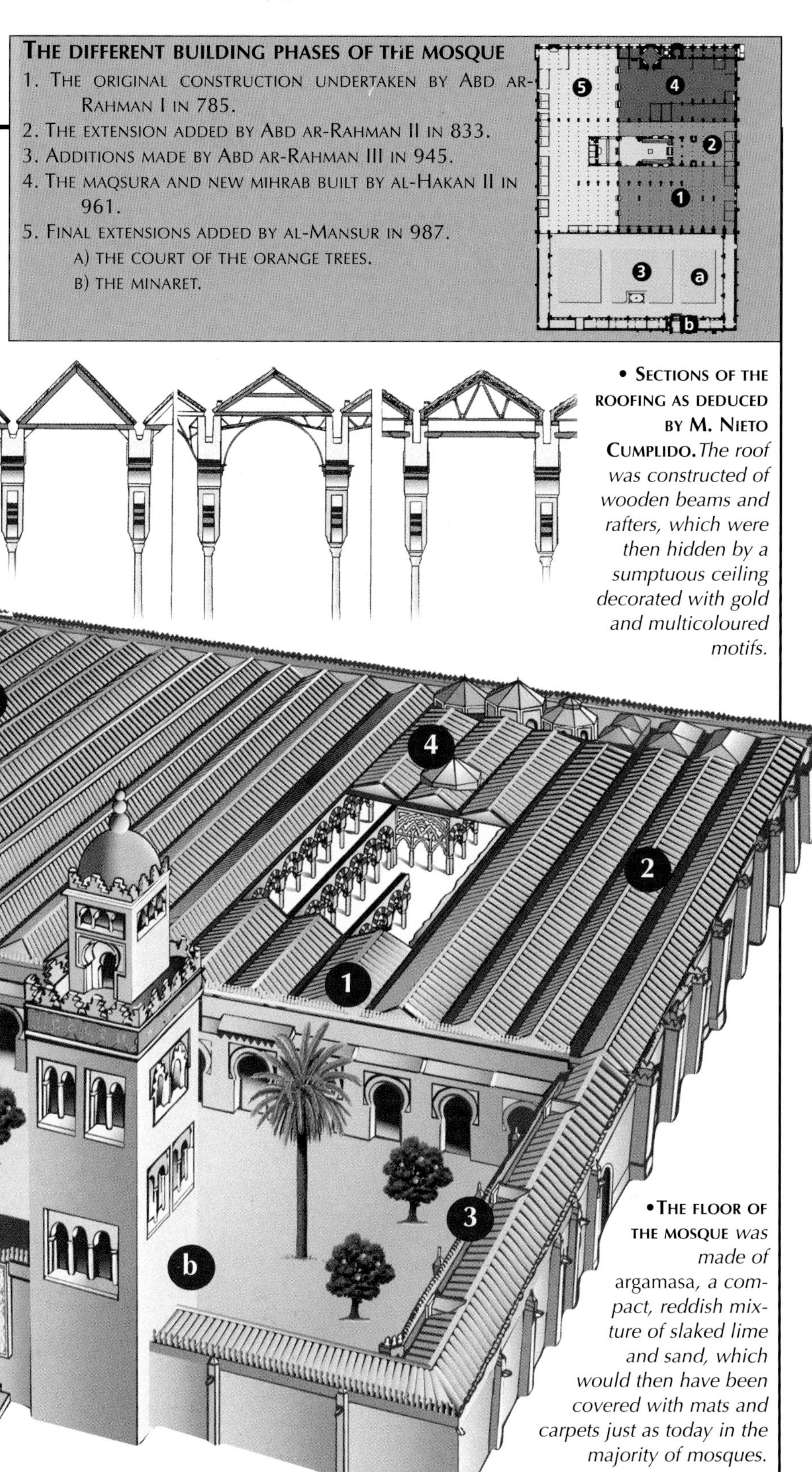

• **SECTIONS OF THE ROOFING AS DEDUCED BY M. NIETO CUMPLIDO.** *The roof was constructed of wooden beams and rafters, which were then hidden by a sumptuous ceiling decorated with gold and multicoloured motifs.*

• **THE FLOOR OF THE MOSQUE** *was made of* argamasa, *a compact, reddish mixture of slaked lime and sand, which would then have been covered with mats and carpets just as today in the majority of mosques.*

THE INTERIOR OF THE MOSQUE

The interior of the communal prayer hall of the Great Mosque in Córdoba, gives the visitor the sensation of entering into a different world from that which he has just left outside, a world where space expands in all directions and the translucent arches suspended above his head like weightless palms are endlessly interwoven and stretch away to eternity.

"The pillars rise vertically above the capitals like branches striving upward towards the light.

The red and white voussoirs of the arches emphasise the sensation of space repeating itself and expanding towards the unreachably far horizon" (A. Muñoz Molina).

For the Muslim worshipper the perfectly parallel symmetry between the floor and the ceiling flow in unison towards a limitless infinity, a mystical void, the bare simplicity of his personal relationship with God.

The lobulate arches (left), which are typical of Syrian Abbasid architecture, are in fact the strongest elements in the structure. They are subtly interwoven to absorb the many different angles of thrust exerted upon them whilst at the same time giving the impression of lightness and delicacy.

• *XVIII century engraving by Girault de Prangey of the sanctuary behind the* maqsurah.

• **THE STRUCTURE OF THE ARCHES.** *The lower tier of lobulate arches are overlapped by the upper ones, thus sharing the weight where they intersect and directing the final downward thrust into the columns. The interweaving of a multitude of arches indicates at one and the same time the physical screen of the* maqsurah, *whilst the richness of its adornment emphasises the nobility of the sanctuary reserved for the caliph before the* mihrab.

AL-HAKAN II. THE *MAQSURAH* AND THE *MIHRAB*.

Al-Hakam II did not pillage his building materials from elsewhere but had columns and capitals hewn in his own workshops. The lack of light and insufficient ventilation in the mosque prompted him to construct four lanterns in the roof and once again necessity gave rise to an ingenious solution. The stronger supports required for the extra weight seem to be made more graceful by the open spaces they create as they cross the lobulate arches (this page). But this is deceptive as they are interlaced by elegant ribs which bind in a central knot, thus absorbing the many counterthrusts and

increasing the overall distribution of the weight. Above this stone latticework rises the ribbed cupola, which seems to float on its octagonal base of fine ribbing, arched into two squares intersecting at an angle of 45°. This ribbed vault, serving as a sofit to centre the dome, is divided into small segments and was thus much easier to vault over, the vaulting here being made of stone and not brick as it tended to be in Persia some hundred years later (see opposite page).

It is in this small area of the mosque, reserved for the caliph's private prayer, where the art of the Córdoban caliphate can be seen to have reached maturity and where eastern and western traditions combine most successfully.

the lobulate arch and the stylisation of natural shapes.
What was genuinely Umayyad in origin seems to have been the idea of the transept, the rectangular minaret, and above all the rounded cupola unsupport-

Horizontal plan

According to Enrique Pareja, the Arabs inherited the horseshoe arch and the agave capital from Hispano-Visigothic architecture and figurative representation from Byzantine architecture. From their Abbasid rivals they borrowed

ed by ribbing.
The Córdoban contribution to caliphal architecture was the ribbed vault, the *ataurique* vegetal motifs and the honeycombed marble capitals. (Various types of these cupolas are depicted on this page.)

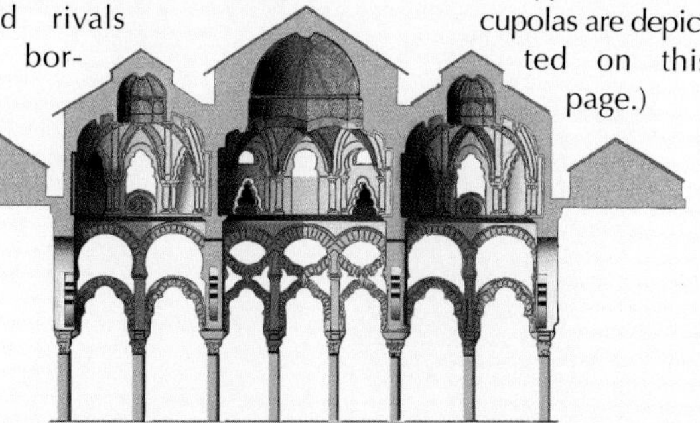

• **THE SANCTUARY BEHIND THE** *maqsurah* **IN AN ORIGINAL PLATE BY C. EWERT.**
Inside the mosque the prayer hall attains height and airiness through two tiers of arches. In the confines behind the maqsurah, *however, lanterns needed to be built into the roof to illuminate the area immediately in front of the* mihrab.

• **IN 961 AL-HAKAN** *built two ribbed domes on either side of the original main dome (see illustration). It is unlikely that ribbed cupolas had their origin in earlier buildings in the Near East; it seems more probable that they were the invention of the Spanish caliphate and may also have gone on to inspire some of the ideas to be seen in Gothic architecture.*

• *Left: cross section of the* maqsurah *precinct.*
The first three bays of the central nave constitute the approach to the oratory of al-Hakan II. In this way the area, or sanctuary, before the mihrab *remains cut off from the rest of the prayer hall by this enormous masonry jalousie, the* maqsurah.

On the double page overleaf, a view of the main cupola from beneath.

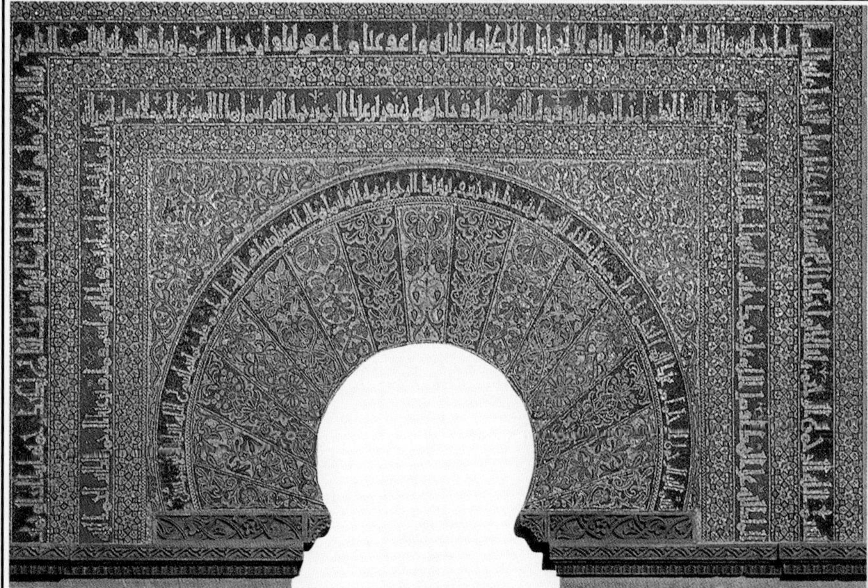

THE MIHRAB

AN ARCH BESIDE THE MIHRAB.

The *mihrab* as such first appeared in the mosque at Medina when it was rebuilt by the Umayyads, but it was in Córdoba that it became most refined and was for the first time incorporated as a niche into the far wall of the prayer hall, indicating the *qiblah,* or direction towards Mecca. The concept of a niche may have owed its inspiration to the Christian apse or the niche in Roman households where their divinities were displayed. But in the Córdoban mosque what had originally been a mere groove cut into the wall to mark the *qiblah* became an octagonal niche with a ceiling sculpted from a single block of white marble into the shape of a scallop shell, the symbol of life, the word of God, beneath which, to celebrate special occasions, a copy of the Koran written out in the hand of Oman himself was placed. Although everywhere is recognised as being sacred and apt for prayer, "Turn wherever you will and you will find the face of God" the *mihrab* became the focus for the faithful to prostrate themselves before their God, a symbolic doorway leading to heaven where they directed their prayers, a symbol of the absolute, an affirmation of the divine within this world. What had originated as a simple reference point to the *qiblah* became in the Great Mosque at Córdoba a focus of enormous religious significance. For this reason the *mihrab* had to be the most sumptuously adorned place in the mosque to attract the eyes of the worshippers. (On the preceding page, a view of the *mihrab*)

•*According to Ibn al-Hazan, al-Hakan II was one of the most learned men of his day. He had a library of 400,000 books containing the whole of human knowledge of that time.*

•**LEFT:** *The chapel at Villaviciosa in an XVIII century engraving by Girault de Prangey*

The Mihrab.

When he was heir to the throne al-Hakan, the learned and extremely pious prince, had overseen the building work on the royal city of Madinat az-Zahra and so it is not surprising that when he ascended the throne his very first royal command was to begin forthwith on the most important reforms that the mosque had ever seen and it is equally certain that his personal intervention in its design had a decisive influence on the growth in maturity of Córdoban art. He had no hesitation in asking the Christian emperor Nicephorus Phocas for advice In the adornment of the *mihrab*, just as the first of the Umayyads had turned to Christendom for help in Damascus 250 years before. Whilst Charlemagne sided with the Abbasids, the Córdoban Umayyads had come to an understanding with the Christian empire in the east. From this alliance the emir received 320 quintales (nearly 15 tonnes) of golden mosaic cubes, together with the services of a master builder to teach the Córdoban artisans the Byzantine technique of mosaic decoration. In the words of Gómez Moreno, *We have to go back to Santa Sofia to find anything comparable to the exquisite elegance of this mihrab.*

• **The façade of the mihrab.**
The intentions of the first architect were completely respected in all the later extensions to the mosque, as can be seen in the use of his scheme to frame the horseshoe arch above the outer door in a closed spandrel (855). Above, to the right: St Stephen's doorway. This design was copied in the façade of the mihrab *(above left), to which Umayyad decoration was added in the shape of Byzantine marble and tiling. Also woven into the design were delicately contrived ribbonwork and* ataurique *motifs of oriental origin, belonging to the so-called second style, which, together with intricate honeycombing in the capitals, became the hallmarks of this apotheosis of Spanish caliphal architecture.*

The stylised vegetal designs on the blind arches within the mihrab and the use of colour are of rare and delicate simplicity.

• **The decoration of the arch before the mihrab.** *The twin red and white colouring of the voussoirs of the arches which meets the eye upon entering the mosque was translated some centuries later on this arch above the entrance to the* mihrab *into a fantastic interplay of* ataurique *designs upon backgrounds of blue, red and gold (left), creating a symmetrical repetition of unidentifiable floral motifs reminiscent of far-off Damascus.*

The date when the line of imposts was finished is inscribed in tiny red Kufic characters upon a gold background as being 965. Inscriptions from the Koran stand out clearly against blue and gold backgrounds around the spandrel of the arch.

Decorative features. *The elaborate floral motifs used in Spanish-Umayyad decoration include leaves and calices, rosettes, palm sprays, clover leaves, pineapples and bunches of grapes. These individual elements are also intricately decorated within themselves and their edges are often jagged or feathered into leaf-like designs.*

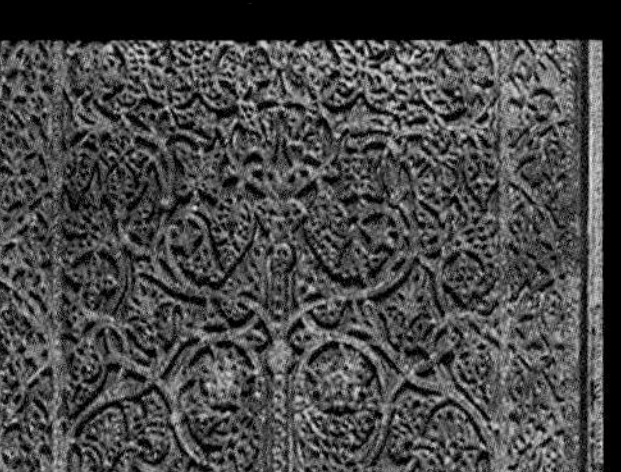

A fragment of the tree of life, originally a Syrio-Persian concept, incised using the so-called "soft-chisel" technique because of the delicacy and precision of its carving.

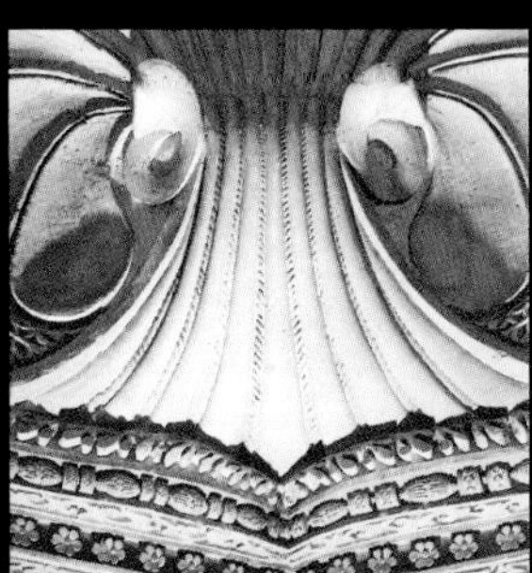

• **The cupola of the mihrab.** *The interior of the mihrab is an octagonal recess crowned by a single white marble dome sculpted into the form of a scallop shell, which symbolises the word of the Koran and is thus related to ancient belief, which identified the shell as the symbol of the source of life. Henceforth it became customary to decorate the* mihrab *with a shell, which had the added advantage of helping to amplify the voice of the imam when leading communal prayer.*

The scallop is also a symbol associated with the Virgin Mary and the Immaculate Conception, the generator of life, and thus Christians are born to a life of grace via baptism by water poured from the shell. It is also to be found in many other cultures because of its connotations with procreation and with water, the giver of life.

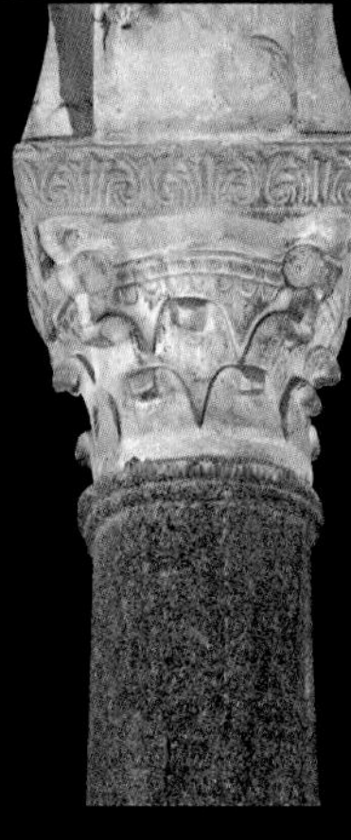

SCULPTURE.

The original mosque contained almost 150 capitals pillaged from other Visigothic and Roman monuments and so they represent a multitude of styles from the preceding centuries. The craftsmanship in them is also fairly disparate, some belonging to very elaborate classical Corinthian and late-Roman periods whilst other Visigothic ones were quite simply and roughly hewn, although often full of ingenious elegance: these are known as agave capitals (left), which are often composite, showing a combination of a basic Corinthian form with stylised Ionic volutes (below left). During the first extension process in the IX century, although some pre-Islamic capitals were also brought in, seventeen new ones, copied from those already in place for conformity's sake, were moulded in Córdoban workshops. Their abacuses are Christian-Visigothic in style and are decorated with typical geometric shapes and vine leaves, among which appear Christian crosses.

Right: the Visigothic altar; its upper section is missing and the horizontal arms of the Christian cross carved in relief on its side have been chipped off. Its decoration is typically Visigothic with friezes of simple repetitious geometric motifs. It now forms part of a small display of archaeological finds within the mosque itself.

It can often be seen th because the capitals hav been taken from other build ings they are smaller in dian eter than the columns beneat them.

Left: a caliphal column base moulded in the same style as the honeycomb capitals.

To the left is a translucent, white-marble Roman column, remarkable here because of its vertically fluted shaft.

According to Gómez Moreno the collection of capitals used in the Great Mosque of Córdoba makes it the ideal place to study the evolution of the classical capital and its transformation at the hands of the Visigoths; a veritable living museum of architectural marvels that would not have survived had they not been reused in this way.

The X century capital, used frequently in Madinat az-Zahra, was derived from the Corinthian capital. The stylised acanthus leaves sprouting from the abacus are filled with perforations, giving rise to the so-called "honeycomb" capital, which continued to evolve until the end of the Nasrid dynasty in Granada in the XV century.

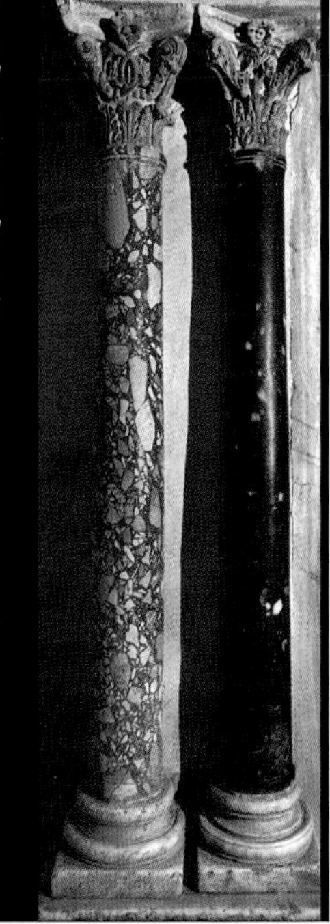

To the right are two of the four columns of black marble and red pudding stone from the Sierra de Cabra, used in the first extension and then re-used by al-Hakan II in the final mihrab.

To the left is a view of one of the aisles belonging to the final extension carried out by al-Mansur, in which the original schemes are repeated but which also illustrates the depth and lucidity achieved with a felicitous combination of arches.

THE COURTYARD OF THE ORANGE TREES AND THE MINARET

The courtyard is fundamental to any mosque and is normally the place where the fountain for ritual ablution is to be found. In Córdoba the courtyard was originally surrounded by a wall (left) but Abd ar-Rahman III built arcades in which much of the daily activity of the mosque took place. The mosque, apart from being a place of prayer was, and indeed still is, equivalent to the town square in western tradition, a place to meet and to talk or just to watch life go by. These porticoes were witness to much of the hustle and bustle of the daily round of city life.

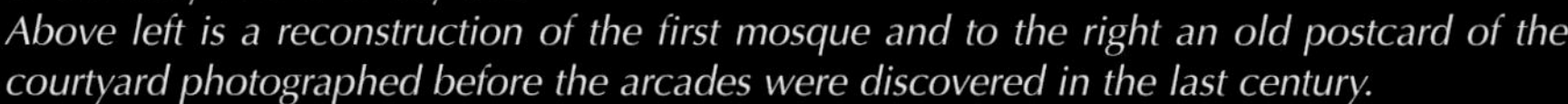

Above left is a reconstruction of the first mosque and to the right an old postcard of the courtyard photographed before the arcades were discovered in the last century.

• A WINDOW IN THE MINARET, *part of which survives today incorporated into the cathedral bell-tower.*

THE MINARET.

The word alminar, *or* minaret, *means in Arabic "the place of light", the place from whence is promulgated the Word which will illuminate the soul as the light dispels the darkness. There has been much speculation about the second minaret erected by Abd ar-Rahman III; some scholars claim that it was crowned by three golden spheres, others say five. What is sure is that it was 47.5 metres high. Félix Hernández left us his drawings, which served as a model for the infographic reproduction on the left. Its shape and structure were reproduced in many later minarets, including those at Marrakech, Rabat and Sevilla (the present-day Giralda), together with other contemporary ones which today are church towers.*

• The Courtyard of the Orange Trees.
This is the sahn of the mosque, enclosed on three sides from the middle of the X century. Its name derives from the fact that the Christian conquerors planted orange trees here, although in Muslim times there had been other types of trees there.

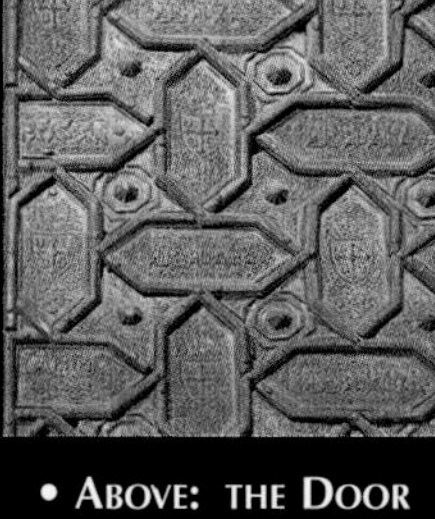

• Above: the Door of forgiveniss
The doorways in mosques tend to be very impressive in design and elaborately ornamented.

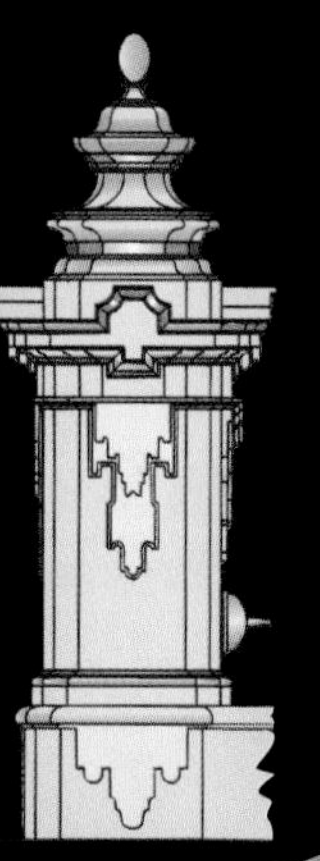

• The Tower
In 1593 Hernán Ruiz the younger built a second storey onto the minaret to accommodate the bells and the clock but later because of repeated earth tremors it was thought advisable to construct an outer strengthening wall, concealing what was left of the original minaret, and that is what we see today. Later still, a third storey was added on top of which stands the Archangel Raphael, guardian angel of the city of Córdoba. The last repairs were finished in 1763 and show the clear influence of the Sevillian late-Renaissance architect Sebastián Herrera.

• The marble bowl for washing before prayer
Such a facility is essential in or beside all mosques to allow the faithful to wash before prayer. The bowl in the Courtyard of the Orange Trees was originally filled from a well beneath it but al-Hakan II built an aqueduct to bring water from the mountains behind the city to fill an aljibe, or cistern. Al-Mansur then dug an even bigger cistern, capable of holding some 600,000 litres of water.

• Below: the basic structure of St. Stephen's doorway (855) follows the original architect's design but later decorative additions have been made in a mixture of both Visigothic and Umayyad styles. The modillions above the doorway and the stepped-pyramid crenellation are Córdoban innovations which were later copied extensively in many other places.

THE ARCHITECTURE OF THE FAÇADE.

The doorways into the original mosque were notable for their harmony of design but of the four doorways in each side of the first building only one remains, that of St. Stephen (San Estebán or San Sebastián) in the western wall. It is a perfect example of the typical Córdoba tripartite, buttressed doorway and with its rich architectural adornment and monumental mien is not only an exceptional work of art but also completely original in design. There is nothing similar to it in contemporary archi-

tecture and according to Professor Torres Balbas we need to go back to late-Roman structures such as Diocletian's Porta Aurea in Split (Dalmatia) to find anything resembling this architectural achievement.

The four outer walls enclose an area of some 22,400 square metres and contain twelve doorways. Those in the western wall, introduced during the reform of al-Hakan II, follow the general tripartite composition of St. Stephen's doorway, with their arches elegantly interlaced, the simple clean lines of the projecting borders around the spandrels and the great variety in decorative motifs. The upper sections of the structure on both sides of the doorway proper are composed of overlapping horseshoe arches and the windows are composite, or lobulate, arches.

The *ataurique* designs are very similar to those adorning the *mihrab* and the stone and brickwork marquetry of the pavement resembles that found in the royal city of

• **DECORATION OF THE EXTERIOR WINDOWS.** *The motifs are a symmetrical repetition of geometric shapes extended towards infinity by multiplying, dividing and rotating them until they become a metaphor of eternity*

• **A MARBLE JALOUSIE** *to one side of St. Stephen's doorway. This is the oldest surviving exterior decoration in the mosque*

• Interlaced arches. *Above the doors themselves there are intricately decorated friezes, with interlaced arches supported upon small marble columns. Chiselled into the stone wall are alternating designs of vine leaves and swastika crosses. The perforated capitals are reminiscent of Byzantine art; they support strong imposts which in turn absorb the downward thrust of the overhanging arches. Right: details of the doorways of al-Hakan II and St. Michael.*

Madinat az-Zahra. The interwoven jalousies reveal the Byzantine influence that shaped the basic elements of this style of Córdoban doorway, although they were

crassly restored by Professor Velásquez Bosco at the beginning of the XX century and substantial changes were made to the upper parts of the doorways, with no real reference being made to the original design. Unnecessary apocryphal introductions were also inserted into the epigraphic texts.

The main doorway, the "Door of forgiveness", is in the northern façade and is clearly Almohad in style. Many of the doorways in the western wall have been sub-

• Ornamentation. *The doors along the side walls of the mosque are very characteristic in their decoration: the arches slightly projecting with heavy keystones, framing multi-lobular, windows filled in with marble. Above: St. Michael's doorway and right: the doorway of al-Hakan II*

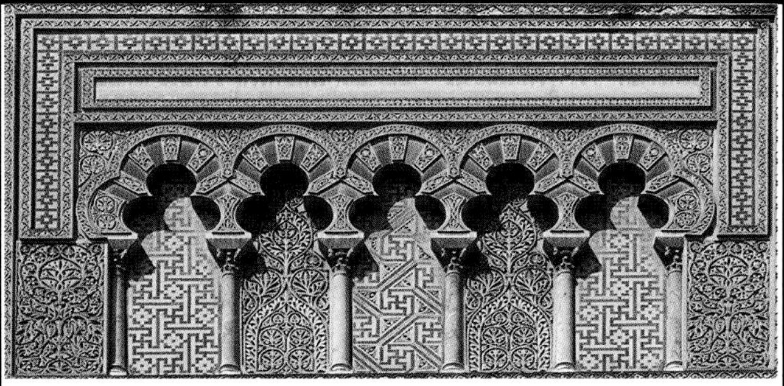

ject to considerable alteration since the XVI century, easily discernible by the Christian details incorporated into the additions, particularly the door of St. Stephen, already described above, and that of al-Hakan II.

There was also a small doorway close to the river that opened onto a passageway crossing over a system of arches connect-

• **Milestone pillars.** *These were genuine Roman milestones used to mark the distance along their roads.*

• **A reconstruction of the Sabat doorway built by al-Hakan,** *according to the scheme proposed by L. Golvin, based upon contemporary accounts that speak of a door leading to a walkway above street level supported upon five arches and divided into five separate "rooms" along its length.*

• **The eastern façade, built by al-Mansur.**

• **The eastern façade,** *built by al-Mansur. To the right are the six doors which were over-restored by Velázquez Bosco at the beginning of the XX century.*

• **Right: view of the Door of Forgiveness**

ing the mosque to the caliphal citadel, the alcázar. According to the contemporary writer Ibn Hayyan, there was a raised walkway known as the *sabat,* which resembled a covered bridge supported by one or more arches, spanning the gap (nowadays Torrijos street) between the two buildings. When al-Hakan II extended the mosque he did away with this original passageway, building himself a new one, which existed until 1622, when it was demolished during restoration work on the bishop's palace.The whole of the original eastern façade was knocked down by al-Mansur, including some of the doorways made during al-Hakan's reforms 120 years before. Nevertheless, sufficient remains still exist of one of al-Hakan's doorways, now inside the mosque and known as the "Chocolate Gate", to appreciate the beauty of its *ataurique* designs and marquetry. Although al-Mansur did not skimp on materials in his extension to the

•**An inscription by Abd ar-Rahman III** *beside the Arch of Blessings.*

• **A RECONSTRUCTION** *of the western façade of the mosque before its restoration at the beginning of the XX century by Velásquez Bosco.*

mosque, he confined himself to copying the earlier designs both on the inside and in the six gateways, which he modelled on those of al-Hakan before him, but of much mean-

• **XVIII CENTURY ENGRAVINGS** *by Girault de Prangey. Left: the western façade and details of some of the doorways before their restoration.*

er design. His only slight innovation in the doorways was in the incorporation of twin horseshoe arches, although this design had first been seen in the minaret of Abd ar-Rahman seventy years earlier.

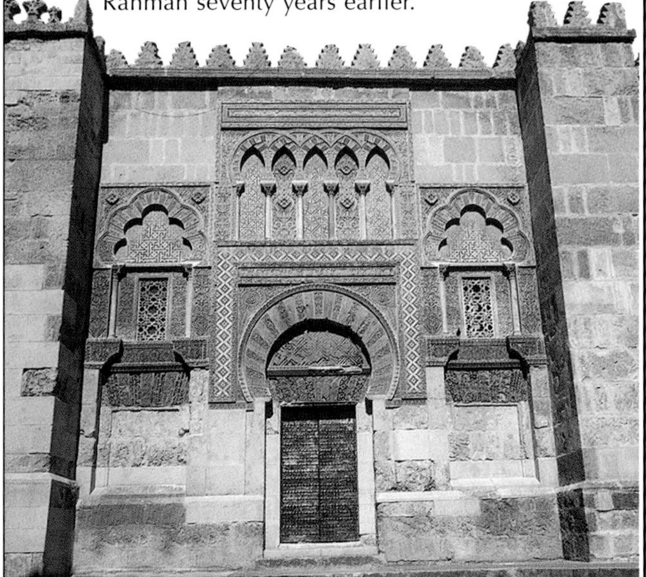

• *Left: the Doorway of the Holy Ghost, which was totally restored by Velásquez Bosco.*

• **THE CUPOLA.** *View of the oval cupola in the late-Gothic transept, in the style of Francisco Herrera.*

CÓRDOBA CATHEDRAL

After the reconquest in 1236 and the subsequent christianisation of the Great Mosque no immediate alterations were made to the building itself. It was not until 1523 nearly 200 years later, that Bishop Alonso Manrique obtained permission from his uncle the Emperor Charles V to build a cathedral inside the mosque. Afterwards the emperor regretted his decision, when on a visit to the city during his honeymoon in 1526 he saw what his avuncular benevolence had led to. But it was too late to stop the work, which went on for nearly a hundred years under the supervision of Hernán Ruiz the elder and then Hernan Ruiz the younger and Juan de Ochoa. The building was not in fact finished until 1766 and architectural tastes and concepts had obviously changed during those 250 years. The Hernan Ruízs, father, son and grandson, watched over the

• *Left: page from a* **BOOK OF BALLADS** *of Alfonso X the wise. Above: a page from a choral missal.*

•**AN ENGRAVING OF THE ROYAL CHAPEL** *and in the photograph a view of the Christian Cathedral within the Great Mosque . Below: a lion's head belonging to one of the pulpits carved by Miguel Verdiguier.*

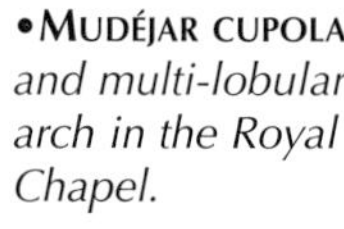

transition from the late-Renaissance to the Plateresque and then to the most elaborate Spanish Baroque, the Churrigueresque. The main chapel of the cathedral is a prime example of this mixture: the arches in the form of the Roman cross are Gothic whilst the vaults over the central nave and the transept owe their style to Francisco Herrera. The altar screen dates from 1618 and is the work of the Jesuit master craftsman Alonso Matías. It is carved from red marble and jasper from the Córdoban quarries of Carcabuey and Cabra, which also frame the paintings of Palomino. Worthy of attention are the two pulpits by Verdiguier, carved in mahogany and supported by symbols of the four evangelists, each sculpted in differently coloured stone (left: the lion of St. Mark in red jasper). But most outstanding of all is the choir, carved in mahogany from the West Indies by Pedro Duque Cornejo in the middle of

•**MUDÉJAR CUPOLA** *and multi-lobular arch in the Royal Chapel.*

• **Above: layout of the different chapels within the cathedral.**

the XVIII century. In a masterly display of craftsmanship he includes a whole range of religious themes ranging from biblical scenes to images of Córdoban martyrs. The choir stalls are fairly uniform except for the magnificent bishop's throne in which the whole repertoire of Baroque rhetoric is displayed to its full effect and symbolism: the Ascent of our Lord amongst the apostles, crowned by the Archangel Raphael, guardian angel of Córdoba, is surrounded by St. Theresa and St. Mary Magdalene, whose exemplary lives exert great doctrinal authority (left). The cathedral also contains more than fifty chapels, most of them occupying recesses in the walls, among which the Chapel of Cardinal Salazar, also known as the Chapel of St. Theresa, is noteworthy because of its splendid sculpture of St. Theresa, carved by José de Mora. Apart from being the sacristy it is also the chapter house, a typically octagonal Baroque structure, decorated by Hurtado Izquierdo, another of the last great masters of the Baroque along with Duque Cornejo and Palomino, who painted many of the portraits in the cathedral. Beside the chapter house is the treasury; its most valuable item is the early-XVI-century Gothic-style reliquary belonging to Enrique Arfe, measuring 2.63 metres and weighing more than 200 kilos. Among the many precious religious relics kept in the sacristy are a crucifix belonging to the Granadan architect and artist Alonso Cano and another of unknow origin from the XIII century.

•**The choir stalls.** *The most outstanding work of Pedro Duque Cornejo y Roldán are the 109 stalls carved from mahogany from Cuba and Santo Domingo in the West Indies. The ground plan of the choir is square and overlooked by a high frontispiece where the prelate's throne is situated (above left), also watched over by a statue of St. Raphael, guardian angel of the city of Córdoba. On this page there are several views of the choir.*

• **The festival of the courtyards** *and the springtime crosses. On 3 May Córdoba celebrates the festival of the cross when the whole city is filled with set pieces of crosses garlanded with flowers and a multitude of other traditional adornments. A week later there is a festival for individual courtyards, the best decorated receiving a considerable prize. Shortly afterwards is the festival of Nuestra Señora de la Salud.*

Córdoba's domestic courtyards

The megaron in ancient Greece and the atrium in Rome were open courtyards within the private house, often serving as a reception centre or business area for a patrician citizen. Family life would have gone on around these courtyards.

• **The typical decoration of a Córdoban courtyard.** *The most important elements were the spring or well and the surrounding plants, but over the centuries the courtyard developed and became more ornate with elegant wrought-iron grilles and lamps, ceramic tiling and above all flower pots of all shapes and sizes.*

•**SPRINGS AND FOUNTAINS.** *The spring in a courtyard offers an oasis of freshness in the torrid heat of the Córdoban summer and without doubt the gentle murmur of flowing water is the sweetest of melodies in the baking silence of an August afternoon.*

What used to be an intimate space in family life has come over time to be the centre of social life among Córdoban neighbours. The potted plant, originally an idea conceived by desert nomads so as to be able to carry with them a small piece of living nature (those same nomadic Berbers who conquered and inhabited Córdoba in the VIII century), became the centrepiece of domestic decoration, beneath the shade of the inevitable grape vine or fruit tree overhanging the courtyard.

•**CÓRDOBAN COURTYARDS**, *direct descendants of caliphal courtyards, share their design of shady arched porticoes, which alleviate the heat of*

summer and also capture the warmth of the winter sun.

•XIV CENTURY SYNAGOGUE. *One of the three mediaeval synagogues to have survived in Spain. Below: the seven-branched menorah.*

•MAIMÓNIDES. *A great Spanish-Jewish philosopher, scientist and physician, was forced to flee with his family from persecution in Spain under the fanatical Almohads to Fez in north Africa and thence to Egypt, where he became personal physician to the sultan Saladin.*

THE JEWISH NEIGHBOURHOOD

There are records dating from the III century A.D. testifying to Jewish settlements in the Iberian peninsula, of the persecution that they suffered under the Visigoths and of their alliances with the Muslims after the Arab conquest. But it was in the X century that they began to play an important role in Spanish Muslim society as administrators, doctors, businessmen and functionaries. Al-Hakan II was in this respect a very tolerant ruler and was known as the lord of the three religions.
In Córdoba, as in the majority of medieval cities, the Jews tended to live in their own neighbourhoods, apart from the rest of the townspeople. The Jewish quarter must have been quite extensive and considerably important, close as it was to the wall surrounding the royal apartments and to the centre of administrative power. What remains today of the Jewish quarter, despite being considerably reduced in size, is little changed from how it must have been in the days of the caliphate: a maze of narrow, winding, whitewashed streets, which lead into shady alleyways with glimpses of deliciously cool courtyards, or suddenly open out into peaceful, tree-lined squares, a delight for visitors and residents alike.

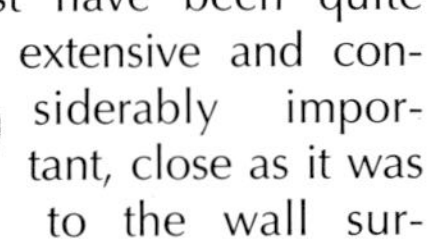

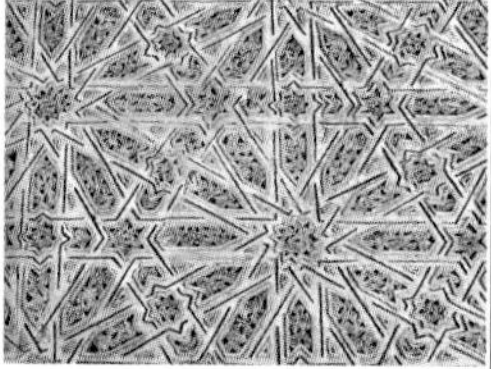

• THE SYNAGOGUE.

The original synagogue is to be found in *calle Judios* (the street of the Jews) and is entered via a small courtyard and a narthex below the women's gallery. It was built in 1315 during the reign of the Christian king Alfonso XI in the Mudéjar style and decorated with stucco adornments which follow clearly in the tradition of Nasrid architecture in Granada. Within the heart of this thriving community one of the greatest Jewish theologians and philosophers of all time was born and educated. The writings of Moses ben Maimon (1112 - 1185), more widely known as Maimónides, were prolific and covered a vast range of subjects. Before the age of 33 he had summarised the teachings of Judaism in a creed of Thirteen Articles of Faith. His magnum opus, however, is undoubtedly his commentary on the Torah, Mishne Torah, in which he systemises all of Jewish law and doctrine.

• DETAILS OF THE XIV CENTURY SYNAGOGUE

The inscriptions. above the Mudéjar ataurique *motifs show that the Jews never developed an art form proper to themselves but simply adapted the styles of the time to their own needs.*

• *Above: public baths from caliphal times in* Velázquez Bosco street. *Below: The Church of St. Bartholomew.*

OTHER POINTS OF INTEREST

One of the most attractive features of Córdoba is the way in which a visitor can allow himself to be lead by his instincts and be surprised at every turning by hidden corners, courtyards and little squares, wander through the narrow, twisting alleyways surrounding the mosque, streets which from Moorish times have changed their route according to the needs of the houses and their residents rather than imposing their will on the whole shape of the city, as we can see in the streets and avenues of some modern cities. Muñoz Molina comments that its streets seem to be designed especially for visitors who are in no hurry, and their twists and turns increase the pleasure of strolling and observing.... *La calleja de las Flores* (Blossom Lane, below) typifies the synthesis of perfumes and colours in these streets, and, with the cathedral tower emerging from a background of geraniums hanging down from the wrought-iron balconies, is a classic example of their beauty. The XVI century theatre was in the adjacent *Comedias street.*

• **DETAIL OF THE SHIELD IN THE PLAZA DE LAS FLORES (BLOSSOM SQUARE).**

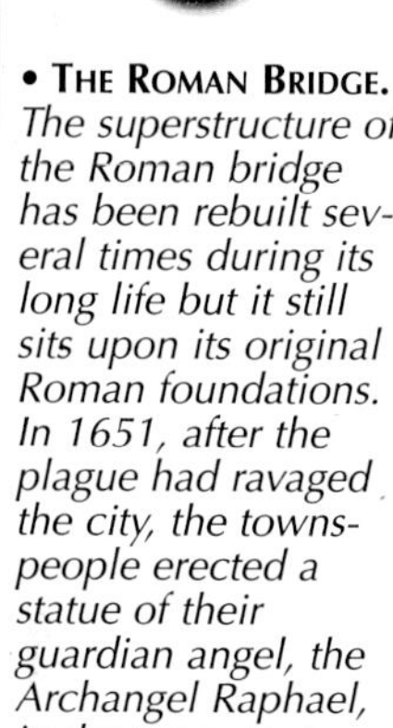

• **The Roman Bridge.** *The superstructure of the Roman bridge has been rebuilt several times during its long life but it still sits upon its original Roman foundations. In 1651, after the plague had ravaged the city, the townspeople erected a statue of their guardian angel, the Archangel Raphael, in the town centre.*

Also nearby are the streets of San Fernando (popularly known as *La Feria*), an avenue of orange trees with its Baroque fountain, and the Arco del Portillo, an archway which opens onto Cabezas street. At the southern end of the long Roman bridge, over which ran the Via Augusta, in the Campo de la Verdad, stands the Calahorra Tower, built by Alfonso XI upon the remains of an old Arab fortress almost a century after the reconquest. Enrique II, the first of the Trastámara dynasty, added a further storey to the tower in 1369 during the civil war which he waged against his step-brother Pedro the Cruel. Nowadays it houses the Museum of the Three Cultures with exhibitions and an audio-visual presentation explaining how daily life might have been in Córdoba when it was a multi-religious, cosmopolitan, mediaeval city.

Photograph by Lewis, 1891.

• **AVERRÖES.** *Author of scholarly treatises on medicine, mathematics, astronomy, ethics and above all philosophy, which had a deep influence on Christian Europe of the time.*

The walls of mediaeval Córdoba were built upon the old Roman wall and during the final years of the caliphate were 22 kilometers long, encompassing an area of some 5,000 hectares. There were seven gates; according to Dr. Juan B. Carpio, starting from the south-east and going clockwise, these were: the Roman Bridge Gate (the Triumphal Arch), across which the Via Augustina ran; then came the XIV century Sevilla Gate, the Almodóvar Gate, the Gate of the Gallicians, the Cemetery Gate (Gate of the Jews, of Talavera ...), the Toledo Gate (The Iron Gate, Gate to Rome, St. Salvador ...), and coming round towards the east once more, the Zaragoza Gate (New Gate). The Sevilla and Almodóvar Gates are flanked by statues of Córdoba's most eminent philosophers Averroës (left) and Seneca.

THE CITADEL.

In 1328 Alfonso XI ordered the construction of a Christian fortified palace upon the remains of earlier Roman and Arab buildings close to the mosque. It was to be known as the House of the Christian Monarchs in order to distinguish it from a similar citadel in the vicinity which had been the palace of the Muslim caliphs. It is a square fortress with towers at each corner and encircled within by a gallery flanked by numerous valuable archaeological treasures, among which are a well-pre-

The Sevilla Gate (below) in a stretch of the original medieval wall.

served, third-century, Roman, marble sarcophagus with portraits of the dead and their protecting spirits carved upon it (below). In the great hall, decorated throughout with mosaics,

there are likenesses of Polyphemus and Galatea, justly famous for their beautiful colouring, and some excellent, minutely carved bas reliefs (above right: Pegasus).

•**THE ALCÁZAR MUSEUM.**
This living museum contains various artefacts from Roman times and some tessellated floors found beneath that of the present-day Plaza de la Corredera. *Also to be seen here are the well-preserved Islamic steam baths and a Mudéjar courtyard. Surrounding the museum are traditional Moorish-Andalucían gardens with many examples of local flora.*

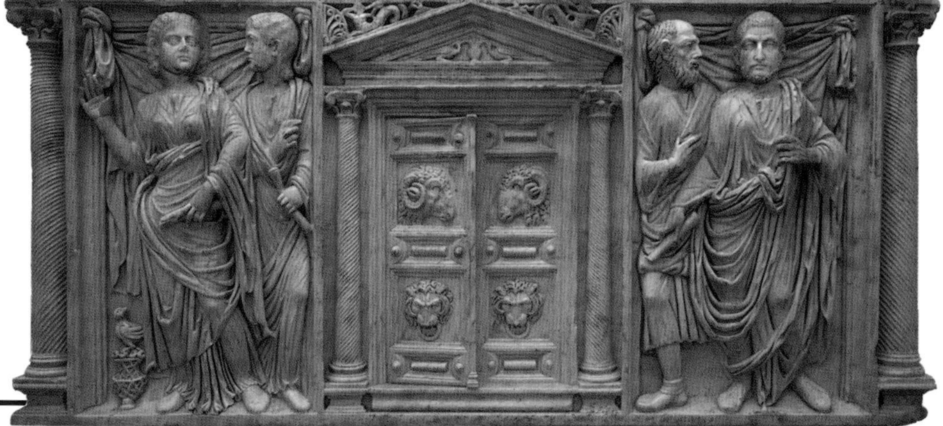

• *Right:* **THE TRIUMPH OF ST. RAPHAEL** .
• *Below:* **THE TOWER OF ST. NICHOLAS DE LA VILLA,** *one of Córdoba's most famous towers. Dating from 1496, it was used as the symbol of Córdoba in the World Exhibition in Sevilla in 1992.*

• *Below:* **THE TEMPLE OF CLAUDIUS MARCELLUS.** *The abundance of Roman relics constantly coming to light gives us some idea of the importance of this capital city of Baetica. Right: the Bridge Gate.*

WALKING AROUND

THE BRIDGE GATE *(Triumphal Arch)*. The present-day gate replaced the older one which formed part of the city wall. It was built by Hernán Ruiz at the behest of King Phillip II and is the epitome of Renaissance style. For centuries the TRIUMPH OF ST. RAPHAEL, guardian angel of Córdoba, has presided over the most important public and private squares in the city, witness to the devotion the townspeople feel for their archangel.

In 1651 he is credited with having rid the city of the black death. The most impressive of these statues to St. Raphael is that sculpted by Verdiguier at the end of the XVII century (above), which stands between the Great Mosque and the Roman bridge. The archangel stands majestically upon a slim column rising from a figurative, ornate pedestal, typical of the high Baroque period.

THE TEMPLE OF CLAUDIUS MARCELLUS. At the very heart of the city stand the bare pillars (left) reconstituted from what was once a Roman temple

•Below: different courtyards within the gardens of the Palace of Viana. Left, main façade.

bearing the name of the founder of the original colony here, later dedicated during the first century B.C. to the newly deified emperor Augustus.

THE CHURCH OF ST. LAWRENCE. After the Christian reconquest in 1236 King Ferdinand III organised the new Christian city into fourteen parishes, which were popularly known as *parroquias fernandinas* in recognition of this fact. Each had its own church, built in the architectural style of the transition towards the Spanish Gothic, although they all retain certain fortress-like features typical of the Romanesque period. The most outstanding of these *fernandina* churches is that of St. Lawrence (below).

THE PALACE OF VIANA. This palace, built during the XVI century, is an outstanding

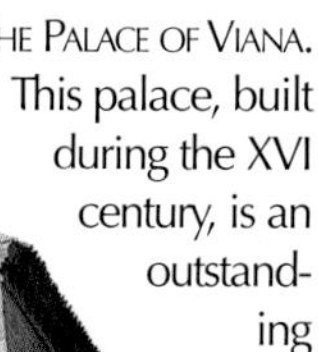

•Left: church of St. Lawrence.

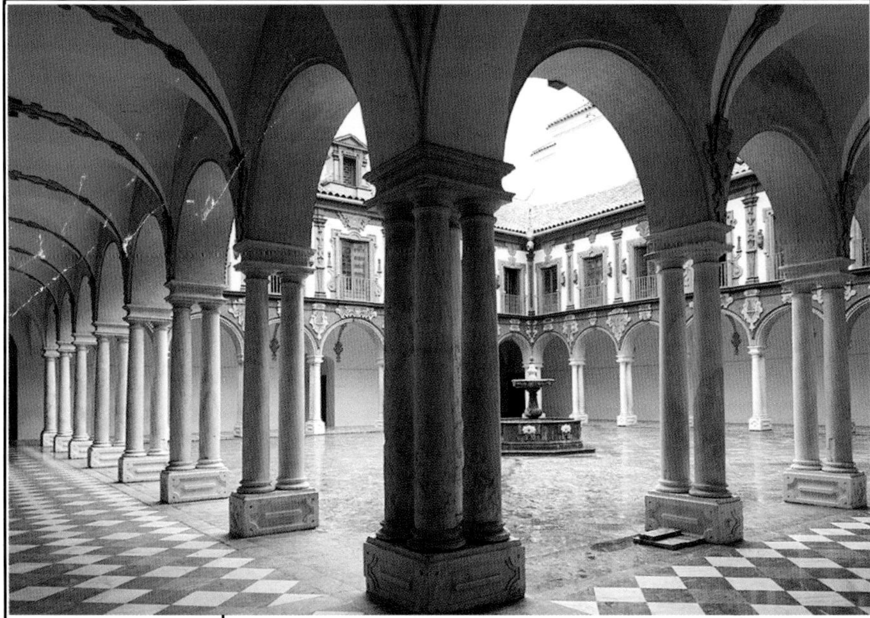

• Courtyard of the old Convent of la Mercy.

example of a noble Córdoban mansion. All visitors to Córdoba admire the courtyards tucked into the narrow streets in front of simple town houses, but this mansion can boast of twelve such courtyards and also one of the oldest designed gardens in the city. On show inside is a collection of splendid ceramics and examples of the important Córdoban craft of intricate silver filigree (It isn't open during the weekends).

The Convent of Mercy (La Merced). This convent was also founded by King Ferdinand in the XIII century but was completely reconstructed in 1757 at the height of the Baroque period, to which so many buildings in the city belong, although none of them can rival this one. The façade was painted only 30 years ago, but what is of real interest is its beautiful court-

• La Torre de la Malmuerta.
This is a flanking tower built onto the main wall of the city in the XV century. Legend has it that It was constructed by a forlorn husband who had killed his wife, suspecting her of adultery, only to find later that she was completely virtuous.

Left: *Plaza de Zocodover*

• *Below:* **THE COURTYARD OF THE SOUK** (*Patio del Zoco) is one of the remaining corners of the town to retain the traditional style of Spanish-Moorish building.*

yard (above), its grand stairway and above all the church, which contains the finest example of a Baroque altar piece in the whole of

Córdoba. The palace is now home to the offices of the provincial council.

THE CONGRESS PALACE. This conference centre is housed in the old Hospital of St. Sebastian, situated opposite the Great Mosque Its building, in late flamboyant-Gothic style (sometimes also known as Isabeline), was overseen by Hernán Ruiz the elder. Of greatest interest are the cloister and surrounding buildings.

• Below: the Jewish quarter near the Taurine Museum

• Facing page below: the Hospital of St. Hyacinth (XVI century), originally known as the Hospital of St. Sebastian .

•JULIO ROMERO DE TORRES (1874 - 1930).

This artist is considered by many to be the painter who captured the soul of Andalucían women, but he has also been criticised by others who consider that he used his talent only to reflect the worst clichés of a tragic Spain wrapped in its own secret self. His daring subjects, above all the frank realism of his nude figures, provoked a considerable degree of scandal in his day and resulted in the rejection of his portrait Vividores del Amor from the Spanish National Exhibition of Fine Arts in 1906.

MUSEUMS OF CÓRDOBA

The most interesting museums in the city are to be found near to the mosque, in the famous Plaza del Potro. The most visited is in fact that devoted to Julio Romero de Torres. The museum is the studio of the artist and shares its entrance through a garden courtyard with the Provincial Museum of Fine Arts alongside it. Both museums occupy the old Charity Hospital, with its fine Renaissance portico. The Romero de Torres Museum itself is both house and museum in which the furniture and ornaments give an authentic feeling of middle class

life between the end of the XIX and beginning of the XX centuries in Andalucía. It has on show some of the artist's most famous portraits, including "La Nieta de Trini", "Naranjas y Limones", Cante Jondo", "La Chiquita Piconera" and "El Pecado", among others. In the downstairs rooms there are

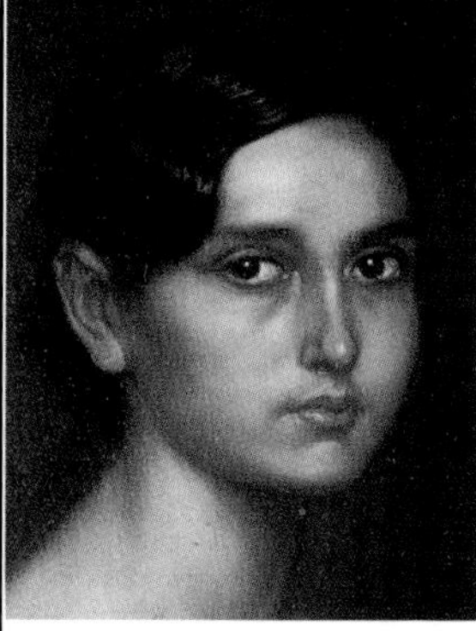

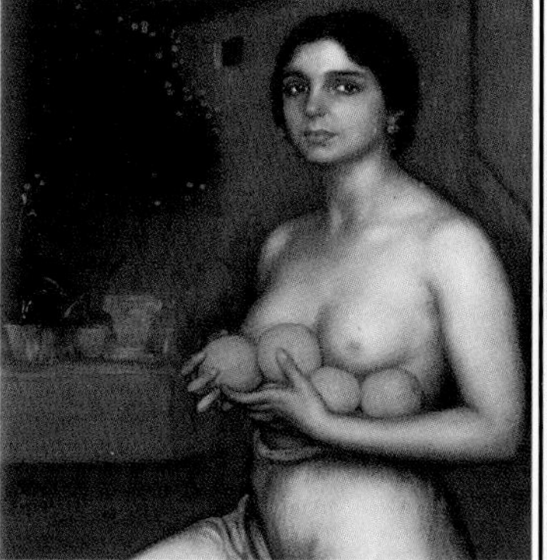

• *Above: paintings by* **JULIO ROMERO DE TORRES.**

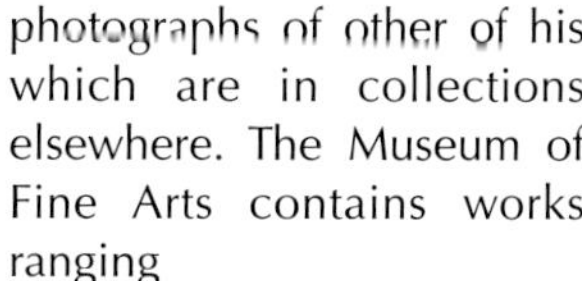

photographs of other of his which are in collections elsewhere. The Museum of Fine Arts contains works ranging

from the late Gothic to the XX century, including Antonio del Castillo, Valdés Leal, Zurburán, Rusiñol and Zuloaga, amonst many others. La Plaza del Potro (The Square of the Colt) is a long square of great character and nobility with a fountain crowned by el Potro, the statue of a young horse, from which it derives its name. Apart from the museums, amongst the buildings that surround it is the el Potro Inn (see the double page overleaf), records of which go back until at least 1435. Cervantes immortalised it in Don Quixote de la Mancha, referring to it "as a den of thieves".

The Diocesan Museum of Fine Arts, in what used to be the bishop's palace, contains an outstanding collection of sculptures and paintings from the XIII to the XV centuries and rooms exhibiting more recent Córdoban painters.

• *Paintings from the* **MUSEUM OF FINE ARTS.**

MEDINAT AZ-ZAHRA

Abd ar-Rahman III imitated the Abbasid caliphs in Baghdad in building a royal city just outside the city of Córdoba itself. He chose the hill of al-Arus, where he erected a whole palatial town, which took forty years in the building only to survive thirty-four years thereafter. Extant chronicles of the day speak of 10,000 labourers, 6,000 blocks of stone hewn every day, and more than 4,000 columns brought from the four corners of Muslim Spain. These figures, although often taken to be exaggerated, do in fact seem to be confirmed by scholarly and archaeological research. It would appear that al-Hakan himself oversaw the work, both as prince and later as caliph, and that he managed to assimilate and synthesise eastern motifs and techniques from Syria with Byzantine influences to create a new and exquisite original style peculiar to the height and maturity of Spanish caliphal architecture. The walls of Madinat az-Zahra ran 1,518 metres from east to west and 745 metres from north to south and the town was situated on three different levels, or terraces, to allow for the steep slope of the land (some 70 metres from top to bottom).

The upper terrace was the site of the caliph's palace, from whence he could survey the whole of the town and his court. The middle terrace was given over to houses for important administrators, offices and court buildings and gardens. The lower terrace was where the lesser functionaries, artisans and soldiers lived; it was also the site of markets, public baths and the mosque. In the very centre of the highest terrace was the main hall, surrounded to the east by three chambers designed for official receptions and beyond these an octagonal throne room with eight doors. According to a chronicler of the day, at the centre of the city is the great square

• THE GARDEN PAVILION. *Extending before the Royal Reception Hall was a long pool, the remains of which can still be seen (left). The water would have reflected the pavilion and the other buildings surrounding the gardens, just as we see in other Muslim palaces.*

of the central terrace with walls 100 metres long. To its north is the pool before the great hall (Salón Rico), also known as the Hall of Abd ar-Rahman III, which is rectangular and comprises five aisles, the three central ones lined by arcades (left) and the other two in naves behind the rear wall of the building. This hall contains the most refined of caliphal decoration, from the adornments of the bases of the columns and the alternating reds and greens of the columns themselves to the very sophisticated honeycombing of the capitals.

• THE ROYAL RECEPTION HALL (DAR AL-MULK).
Legend has it that this hall was so elaborately decorated with gold and silver, diamonds and other precious stones that on entering it all visitors, alike royalty, statesmen, poets, scholars, musicians or dancers, were utterly bedazzled by the sunlight playing a game of enchantment with lights and reflections upon them ... arches of ivory and ebony, walls of multicoloured marbles and translucent jasper, the dome of the roof covered with gold and silver tiles and lined with gilded mosaics.

• X CENTURY DISH. *The people of al-Andalus made the same kind of lustre pottery that they had brought with them from Iraq, and in Madinat az-Zahra shards of this type of ceramic ware have been found with the characteristic caliphal design inspired by manganese-green fabrics.*

• JALOUSIES. *The jalousies were made of wood, except for especially sumptuous examples which were ceramic or carved from marble.*

• **MADINAT AZ-ZAHRA.** Abd ar-Rahman III built this royal city some eight kilometres from Córdoba for his favourite, Azahara. She missed the snowy mountains of her home in Syria and so Abd ar-Rahman promised her, "It will snow for you, Azahara my love, I shall make it snow for you", and he covered the surrounding hills with white-blossoming cherry and almond trees.

• **THE MOULDED VEGETAL DESIGN** *in the centre of this panel from the frieze on a door jamb is separated into two rows, each bearing five bunches of leaves surrounded by entwined branches of grape vines, which represent the tree of life.*

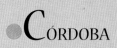

CAPITAL AND BASE. *The exquisitely worked ornamentation reached its highest point of achievement in the carving of the bases and capitals of the columns. The capital is of the Corinthian order and has two tiers of acanthus leaves. The very freely designed vegetal motifs covering the surfaces are deeply incised. The same is true of this reconstructed column base.*

• **THE HOUSE OF THE VIZIERS** (also known as The House of the Army) stands to the north of the royal residences close to the lower portico and next to the five-metre-thick surrounding wall. All the archaeological excavations at Madinat az-Zahra have been conducted only recently during the twentieth century because its precise location was unknown until then, and so only a tiny part of what might lie hidden beneath the ground has been revealed. From what has been unearthed so far, however, it seems that we may be lucky in that later looters were only interested in building materials and might have left a lot of interesting decorative ornamentation and day-to-day artefacts behind.

• **THE MILITARY BARRACKS (DAR AL-YUND).** *A central axis of three long naves procedes through arcades to a portico, which separates them from the residences of the nobility.*

• **CIVILISATION IN CÓRDOBA DURING THE REIGN OF THE CALIPH ABD AR-RAHMAN III.** *Above: a painting by D. Baxeiras (1862 – 1943) depicting a reception of ambassadors from Byzantium at Madinat az-Zahra during which they were presented with books about botany (University of Barcelona).*

• **AL MUGIRA'S FLASK.** This marble flask forms part of a series of jars with domed lids which were found at Madinat az-Zahra.

• Sierra de la Horconera. *Whitewashed farmhouses peep out through the olive groves lining the roads between Priego, Rute and Iznajar.*

• Streets and courtyards of Priego de Córdoba *The La Villa quarter forms a small labyrinth of narrow streets, its windows closed with elegant wrought-iron grilles overhung with a profusion of flowers.*

• Main façade of the church of the Assumption and our Lady of the Dawn in Priego.

The Province of Córdoba

The north of the Province of Córdoba lies in the heart of the Sierra Morena, deep mountainlands, home of the native Iberian holm and cork oaks, where sheep and Iberian, blackhoofed pigs forage at their will. This is part of the "acorn area" of western Spain, stretching down to Huelva in the south and running west and northwards through the hillsides of Extremadura to Salamanca in the north. Its pork products are famous throughout Spain, particularly the hams cured in Jabugo and Guijuelo. The most important towns in this part of the province are Pueblo Nuevo Peñarroya and Fuente Obejuna (of literary fame) on the meseta, and Pozoblanco and Hinojosa in the district of Pedroches. The centre of the province is a great cultivated plain contained within the basin of the river Guadalquivir with its riverside towns of Montoro and Palma del Río; green and sparkling in spring, in summer russet with the iridescent yellow glow of sunflowers and the scarlet flash of poppies in the wheat fields. To the

south-west the area of fertile plains, sheltered by the foothills of the Horconera, Alcaide, Gaena and Rute mountain ranges, with villages such as Luque, Baena, Doña Mencía, Cabra, Rute, Iznájar and Priego de Córdoba nestling in their folds, is now a national park. This district forms the western end of the Jaén and Granada mountain ranges and is one of the wildest and most beautiful areas in the whole of Andalucía. It is also the place where Spain's finest olive oil is produced. In the far west of the province, between the towns of Lucena and Puente Genil and the wheat fields and the olive groves, lies the district of Montilla, an undulating stretch of greyish marls densely covered in vineyards that produce fullbodied, sweet and dry white wines, which are justly famous throughout Spain. Although the name of origin of these wines is strictly Montilla-Moriles, the vineyards extend through areas such as Montemayor and climb up the hillsides of Monturque and Espejo, fortified villages that still betray their ancient role of strategic military posts

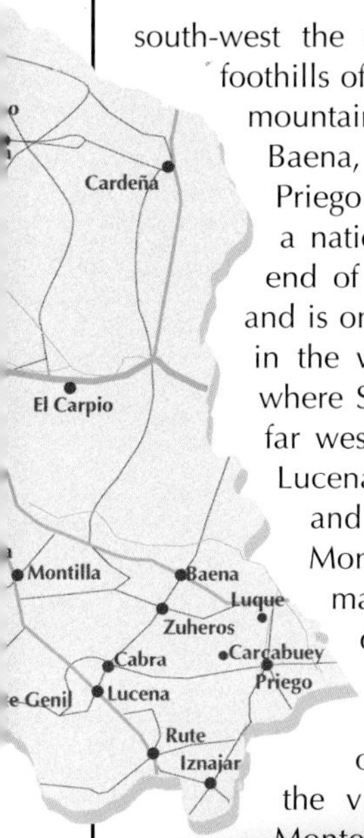

•**DURING THE FESTIVALS OF THE 3 MAY** *(the Day of the Cross) and Corpus Christi (see above) the old quarter of la Villa in the town of Priego de Córdoba decks itself out with flowers. The parish church of Our Lady of the Assumption was declared a national monument in 1932, particularly because of its Chapel of the Holy Shrine with an XVIII century dome.*

•**CASTLE OF ZUHEROS** *founded in the IX century (above).*
•**CASTLE OF LUQUE** *(below).*

• **The Iznajar** *reservoir is fed by the river Genil.*

during the border wars between Muslims and Christians 800 years ago. Apart from Priego, with its interesting XVIII and XIX artistic heritage, there are other villages in this area, such as Lucena (St. Mathew's Church, below) and Iznájar (below left) and Baena (below), which have always main-

tained a strong tradition of local handicrafts, particularly silk-weaving, villages which have maintained a quiet prosperity amidst the considerable hardship of rural life in Spain, and nowadays, following their tradition of self sufficiency and local agricultural commerce, have managed to produce and sell an olive oil second to none in the world, together with highly palatable wines.

The olives, grapes and cereals, the three basic crops of the Mediterranean basin from time immemorial, are of such quality in this region as to be renowned throughout the oil- and wine-producing lands from here to the Near East.

The town of Baena, apart from being known as "the olive-oil town" is also called "the town of drums": more than 2,000 religious brothers in fierce competition turn Easter week into a thunder of drums and "cry sleep to death" as they enact the scenes of the Passion of Christ throughout the streets.

• **Hand-made leatherware.** *From the time of the caliphs there has been a great tradition of leatherworking in Córdoba, and in fact the famous illustrated ceilings in the Alhambra in Granada are painted on Córdoban leather. The craft thrives to this day thanks to Córdoba's saddlers and harness makers.*

GRANADA

With good reason Granada is known throughout the world as the jewel of Andalucía, the town which visitors to Spain have always sought out first and foremost and have taken home with them in their hearts. It lies almost surrounded by mountains, most spectacularly the snowy peaks of the Sierra Nevada. To the west a fertile irrigated plain has always been Granada's garden. Andalucía was home to the first humans in Europe, who crossed the land bridge from Africa and it is in the province of Granada that the earliest signs of human habitation have been found, going back more than a million years. Granada occupies two hills, the Albaicín and the Alhambra, separated by the river Darro. The Albaicín is clearly the oldest inhabited site, where some two-and-a-half thousand years ago a settlement called Elibyrge formed part of a sophisticated Iberian civilisation in southern Europe. During the Roman occupation of the Spanish peninsular Illiberis Florentinum was the capital of the eastern part of Baetica. The early centuries of Arab rule in Spain saw the town play a secondary role to Córdoba, the seat of the caliphate, but soon after the caliphate disintegrated the city (still not known as Granada) became the capital of the last Islamic stronghold in Europe. Córdoba, Sevilla, Jaén and Murcia all fell in succession to the Christian reconquest when Abu Abd Allah ibn Yusuf ibn Nasr al Ahmar, a Spanish aristocratic Mulim, agreed to pay homage to King Fernando III of Castilla in exchange for leave to rule over the kingdom of Granada. There followed 246 years of splendour for Granada. The Nasrid dynasty built the Alhambra palace on "the red hill" (from whence its name), the most outstanding example of Islamic architecture surviving in the western world. And Granada gained its modern name from the Arabic "Gharnatah", meaning "hill or town of the newcomers", although popular belief would like mistakenly to relate the name to the granada, or pomegranate, the symbol of the city.

In 1492 the Muslim kingdom of Granada finally fell to the Catholic Monarchs, Isabel and Ferdinand and for a short time, particularly under their grandson the emperor Charles V, it became the artistic and social capital of Spain accumulating a wealth of architectural styles from the Gothic through the Renaissance to the Baroque. Today a visitor can spend days just wandering the streets of its old quarters, appreciating the passage of time and the variety of cultures with which the history of Granada is imbued.

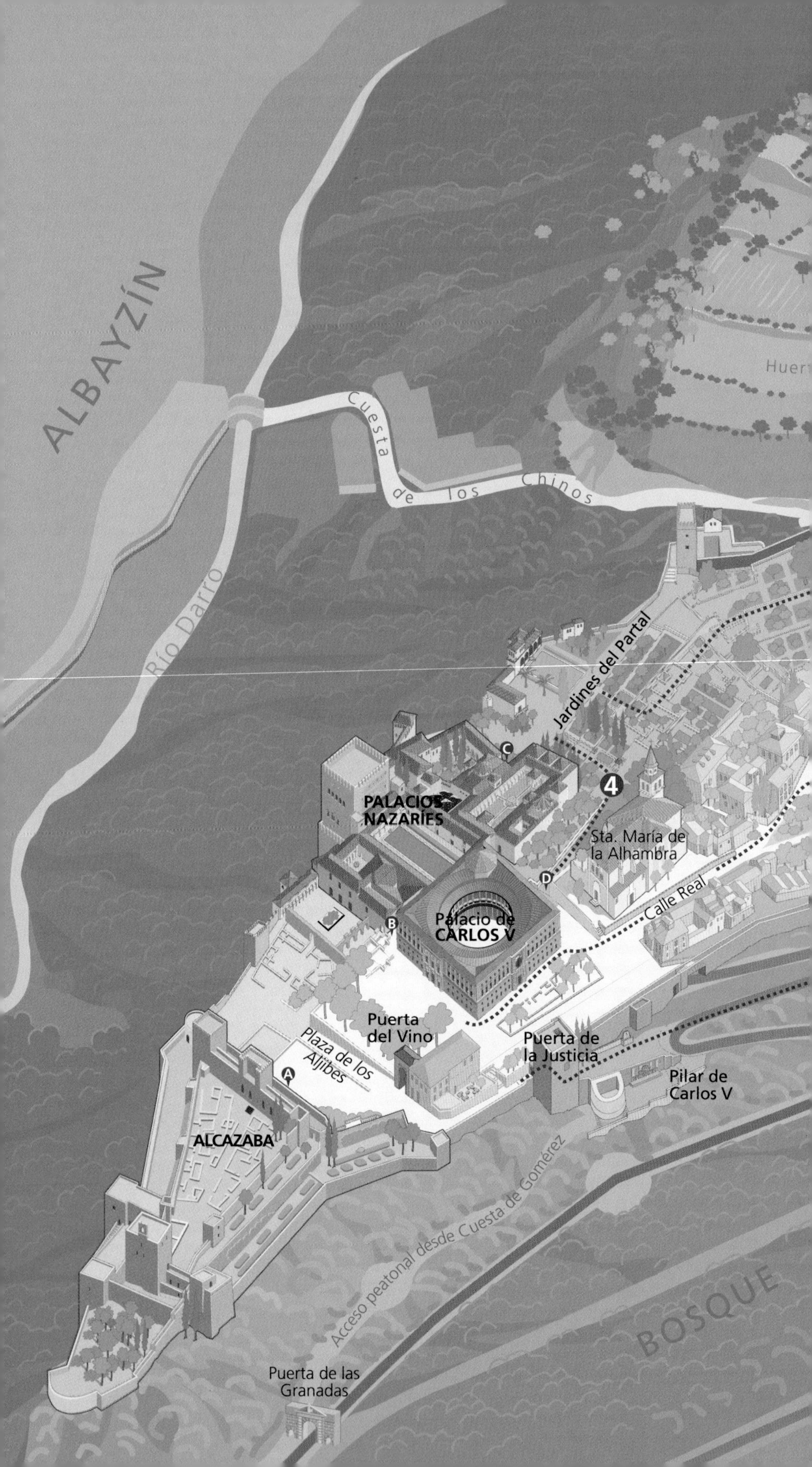

ALBAYZÍN
Río Darro
Cuesta de los Chinos
Huer
Jardines del Partal
PALACIOS NAZARÍES
4
Sta. María de la Alhambra
Calle Real
Palacio de CARLOS V
Puerta del Vino
Plaza de los Aljibes
Puerta de la Justicia
Pilar de Carlos V
ALCAZABA
Acceso peatonal desde Cuesta de Gomérez
BOSQUE
Puerta de las Granadas

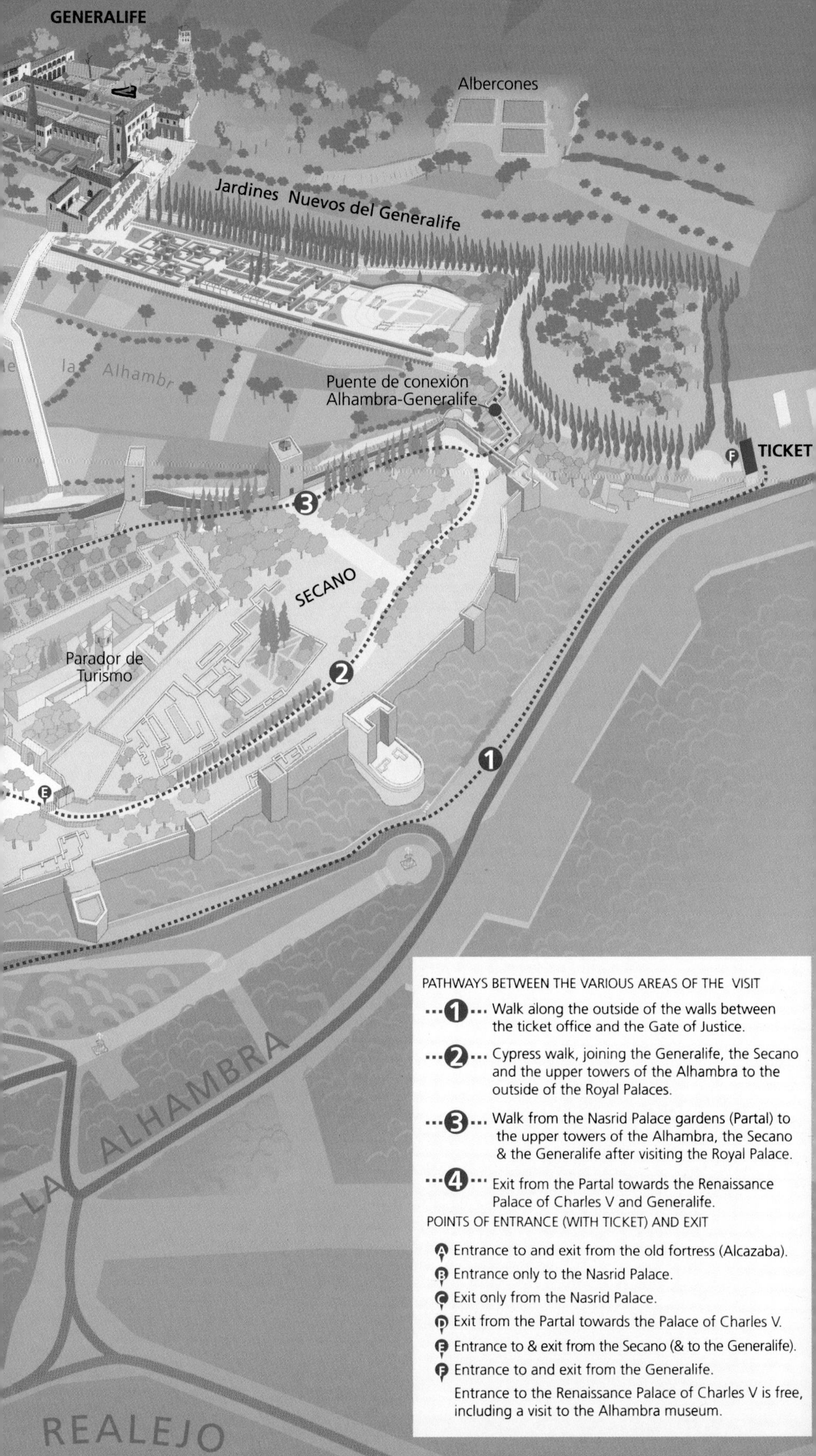
GENERALIFE
Albercones
Jardines Nuevos del Generalife
Puente de conexión
Alhambra-Generalife
TICKET
SECANO
Parador de
Turismo
LA ALHAMBRA
REALEJO
PATHWAYS BETWEEN THE VARIOUS AREAS OF THE VISIT
1 Walk along the outside of the walls between the ticket office and the Gate of Justice.
2 Cypress walk, joining the Generalife, the Secano and the upper towers of the Alhambra to the outside of the Royal Palaces.
3 Walk from the Nasrid Palace gardens (Partal) to the upper towers of the Alhambra, the Secano & the Generalife after visiting the Royal Palace.
4 Exit from the Partal towards the Renaissance Palace of Charles V and Generalife.
POINTS OF ENTRANCE (WITH TICKET) AND EXIT
A Entrance to and exit from the old fortress (Alcazaba).
B Entrance only to the Nasrid Palace.
C Exit only from the Nasrid Palace.
D Exit from the Partal towards the Palace of Charles V.
E Entrance to & exit from the Secano (& to the Generalife).
F Entrance to and exit from the Generalife.
Entrance to the Renaissance Palace of Charles V is free, including a visit to the Alhambra museum.

Granada

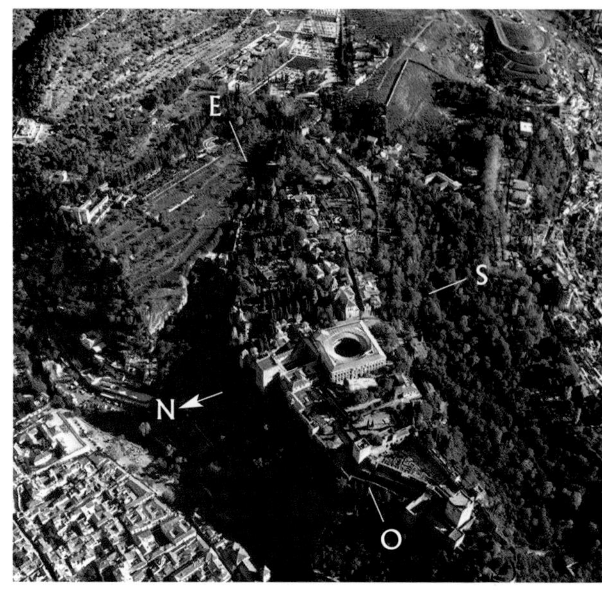

The royal city of the Alhambra stands proudly above Granada upon the hill known in the middle ages as the Cerro de la Sabika, the Hill of Gold. It is one of the most important architectural structures of the Middle Ages in Spain and the finest example of Islamic architecture left to us in the western world.

The steep scarp upon which the Alhambra stands forms a rough triangle; at its eastern end is the Cerro del Sol (Hill of the Sun), crowned by the Generalife, the private retreat of the Nasrid royalty, and a small fortress known as the Seat of the Moor. Running beneath its abrupt northern flank is the valley of the river Darro; at its western extreme stands the Alcazaba citadel and to the south runs a deep valley separating the Alhambra proper from the Mauror Hill and the Vermilion Towers, where a path climbs through woods to the gates of the Muslim citadel.

The hill is composed of reworked detritus from the Sierra Nevada, mainly schists and quartz, deposited some six million years ago in an alluvial fan delta. Subsequent tectonic activity left it staggered into four distinct terraces, the Alhambra itself standing on the third one down. The deposits are in fact grey, the distinctive red colour which gives the hill its name being due to a thin covering of oxidised palaeosoil. At its highest point it is some seven hundred metres above sea level.

The shape of the whole citadel resembles that of a boat with its prow, the Alcazaba, set on a tireless course towards the city. It is seven hundred metres from its stem, the Alcazaba, to its stern, the Cabo de la Carrera tower, and two hundred metres in the beam at its widest. In all it covers an area of some thirteen hectares and is enclosed by more than two kilometres of walls reinforced by some thirty towers, many of which are now in ruins.

With the exception of occasional passing references, no contemporary text speaks in any detail of the Alhambra as such. Occasionally one of the kings of Granada might make some such allusion as "I write to you from the Alhambra, may Allah preserve her!", but little else.
The Alhambra has not always been appreciated for the architecture itself. We all seem to become mere tourists in the Alhambra. A group of Spanish architects wrote in 1953 in the Manifiesto de la Alhambra that "The Alhambra is a monument that has never been looked at properly from an architectural point of view; it is curious: not even by those architects who sharpen their professional eye (if we might put it like that) before the Escorial; when they come to the Alhambra they let go the reins of their critical perspicacity to become tourists like any other, even to the extent of excusing their complacency by alleging a clear distinction as far as their emotions are concerned: Yes, I like this a lot, but not as architecture." Later in the same text they add, "The relationship between this building of the XIV century and the most advanced modern architecture is in some respects astonishing: they coincide with us in their reducing things to a human scale, in their asymmetric yet organic way of laying out the different levels, in how they managed to incorporate the gardens and landscape into the buildings themselves, in their strictly uncluttered use of materials and in so many other aspects which would be laborious to enumerate." And it is true, that the Alhambra, for all its great age, is in both its design and construction a very modern architectural concept.
The Swiss architect Le Corbusier found his view of modern architecture already defined in this monument as "the intelligent, just and magnificent interplay of volumes made harmonious by daylight ". He went on to express this as his ideal in his Cité Moderne (1922). They tried to bring the garden and the landscape into their buildings and they always maintained their scale within human bounds.
Francisco Prieto Moreno, who was for many years the architect in charge of restoring and preserving the monument, said, "The Alhambra combines in its various buildings many architectural precepts which are still valid today, and are of course considered as masterpieces". Another great achievement in its construction is that although it was built over different periods and on a very uneven site the builders still managed to keep the axes and vertices of its courtyards symmetrical, thus imparting an overall impression of complete regularity and harmony.
And so it was: the Alhambra was not planned out entirely from the start; it grew outwards over the centuries from the original IX century fortress, the Alcazaba, gradually increasing in splendour as the years went by. In the XIV century, during the reigns of the great builders, the sul-

tans Yusuf I and his son Muhammad V, the Alhambra stood out like a blaze of white light against the terraced gardens of the Generalife silhouetted against the Hill of the Sun. But if the Alhambra was white, why is it called "the Red"?. The most widely known explanation is one originally offered by Yusuf's vizier, Ibn al-Khatib, who attributes the name to the colour of the

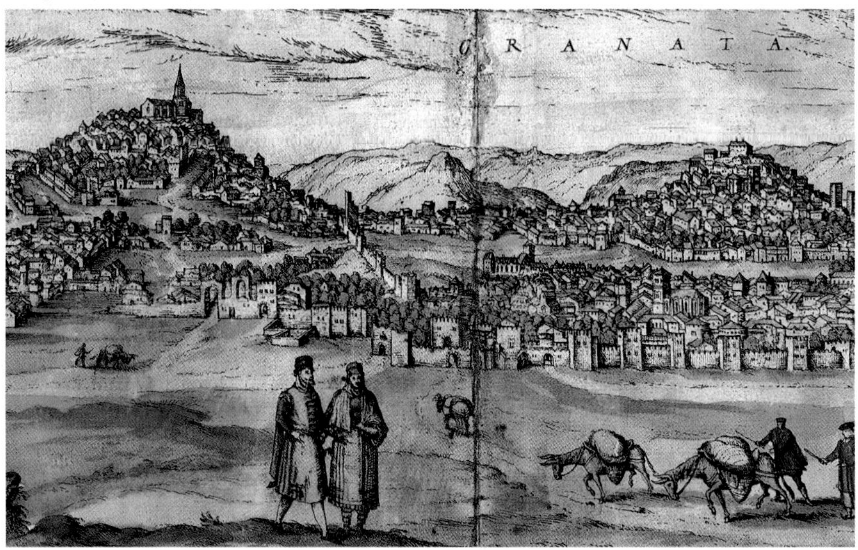

light given off by the torches at night during the hurried construction of the surrounding ramparts. According to Ibn al-Khatib, to those living in the plain below the whole palace seemed to glow red in the dark and so they called it al-Hamra (the Red). We ought to bear in mind, however, that Ibn al-Khatib was also one of the most renowned poets of his time and so we might do well to suspect that this account is a "poetic" version of the truth. More probably the name refers to the red colour of the soil of the hill itself and also includes a pun on the nickname of the first Nasrid emir "al-Hamar", or "the Red".

Titus Burckhardt comments, "The Alhambra was more than a palace, it was a complete city, albeit on a small scale, with its dwellings, administrative offices, garrisons, stables, mosques, schools, baths, cemeteries and gardens. Of all this there only remains the part corresponding to the royal palace itself. And it is almost a miracle that even this has survived, because despite its splendour it was built so insubstantially it almost seems that the builders didn't care. The fortifications as such are strong indeed - they had to be - but the buildings inside the city walls were not built to endure. This would reflect Moslem thought and their ideas about the transitory nature of things: the house of the king is only a temporary dwelling place. This is but one of the many contradictions that the Alhambra offers us if we look at it in the light of the rules concerning the construction of princely dwellings which we take for granted in the rest of Europe. But it is precisely in this "difference" that the hidden meaning of Granadan architecture lies.

In contrast to all the royal residences in Christian Europe, the Alhambra has no façade; it has no main axis about which the buildings are disposed; the rooms are not aligned in such a way as to pass from one to another, from the prelude to the final apotheosis. Instead, at the ends of elusive corridors one finds oneself in hidden courtyards around which rooms are grouped as though by chance"

The Alhambra is not a single building born complete and perfect at a particular moment in time; it is much more the product of three centuries of construction at the end of Muslim rule in al-Andalus, and continued throughout the Christian period almost until modern times. As the outstanding example of Islamic art it is a tree whose roots extend deep into times before al-Andalus, to earlier models in Persia and northern Africa. The Christian influence also began to be felt even before the conquest of the Catholic monarchs, during a period in the middle ages in Spain when the exchange of ideas between Christian and Muslim cultures was almost certainly not so radically proscribed as has often been suggested. Some knowledge of the history of the peoples who shaped the Alhambra is essential to an understanding of its multivariety.

It is not certain whether the mysterious masks are meant to represent Granada's three rivers, the Genil, the Darro and the Beiro, or three seasons, symbolised in the vegetal ornaments: ears of wheat for summer, flowers for spring and grapes for autumn. Whatever their intended significance, they are later Baroque additions to the fountain.

The Charles V Fountain reflects the desire of the conquerors of Islam to christianise the Nasrid city without detracting from its past glory and to emphasise its importance as the new imperial capital. Within this context of respecting the old whilst affirming the reality of the new, this magnificent fountain was placed at the entrance to the Alhambra. It was designed by Pedro Machuca and sculpted by Niccolao da Corte in 1543 to define a new era in the history of the Alhambra.

The Alhambra woods
In order to facilitate its defence the hill surrounding the Alhambra was originally stripped of all vegetation, and thus it appears in contemporary engravings. During the reign of Charles V poplar trees were planted alongside the roads but it wasn't until the XIX century that the Duke of Wellington planted a woodland of new trees, including horse-chestnuts, elms and planes, which survive to this day to give welcome shade to those who walk up the hill to the Alhambra.

Puerta de la Justicia

THE JUSTICE GATE

This gate is today almost the only entrance to the walled confines of the Madina al-Hamra (The Citadel of the Alhambra). It forms a projecting square tower with its rear edge butting against the city wall. Without doubt the most important gateway to the whole royal city, it stands imposingly at the top of a long slope. It still retains its erstwhile majesty in defiance of time, centuries of neglect and modern-day Easter fireworks.

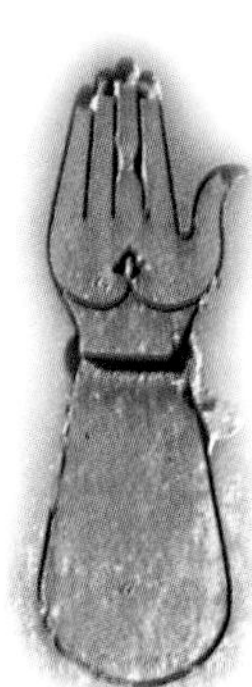

The raised open hand carved into the keystone of the outer arch has been subject to various interpretations; the most plausible of these would seem to be that it represents the five fingers referred to by Muslims as al-Hamza, the five basic precepts of Islam: a belief in one God and in his prophet Muhammad, to pray five times every day, to give alms, to fast during Ramadan and to go on a pilgrimage to Mecca at least once in one's lifetime.

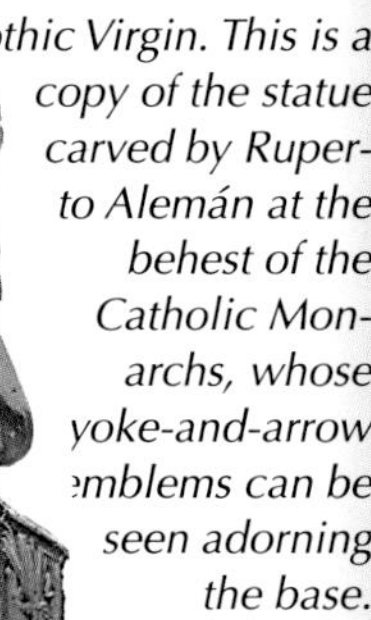

Gothic Virgin. This is a copy of the statue carved by Ruperto Alemán at the behest of the Catholic Monarchs, whose yoke-and-arrow emblems can be seen adorning the base.

"This gate, called Bab al-Sari'a, *was erected by the emir of the Muslims, the righteous warrior sultan Abu-l-Hayyay Yusuf. The work was finished in the month of the Glorious Nativity of the 749th year (June 1348)".*

The tasselled key, *carved on the inner arch, has also been interpreted in various ways; it may have been part of the arms of the Nasrid dynasty in Granada, as claimed by Hurtado de Mendoza, a Christian commander of the time, or else a general symbol of peace and welcome to the well-intentioned. It is repeated on the nearby Wine Gate and in the Polo Courtyard at the entrance to the Generalife.*

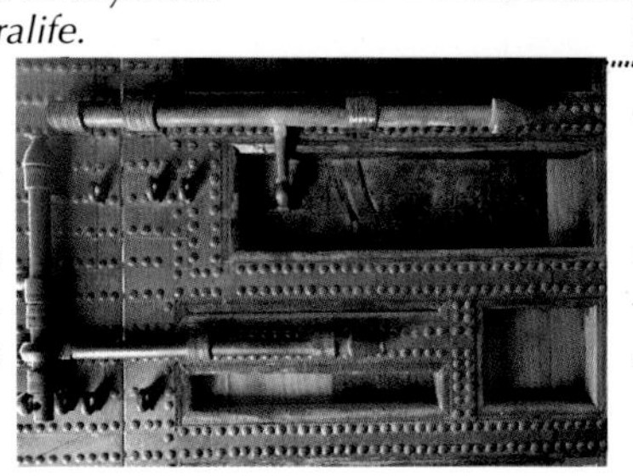

Just inside the inner arch hang two massive ***iron-bound*** *doors, with their original locks and bolts.*

Marble Capital *belonging to the inner arch; in its day it would have been polychromed as would the rest of the doorway*

Between the outer arch, which was probably never closed by doors, and the inner arch there is a confined ***defensive area****, typical of Nasrid military building, where those defending the gate could hurl rocks, boiling oil or molten lead from the tower above onto any assailants trying to break down the door to the inner arch below them.*

Beyond these arches THE ENTRANCE CONTINUES TO RISE *in the form of a ramp with four right-angled corners covered by squinched vaults with lunettes to provide light.*

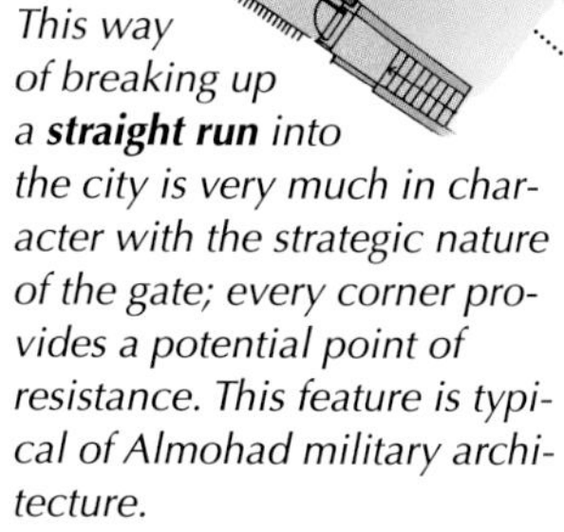

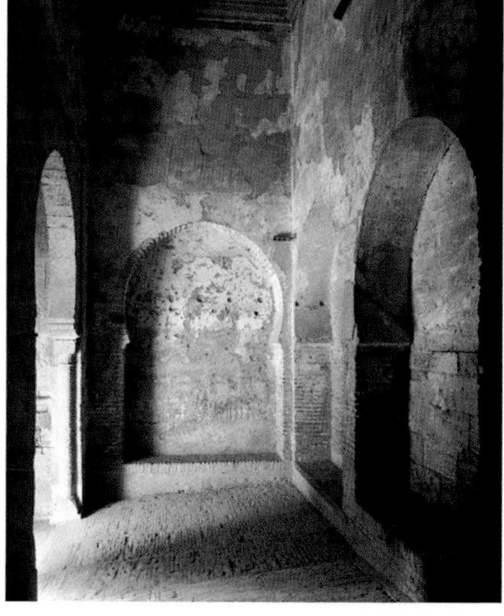

This way of breaking up a ***straight run*** *into the city is very much in character with the strategic nature of the gate; every corner provides a potential point of resistance. This feature is typical of Almohad military architecture.*

Once past the gate itself an aggressor would arrive at the corraleta, a wide passageway where horsemen would be arrayed waiting to charge downhill against the uphill attack. To the right of the gate there is a pathway which runs between the parapets around the entire city wall, sometimes covered, sometimes open to the sky, but always protected sufficiently to allow the guards to make their rounds on horseback.

Right: part of the wall, reconstructed with head-stones from a nearby Muslim cemetery.

It is generally accepted that the name of this gate derives from the tax-free wine that was sold inside the portal from 1554. There were other gates nearby but within the intricate labyrinth of the mediaeval city this was the gate which gave most direct access to the higher reaches of the city, home to some 2,000 inhabitants. At this point the Royal Way, the main artery of the medina began; it was also a crossroads and the dividing line between the military and civil areas of the town.

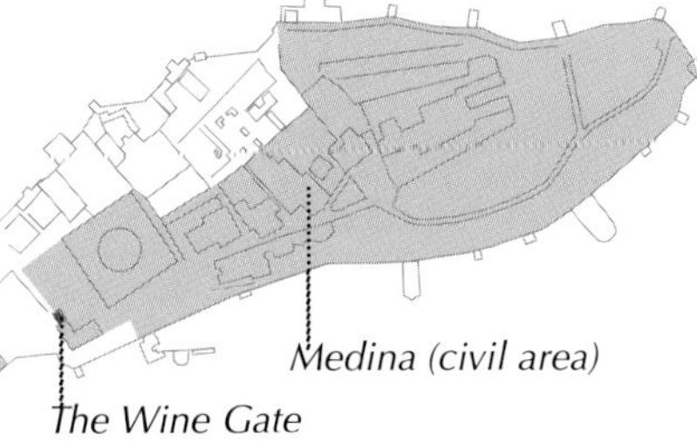

*The **eastern façade** is the most interesting and ornamental. It contains fine ceramic tiling, painted and fired using the dry-cord technique, elaborate decorative gesso (left) and vestiges of stucco-work with hints of polychroming.*

*The **straight entrance** through this gate with no corners to hinder an attacker and the window with its jalousie lend support to the idea that it was intended for civil rather than military use.*

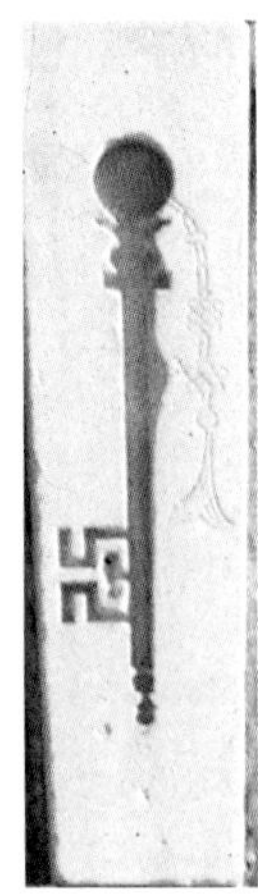

*The **western façade** (right) is older and more roughly executed. The gateway itself has one of the few still extant pointed horseshoe arches. It is also emblazoned with the mysterious symbolic key*

*Inside the **gate** are the typical benches where the guards would have sat, protected from the elements. The small room thus formed is covered by a magnificent groined vault similar to that in the Gate of Arms in the northern wall of the Alcazaba.*

Alcazaba

The Alcazaba, unjustly forgotten by all those who after the Christian conquest wrote in dazzling terms about the Nasrid palaces, is the solitary forbear of an entire aristocratic city, which would later come to be known as Madinat al-Hamra (The citadel of the Alhambra). It is referred to in the accounts of the civil wars in the IX century and battles against the invading Almoravids and Almohads by various different names such as the fortress of Elvira or Granada Castle until, from the XIII century onwards, the name qa'lat al-hamra (the red castle) becomes fixed and it is by this name that we know it today.

Granada

Torre del Homenage *(the keep). This is one of the oldest towers of the Alcazaba, probably dating back to the caliphate. Archaeological comparisons between the building materials of the actual tower and those in its foundations suggest that it may have been rebuilt by Muhammad I upon the ruins of a previous IX century structure.*

Puerta de las Armas *(The Arms Gate). This gate used to be the main entrance to the Alcazaba. It butts onto the inner precinct of the Alcazaba as a flanking tower to the Watchtower.*

Torre de la Vela *(The Watchtower) This tower was originally built by the founder of the Nasrid dynasty, Muhammad ibn Nasr "al-Ahmar" (ruled 1238-73), as his feudal residence.*

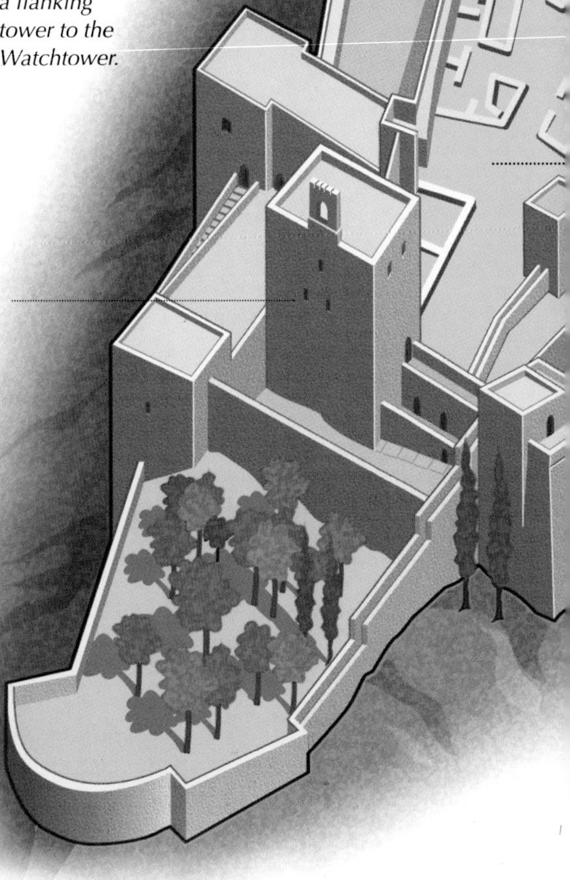

CUBO DE LA ALHAMBRA (THETUB). *This round, squat tower houses the Puerta de la Tahona (Bakery Gate), a XVI century renaissance addition after the Christian conquest.*

TORRE QUEBRADA *(The Cracked Tower), known thus because of the great crack in its wall, stretching like a wound from top to bottom, which can be seen from the Plaza de los Aljibes. The tower has been filled in up to the height of the city wall but has two more floors above this level.*

Ticket

THE CISTERN SQUARE

THE WINE GATE

PLAZA DE LAS ARMAS *(The Parade Square). From the top of a cobbled slope a central street containing buildings of a multitude of uses led away from this square .*

TORRE DE LA SULTANA *(The Sultana's Tower). As the photograph below shows, this tower rises majestically above the Jardín del Adarve. It must have lost some of its slender elegance, however when the deep fosse was filled in to make the garden.*

JARDÍN DEL ADARVE *(The Parapet Garden) A deep fosse separated the outer and inner ramparts until the beginning of the XVII century, when it was filled in with rubble and earth by the Marquis of Mondejar to make this garden.*

TORRE DE LA PÓLVORA *(The Gunpowder Tower). From here a pathway spans the deep ravine of the Cuesta de Gomérez across the top of a gate, thus linking the citadel to the Vermillion Towers on the other side.*

W

The top of the Watchtower offers the visitor magnificent, uninterrupted views all around.

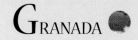

This is the Granada that Gautier called "Celestial Jerusalem" and that which the Córdoban al-Saqundi praised as being "nourishing to the eye and uplifting to the soul".

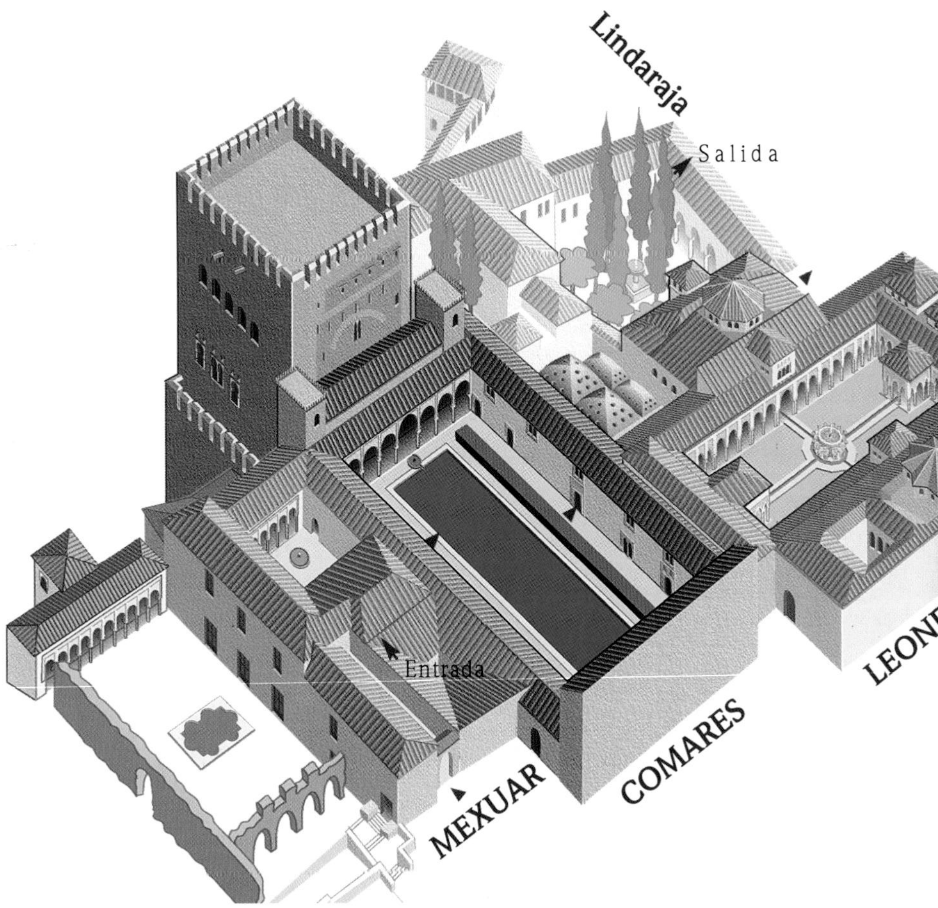

THE OLD ROYAL HOUSE

Not long after the Christian conquest the Nasrid palaces were referred to as the Old Royal House in order to distinguish them from the New Royal House, the palace that Charles V intended to build as the great residential, administrative and political centre of the new Spanish empire. This distinction implied a clear intention to integrate the Nasrid buildings into the projected scheme of the new Alhambra. The Catholic monarchs had no fixed residence and so when their grandson, Charles I of Spain, later the emperor Charles V, chose the Alhambra as the site of his own palace he unwittingly saved it for posterity.

The Old Royal House comprises today, as it did then, the most important focal points of the Alhambra: the Mexuar (council chamber) and the two palaces of Comares and the Lions, together with their annexes and outbuildings, all of which merit individual explanation within the context of the palace complex as a whole.

References have been made to seven palaces within the citadel and there is no doubt that only a small part of the original royal town and some vestiges of the medina remain today, but sufficient to give us some idea of the splendour and majesty of a civilisation at its cultural height, although politically in decline.

The Alhambra has justly been declared a monument of human heritage. Beyond the purely architectural it is a creation of space, air and light. But it is not a space filled within a void; it is rather a captured amalgam of brightness and shadow, streams and flowers, enveloped in verse and sensations which transcend time.

LOS PALACIOS NAZARIES

THE NASRID PALACES

MEXUAR

COMARES

LEONES

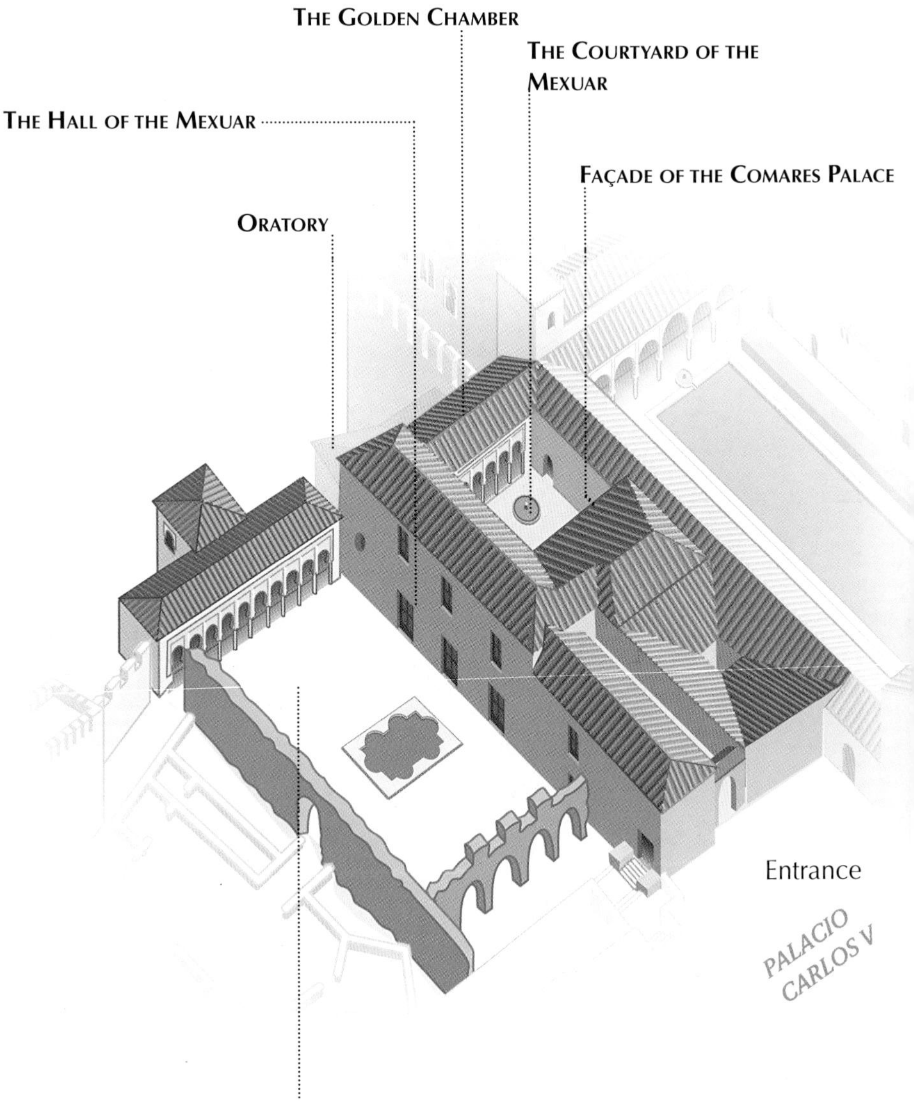

THE GOLDEN CHAMBER

THE COURTYARD OF THE MEXUAR

THE HALL OF THE MEXUAR

FAÇADE OF THE COMARES PALACE

ORATORY

Entrance

PALACIO CARLOS V

MACHUCA'S COURTYARD

This courtyard is named after the famous architect Pedro Machuca, who designed the Palace of Charles V and lived in the tower with an arched portico on the north side of the courtyard overlooking the river Darro. On the opposite side of the courtyard there was an identical gallery, of which only vestiges remain in the ground.

Mexuar

Lewis, 1835

This is without doubt the area of the palace complex that has undergone most transformation since its earliest days, changes which were largely made by the Christian governors in the name of their king to adapt it to new roles and functions. Thus its original shape has been altered considerably, sometimes to the detriment of original structures, and so it is quite difficult nowadays to establish exactly where the entrances to this part of the palace really were.

Granada

The Hall of the Mexuar

This is almost certainly the oldest surviving part of the royal palaces but it has undergone substantial alterations. It was here that the royal court of justice is believed to have convened. After the conquest the Christian monarchs installed their chapel here, changing the shape of the room.

*The **small door** guarding the entrance today is a later introduction brought from elsewhere. It has fine carved surrounds and is sheltered by overhanging eaves supported by elegant corbels.*

*The **original hall** was illuminated by daylight filtering through the stained-glass panes of a lantern window in the roof. This was later replaced by a radial, wooden ceiling.*

*An **original wall** at the northern end of the hall, which closed it off from either a small yard or a street, was demolished to amplify the hall. The decorative gesso covering the original wall was saved and used on the new wall, which contains a doorway leading to the erstwhile oratory.*

*The present-day wooden **balustrade** represents the remains of a choir, which was added in the space gained when the exterior yard was included within the hall.*

*The **eastern wall** was reinforced to support the weight of a new floor added above the hall. Great windows with wrought-iron grilles were opened up to give more light to the room.*

The council met within the square formed by the four columns to decide upon important judicial matters. At the door there was a tile which reads,

"Enter and ask. Do not be afraid to seek justice for here you will find it."

THE COURTYARD OF THE MEXUAR

*This small courtyard used to be called, for no good reason, the Courtyard of the Mosque. On its southern side is an impressive façade, always accepted as having been the entrance to the Comares Palace. Opposite, on the northern side, with a portico in front of it, is the so-called **Golden Chamber.***

***Engravings** of this patio from centuries past should be evidence enough to exonerate later restorers from any feelings of blame we might bear towards them; as far as this courtyard is concerned, the extensive restoration work has been well carried out.*

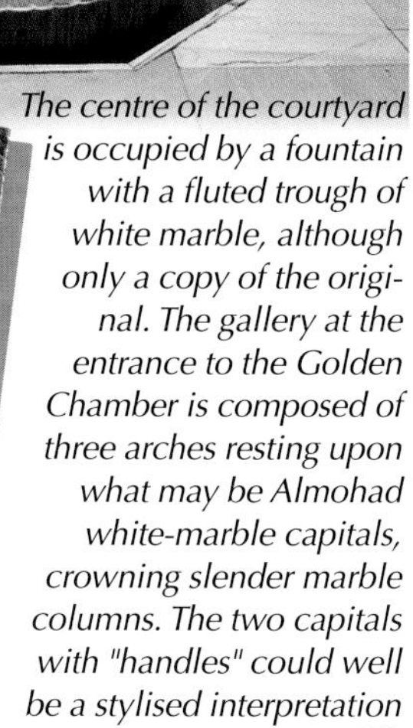

Above: a drawing of the Mexuar Courtyard by Owen (1842) and right: a lithograph by Taylor (1835)

The centre of the courtyard is occupied by a fountain with a fluted trough of white marble, although only a copy of the original. The gallery at the entrance to the Golden Chamber is composed of three arches resting upon what may be Almohad white-marble capitals, crowning slender marble columns. The two capitals with "handles" could well be a stylised interpretation of similar zoomorphic capitals to be found in Persepolis (above).

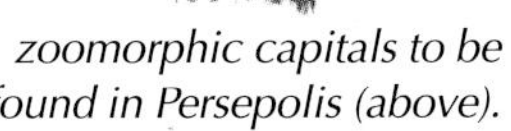

The eastern wall of the courtyard houses the entrance to a long tunnel, which leads eventually to the Comares Palace bathhouse after passing small rooms on either side that must have served as soldiers' quarters or guard rooms.

Fachada de Comares

This façade of the Comares Palace was considerably restored in the XIX century. Its ataurique (foliate and vegetal) decoration becomes more intricate as it goes upwards, possibly in imitation of the ascending order of classical design

"My position is that of a crown and my door is a parting of the ways: the West believes that in me is the East. Al-Gani bi-llah has entrusted me to open the way to the victory that has been foretold and I

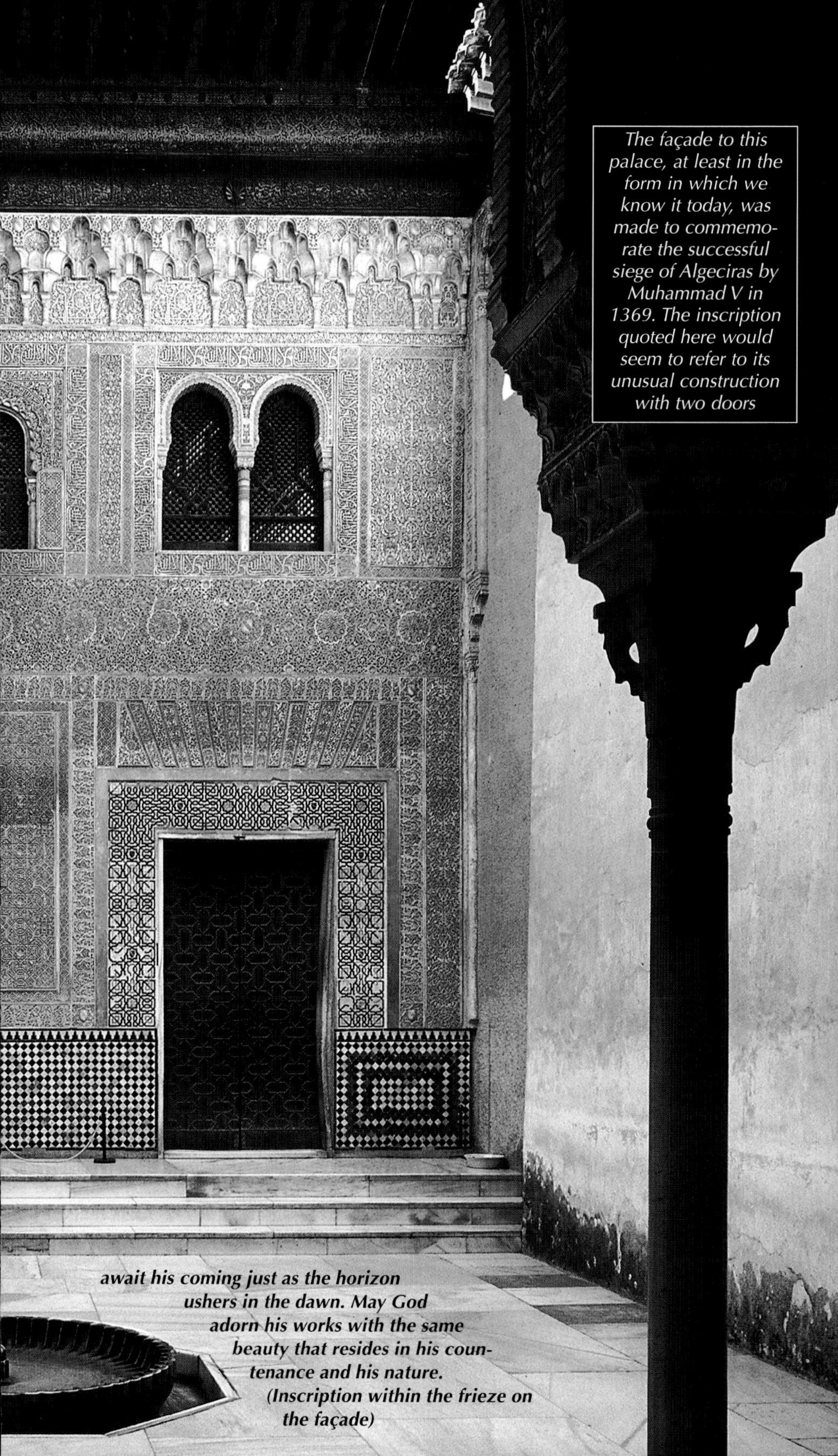

The façade to this palace, at least in the form in which we know it today, was made to commemorate the successful siege of Algeciras by Muhammad V in 1369. The inscription quoted here would seem to refer to its unusual construction with two doors

await his coming just as the horizon ushers in the dawn. May God adorn his works with the same beauty that resides in his countenance and his nature.
(Inscription within the frieze on the façade)

GRANADA

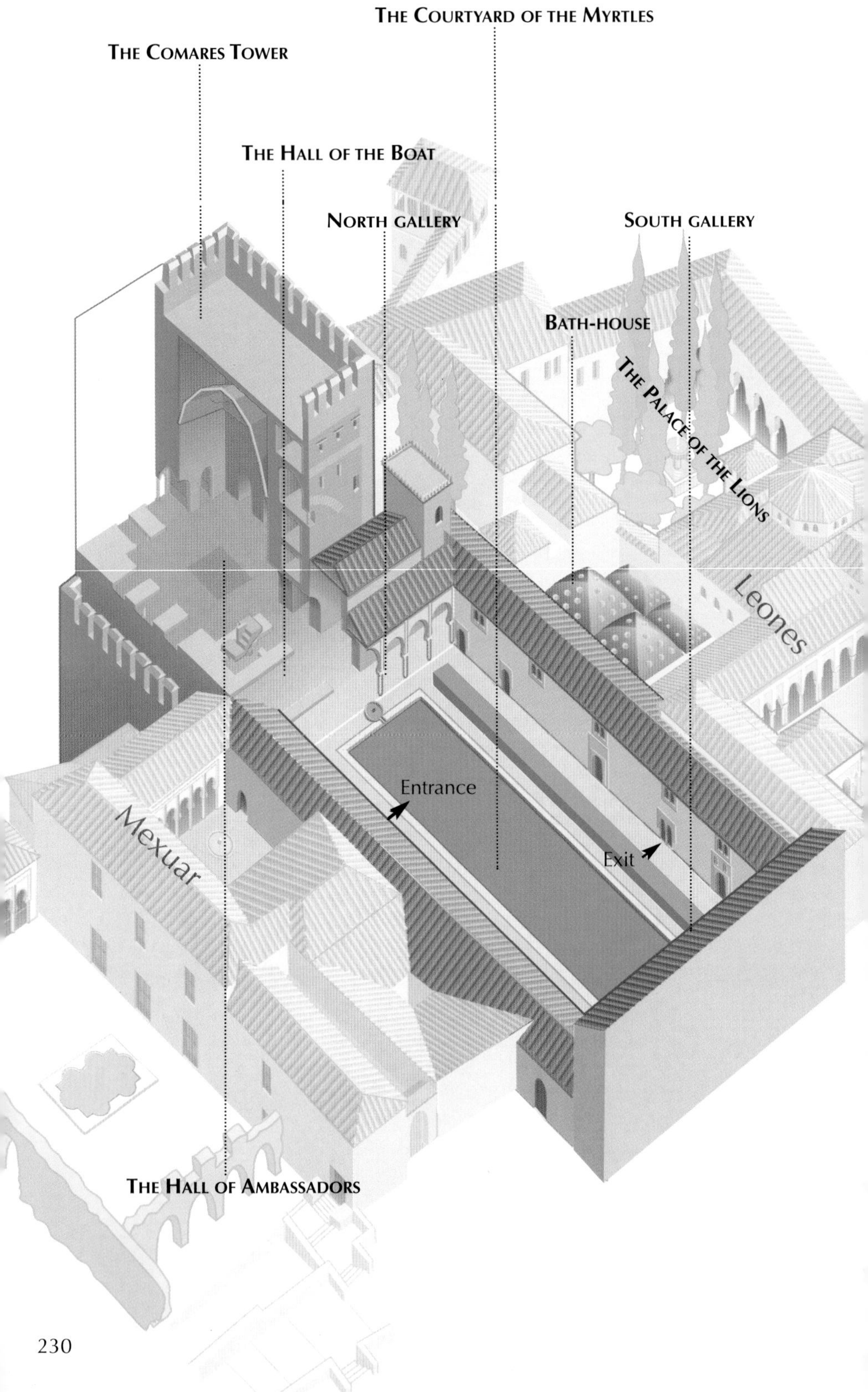

The Courtyard of the Myrtles
The Comares Tower
The Hall of the Boat
North gallery
South gallery
Bath-house
The Palace of the Lions
Leones
Entrance
Exit
Mexuar
The Hall of Ambassadors

Comares

Taylor, 1832

This palace complex, including the Hall of the Ambassadors, or Throne Room, forms the most important nucleus of the Alhambra. The simplicity of its lines and its balanced proportions lend the courtyard a feeling of such serene majesty that we still breath in the air of noble grandeur of the kings who presided over its building.

This was the focal point of diplomatic and political activity in the Alhambra and without doubt the place where great receptions for ambassadors were held. It was also where important visitors waited to be received by the sultan. Until recently the whole of this part of the building, apart from some of the decorative work corresponding to his son Muhammad V, to whom there is a panegyric on the wall of the north gallery, had been accredited to Yusuf I. A study by Emilio García Gómez, however has shown fairly convincingly that Yusuf I (1333-54) built the gallery and Hall of the Boat, the Comares Tower and the baths, whilst the rest was built during the reign of his son Muhammad V.

*The **myrtle** (myrtus communis) was frequently found in the gardens of al-Andalus. This courtyard owes its name to the myrtle bushes that border the central pool. They are evergreen and give off a very pleasant smell when their leaves are rubbed in the hand.*

" ...WHEN THE REST OF EUROPE WAS BUILDING CASTLES IN THE AIR, IN GRANADA THEY WERE CONSTRUCTING PALACES UPON WATER." (JESÚS BERMÚDEZ PAREJA)

*When a visitor crossed the main threshold he was confronted by a **vast mirror of water** reflecting the solid white bulk of the Comares Tower. The slope of the white marble floors allows the water in the pool to reach right up to the plinths of the columns on the north side of the courtyard and so the whole palace, even the tower itself, seems to be floating on water. This use of water to mirror the structure above was used some three centuries later (1630-47) in the Taj Mahal at Agra in India.*

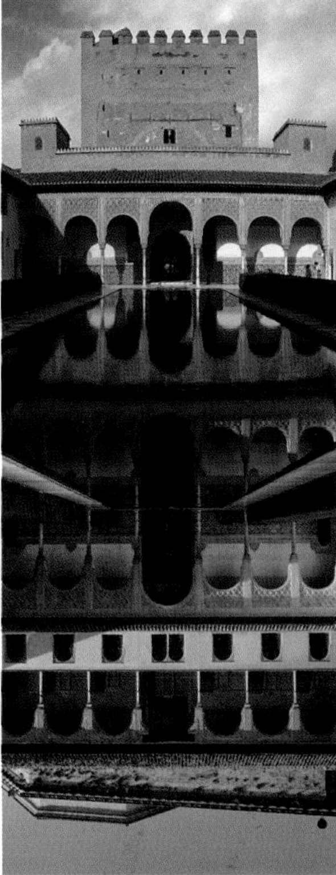

*It can be seen in engravings by XIX century artists, such as that shown above by Lewis (1835), that there were no **small turrets** flanking the main tower and that the roof of the portico did not run smoothly and uniformly into that of the Hall of the Boat. Originally there was only one such tower, to the east, which would have served to protect the door that nowadays allows access to the courtyard. At the time of the engravings this tower was not crenellated, although it may have been in earlier times.*

Galería Sur

The courtyard was an open esplanade during the reign of Yusuf I. His son, Muhammad V, built the gallery to enclose its southern end and thus make a private courtyard similar to the Greek megaton and Roman atrium.

The juxtaposition of the cornice of the Palace of Charles V intrudes upon the delicate, insubstantial lines of the Courtyard of the Myrtles, bearing witness to two completely different ways of understanding shape and space.

The North Gallery

This gallery is very similar to the one on the south side and many of the decorative elements and epigraphs found in the south gallery were copied from this one.

Above the XVI century tiled dado is a poem by Ibn Zamrak written in cursive script, which refers in one of its verses to the heroic deeds of Muhammad V.

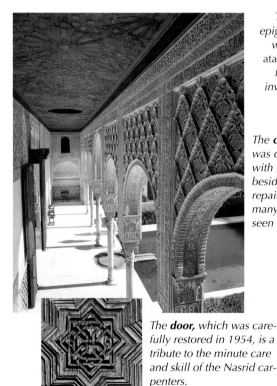

"You conquered Algeciras with the might of your sword, opening a secret doorway to our victory."

*The **tree of life** crowns the line of epigraphic verses written around the wall. This type of design, in which* ataurique *motifs spread downwards from an apex is an allusion to the inverted tree that sustains the celestial bodies in the firmament and buries its roots in paradise.*

*The **coffered ceiling** of this gallery was destroyed in a fire in 1890 along with that of the Hall of the Boat beside it. It has been very skilfully repaired, however, making use of many of the burnt pieces (as can be seen in the photograph on the left).*

*The **door,** which was carefully restored in 1954, is a tribute to the minute care and skill of the Nasrid carpenters.*

*A **detail** of the geometry of the stucco decoration*

This long room lies behind the gallery and serves as an anteroom to the Throne Room. At each end it has two alcoves framed by stilted arches and also a water closet on the west side.

Right: entrance arch in an engraving by Taylor (1855).

The small, beautifully sculpted marble or gesso niches in the jambs of the arches were for keeping jars of water, perfume or vases of flowers, but almost always water as a symbol of hospitality, according to the verses written around them.

Niche made of Macael marble in the intrados of the arch leading from the portico of the Courtyard of the Myrtles into the Hall of the Boat.

According to the inscrip-ions that run along the vall above the tiling in the alcove itself, the central alcove on the north side of he hall was reserved for he throne:

[...] Yusuf [...] chose me to be the throne of the kingdom.

From here the sultan had a psychological advantage over his subjects, who would have felt themselves at one and the same time under the commanding but protective gaze of the political, military and religious leader of their kingdom. Foreign ambassadors too, as they crossed the

hreshold of the Hall of the Boat and walked towards the throne oom, surrounded by brilliant colours and gleaming gold, vould have felt intimidated by he scrutiny of the sultan, silhouetted against the more mysterious light of the stained glass behind him. The sultan himself, ying on his throne, could enjoy he view of Granada and its elegant houses and gardens, the sky and water, which was offered to his eyes like a mirror in the Courtyard of the Myrtles. The stained glass windows of the throne room were destroyed by the explosion of a gunpowder magazine in 1590. The geometric design of these windows were a ransparent continuation of the tiled dado. In he windows; the fine straight lines that criss-cross the ceramics were represented by the

thin strips of lead holding each coloured pane in place. The light thus filtered through the stained glass fell upon a blue and gold tiled floor, some vestiges of which remain,roped off in the centre of the hall. The originals are those tiles in which the blues surrounding the dynastic shields are painted right to the edge and are completely flat, so as to be smooth for unshod feet. The later, post-conquest imitations stick up slightly around the edges of the colours

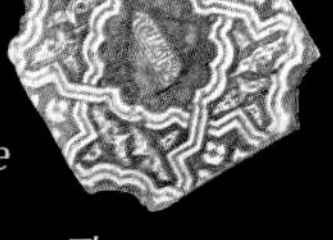

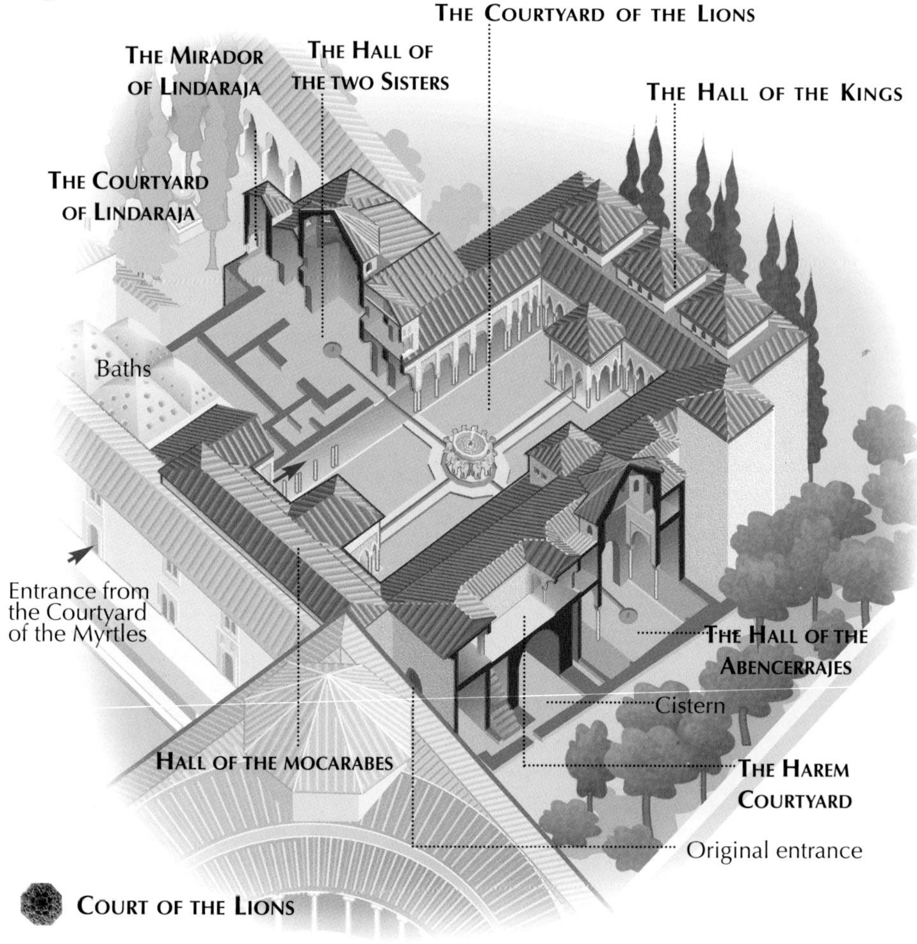

COURT OF THE LIONS

From the original entrance, shown here in the lower corner of the plan, the beauty of this patio progressively revealed itself to the visitor. In either direction that he chose to take around the cloister, he found himself walking through a forest of gilded pillars, which little by little began to appear like "gold fringes of lace hanging from the sky". The cubic capitals were originally polychromed. Their apparent uniformity is deceptive as their motifs are in fact considerably varied. The columns support pilasters, which in turn hold up lintels supporting the upper structure of the walls. The spandrels between the pilasters are filled by small, purely decorative, open-work, or "curtain" arches.

"The original fountain represents an ancient symbol that arrived in Granada from pre-Christian civilisations in the East: the lion spewing water from its mouth is the sun, from whence all life springs. The twelve suns of this fountain are the twelve suns of the zodiac, the twelve months in which we all exist simultaneously. They uphold the sea like the twelve iron bulls in Solomon's temple, and this sea is the basin of heaven's waters. To what extent the Nasrid builders of the Alhambra were aware of this ancient symbolism, however, is im-possible to say." (Prof.Rafael Manzano).

Patio de los Leones

THE PALACE AND COURTYARD OF THE LIONS

Roberts, 1835

This was the focal point of the sultan's private dwellings, within which there were areas set aside for the women of the house. It cannot be called the harem because it wasn't reserved exclusively for female use but was also probably used for some aspects of the sultan's political and diplomatic affairs. It is recorded on December 30 1362 that during the second reign of Mohammad V nothing more existed of the Courtyard of the Lions than the Sala de las Dos Hermanas (The Hall of the two Sisters) and so the buildings that surround it today must have been constructed after this date.

Space in the Alhambra *is as open as in the desert, where intimacy itself is to be found beneath the stars. The Courtyard of the Lions isn't a house with a garden but a garden containing a house, which should be looked at from its corners at floor height (above).*

According to Islamic tradition, the walled garden is an image of paradise, the name of which in the Koran is al-Yanna, a word which embraces the two meanings of "garden" and "secret place". A visitor today must allow his imagination to see the four areas between the streams, today covered with sand, as beds full of flowering bushes and aromatic herbs. The four streams symbolise the four rivers of paradise that run towards the four points of the compass, or flow from them towards the centre). The original fountain represents an ancient symbol that arrived in Granada from pre-Christian civilisations in the East: the lion spewing water from its mouth is the sun, from whence all life springs... They uphold the sea like the twelve iron bulls in Solomon's temple, and this sea is the basin of heaven's waters. (R. Manzano

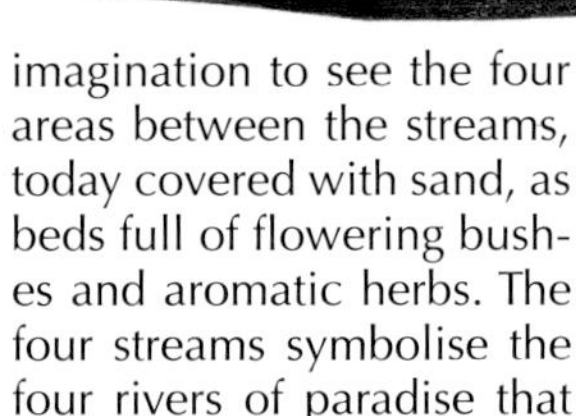

Refreshing water springs *from the mouths of twelve white marble lions in the Fountain of the Lions in the middle of the courtyard. Placed in a circle and bearing on their backs a twelve-sided bowl, their gaze embraces every part of the courtyard.*

An inscription in the Hall of the Two Sisters asks, We have never seen a garden with greater abundance of fruit, nor sweeter, nor more perfumed…" but today its flowers no longer form a carpet on the earth, nor do they climb and twine around the marble columns; what we see is no more than a magnificent skeleton, a dry framework to which greenery once gave meaning and life.The two small pavilions jutting out into the east and west sides of the courtyard, each housing a small fountain, also play a part in the Islamic image of paradise as the high tents (rafraf) or canopies described in the Koran. The model for these pavilions floating above delicate columns derives from further east, in Persian art, of which this part of the Alhambra is so reminiscent.

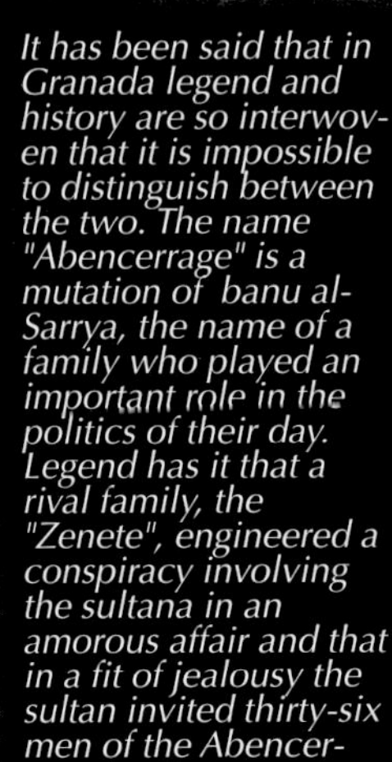

It has been said that in Granada legend and history are so interwoven that it is impossible to distinguish between the two. The name "Abencerrage" is a mutation of banu al-Sarrya, the name of a family who played an important role in the politics of their day. Legend has it that a rival family, the "Zenete", engineered a conspiracy involving the sultana in an amorous affair and that in a fit of jealousy the sultan invited thirty-six men of the Abencerrage family to a celebration in this hall and had them all cut down in front of him. In fact it is not clear when this is supposed to have happened and the story has also been attributed to various sultans.

Mariano Fortuny, a painter of the romantic period of the end of the XIX century, portrayed the slaughter of the Abencerrages in this painting of 1871. A lot of what many visitors to the Alhambra expect to see, and so believe they are seeing, has been created by the imagination of romantic writers and painters.

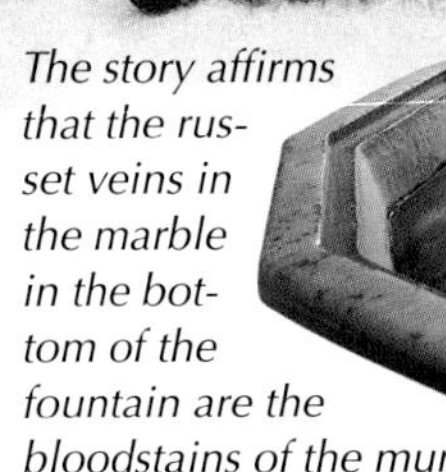

The story affirms that the russet veins in the marble in the bottom of the fountain are the bloodstains of the murdered courtiers.

They are of course oxidisation in the marble itself.

This hall is an ideal refuge in the heat of summer. When the doors are shut the only light to enter the room filters in through the high, star-shaped, lantern windows in the cupola, which also draw out the hot air from below. The water in the fountain, emerging chilly from underground, always keeps the air fresh and cool. Its thick, windowless walls let in no heat and turn it into a pleasant cave in which the temperature of its alcoves never rises much above twenty degrees even during the hottest months of the year.

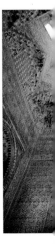

The alcoves, set apart by pillars from the rest of the room, were couches and divans. The step up into these alcoves accentuates their separation from the rest of the room

They usually open onto a courtyard or another room but would have been curtained off for privacy.

The Hall of the Abencerrages by Chapuy (1840).

The "alicatado" tiling was stripped from this hall and taken to the Alcázar in Sevilla (above); the present-day tiles (right) date from the XVI century.

From behind the fountain the perspective is one of a series of different brilliantly lit optical planes. Right in the background, through the The Mirador of Lindaraja in the Hall of the Two Sisters there was a view of the old city framed against the sky. The surface of the fountain reflects the magnificent coffered ceiling, the mocarabes of which form an enormous eight-pointed star.

THE HALL OF THE KINGS

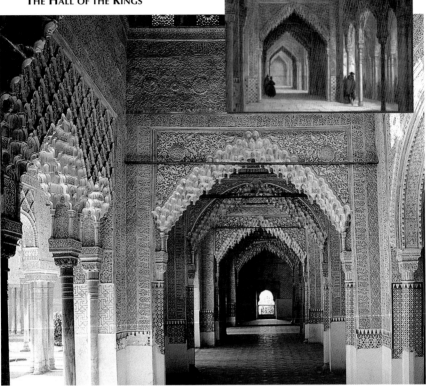

This hall occupies the whole of the east side of the courtyard.

It is divided into five separate areas; three of these are chambers illuminated from porticos giving onto the courtyard and separated from each other by the other two transitional areas, which lie in deep shadow. From either end the hall appears to be a succession of light and shade. Each room is defined by high, pointed stucco arches, all elaborately decorated in different styles. This variety in adornment and the alternation of light and shade renders even such rich and complex decoration soothing to the eye, without producing the fatigue which Baroque design can cause when repeated incessantly.

On the ceiling of the ***central alcove*** *is a painting of ten seated men, who, according to tradition, are the first ten rulers of the Nasrid dynasty.*

THE HALL OF THE TWO SISTERS

Contrary to what was believed until recently, it is now known that this hall is the oldest of all the rooms surrounding the Courtyard of the Lions. What this room was called originally is unknown but its present-day name, the Two Sisters, refers to the twin pair of Macael marble slabs that lie in its centre.

On entering this hall from the Courtyard of the Lions, just as in the Hall of the Abencerrages, one narrow passage branches to the right and another to the left. The one on the right leads to a stairway to the upper rooms and that on the left to a water closet.

The Muslims were far ahead of the rest of Europe in the design and use of lavatories flushed by water. The latrine itself was a tile perforated with a long hole. The closet also contained a separate wash basin and ventilation.

Two sturdy arches on each side of the main entrance from the courtyard provide access to bedroom alcoves. The arch opposite leads out of the Hall of the Two Sisters proper into the Chamber of the Ajimeces (referring to the beautiful mullion windows), which itself serves as an anteroom to the Mirador of Lindaraja. Above these arches there are four more smaller ones, which provide light for the rooms above.

Patio de los Leones

"All the arts have enriched me with their own special beauty and given me their splendour and perfection. You who would see me, judge through me the beauty of a wife who walks towards this jar and asks its favour. When you watch me and contemplate my beauty attentively your eyes are deceived by a vision. Because when you look into my splendid depths you believe that the full moon has abandoned her mansions to live in mine and keep here her dwelling place. I am not alone for from here I look over a lovely garden; no eyes have ever beheld anything similar to it. This is a crystal palace, although there are those who on seeing it have pronounced it a storming, surging ocean.
Here breathe fresh breezes; the air is healthy and the zephyr agreeable.
I join together all beauties in the same way that the stars in the high firmament steal their light from them.
Surely I am in this garden an eye filled with joy and the pupil of this eye is veritably my lord."

Poem inscribed above the mirador.

The Bath-House of the Comares Palace had a very specific function directly related to politics and diplomacy. The position of its door, the first on the left in the eastern wall of the Courtyard of the Myrtles, close to the entrance to the Hall of the Ambassadors, betrays its use: it was a comfortable place to conduct the friendly management of official business. Throughout the history of Islam, the public bath has been second only to the mosque as a focal point of social life and had the same influence on mediaeval urban activity equivalent to the town square in the west or the agora in ancient Greece.

Granada

Musicians Gallery

Once past the entrance the visitor finds what has come to be known as the "musicians gallery". Popular imagination has placed here blind musicians who would charm the bathers without sullying the erotic scenes below with their lascivious gaze. Unfortunately for popular belief it must be pointed out that bathing included certain religious connotations and men and women were never permitted to bathe together.

Rooms assigned to the bath warden

This would have been a man of the utmost trust, who from these rooms could, through a jalousie, keep a discreet eye on the movements of his lord's retinue and visitors. He could call for help to a neighbouring guard-room in case of need.

Water closet

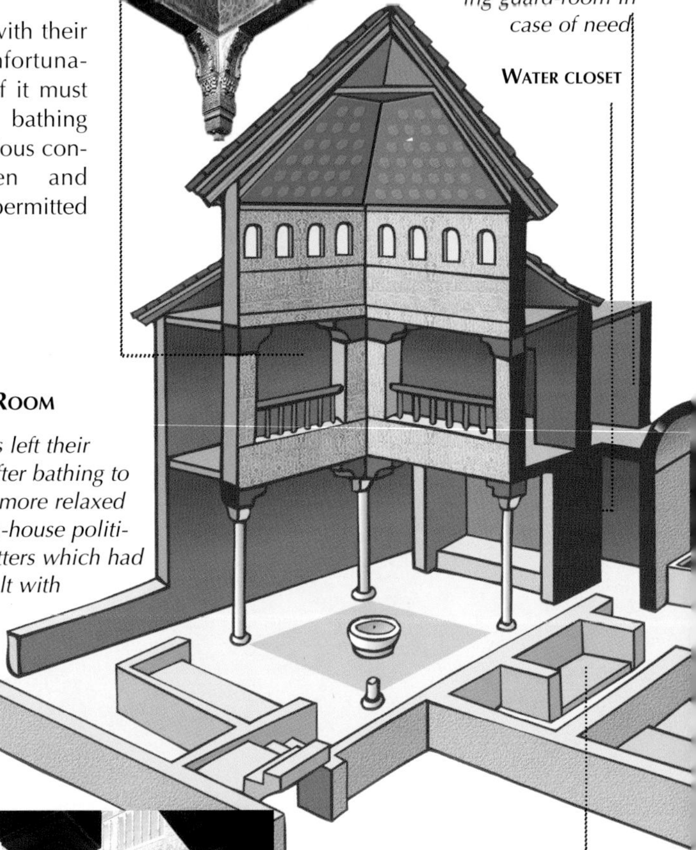

Changing and Rest Room

This was where bathers left their clothes and returned after bathing to rest and discuss in the more relaxed atmosphere of the bath-house political and diplomatic matters which had probably just been dealt with under the greater restraints of protocol in the Hall of the Ambassadors.

Cool Room

This vestibule must have served as a massage room and for general acclimatisation before entering or leaving the baths themselves. The small basin (right) was for personal ablution. The religious aspect of bathing generally required this ritual. The Moorish ceramics on the basin surround are an abstract design representing the reflection of water.

Warm Room

Water ran through a small central channel while heat circulated from the furnace through underground conduits, finally escaping up chimneys hidden within the walls. On contact with the marble, heated from below, the water turned into steam, which softened the skin and opened the pores, cleansing them of impurities and preparing the body for bathing. Seated or lying on daïses behind the pillars the bathers were rubbed down by servants who until then had remained in the room where the bathing equipment was kept. These bath attendants were highly regarded for their skills and enjoyed a social importance second only to the cup-bearers, young servants entrusted with serving wine to the household. All those who had to walk around the various rooms of the baths protected their feet with sandals with thick wooden soles.

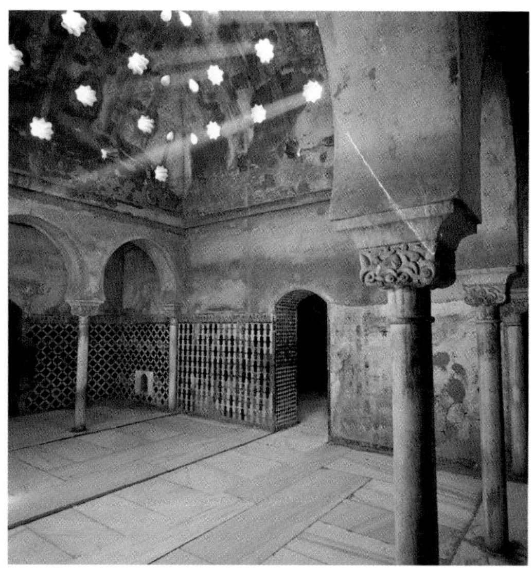

*According to the verse surrounding the marble niche, the **King's Bath** had two spouts, one for hot and one for cold water. Charles V altered this bath to make it suitable for total immersion, a practice not observed by the Muslims.*

Cauldrons

There were three copper cauldrons for hot water, but these were sold some time ago to help pay for restoration work elsewhere in the palace.

Furnace

The furnace, was brick-built and wood-fired. It communicated with the hot and warm rooms via underground conduits.

Hot Room

Many small conduits criss-crossed back and forth beneath the floor of this chamber bringing hot air almost directly from the oven and thus, as might be imagined, the temperature was very hot indeed in this part of the baths.

This cistern was built alongside the furnace to ensure that the water coming from the cauldrons stayed hotter here than in the other deposits. This was the water that was thrown onto the tiling to produce steam.

The Tower of the Ladies

The Tower of the Ladies is a huge mirador from which one can see the Albaicín beyond the river Darro, the orchards of the Generalife and of course the gardens just in front, surrounding the pool in which it is reflected.

Three XIV century ***Muslim houses*** *from the reign of Yusuf I have survived. In one of them there are some interesting, albeit deteriorated paintings.*

Gardens

Torres Balbás recreated these gardens so expertly that no serious criticism has ever been voiced against his restoration work

Exit from the Partal to the Palace of Charles V (round tour). This is one of the alternatives to finishing the tour of the Nasrid palaces, either to leave towards the Alcazaba via the Royal Road or to return down to Granada.

The Tower of the False Cemetery

The path along the walls The citadel of the Alhambra was closed to the north by the ramparts and defensive towers, which served above all to separate the royal city of the Alhambra from the city below (the Granada of today). The path around the walls passes below towers and palaces to appear here as a walkway from which the ramparts could be guarded. Beside it there runs another, deeper, wider track, designed to be patrolled on horseback.

Gardens

Nowadays the path through the gardens bordering the towers provides a delightful stroll from the Partal on the northern side eastwards to the Generalife.

The Palace of Yusuf III

This is one of seven palaces that existed within the walls of the citadel. Little of it remains today except these few ruins, insufficient really to make out its original shape and appearance.

THE TOWERS

Of the thirty or more towers which originally fortified the

ramparts surrounding the Alhambra twenty-two still exist.. The outer walls were built at the beginning of the XIII century, before the palaces themselves, and their role was clearly defensive. Each of the towers, gates and miradors has its own name. Some of these are obviously based on mundane usage and are thus probably contemporary with Muslim and early Christian habitation (the Arms Tower, the Outskirts Tower, the Wine Gate, the Iron Gate, to mention a few).

THE SPIKED TOWER

This tower is easily distinguishable by the masonry corbels jutting out from it, which once supported machicolations, and above all by the spikey, pyramid-shaped merlon on its battlements, both of which may have given the tower its name.

THE OUTSKIRTS GATE

This was the northernmost entrance to the city and the gate that the sultans and their families normally used to come and go between the Alhambra and the Generalife

THE JUSTICE GATE

Built in 1348 by Yusuf I, this was always one of the main entrances into the Alhambra. It is a masterpiece of military engineering and contrasts in its massive solidity and austere grandeur with the fragility of the Royal House (Engraving by Laborde, 1812).

THE WAGON GATE

This gate is angled slantwise through the wall and was opened up after the conquest to allow easy access to the wagons which brought the materials for the construction of Charles V Palace in the XVI century. Nowadays it is still the gate used by wheeled traffic to get into the citadel.

The Tower of the Judge

The Tower of the Captive Princess

The names "the Captive Princess" and "the Princesses" were coined in the XVII and XVIII centuries according to apochryphal stories woven around the supposed inhabitants of these towers.

The Tower of the Princesses

The Tower at the End of the Way

The Water Tower

Apart from its defensive function, this tower played the very important role of protecting the aqueduct to the royal waterway, which carried water to the whole city. The Arabs rarely constructed aqueducts unless for strategic motives, as was the case here.

The Tower of Juan de Arce

The Tower of Baltasar de la Cruz

The Tower and Gate of Seven Floors

This is the tower that suffered most damage when Napoleon's troops blew up some of the ramparts on their withdrawal in 1812. Fortunately its structure had been well recorded in earlier engravings and its appearance today is much as it was before its destruction. Tradition has it that Boabdil left through this gate as he abandoned the Alhambra for the last time and through his express petition the gate thenceforth remained closed "porta castri granatensis semper clausa" (Bucknall Escourt, 1827).

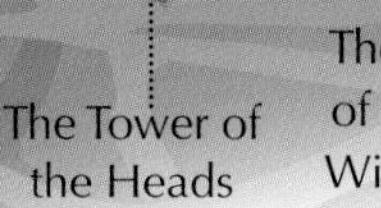

The Tower of the Captain

The T. of the Witch

The Tower of the Heads

The Tower of the Abencerrages

Secano (dry area) *This avenue of cypresses climbs gently from the square opposite the Parado to the entrance to the Generalife, providing a general view of the towers along the south wall of the Alhambra on the way.*

The role of the Generalife, recaptured in these new gardens, was the same as that of the houses known as carmens in the city of Granada, which were used as Autumn retreats.
Autumn is the most beautiful season in this city; the temperature is mild, with neither the suffocating heat of summer nor the dry cold of winter; flowers still linger in the gardens, there is no persistent rain and the sky is blue almost every day.

Generalife

Laborde, 1812.

Of the many private granges and pleasure gardens that once existed on the Hill of the Sun this is the only one remaining. The Generalife was a retreat where the Granadan monarchs could relax, away from the daily toil and bustle of the court. Nevertheless, its proximity to the Alhambra meant that the sultan could still be close enough to palace affairs to attend to any urgent matter which might arise, whilst at the same time be far enough away to enjoy the intimacy of the countryside.

THE CYPRESS COURTYARD

ROMANTIC MIRADOR

THE WATER STAIRWAY

LOWER, OR NEW GARDENS

Planted in 1931 on the site of older orchards

NORTH PAVILION

THE WATER-GARDEN COURTYARD

After a fire in 1958 the original design of this courtyard was discovered and reconstructed. It is the focal point of the whole residence and a perfect example of a Spanish-Muslim garden.

THE DISMOUNTING YARD

ORCHARDS

The land around the Generalife was always cultivated; it took pride of place among many such outlying farmsteads owned by the sultan. Fortunately its orchard terraces have survived relatively unchanged to this day.

According to most scholars the name Generalife derives from the Arab words djennat, meaning "garden", "orchard" or "paradise" (all similar concepts to desert nomads), and al-arif, meaning "architect" or "master builder". Thus the name could be translated as, "The Garden of the Architect".
Nevertheless, other commentators believe they have found evidence in contemporary Arab and Christian writings to translate it as, "Principal orchard" or "The most noble and highest of all orchards".

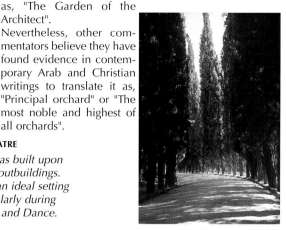

OPEN-AIR CONCERT AMPHITHEATRE

In 1952 this amphitheatre was built upon the ruins of old agricultural outbuildings. The sunken arena provides an ideal setting for ballet and dance, particularly during the annual Festival of Music and Dance.

THE CYPRESS WALK

Cypress trees have always been associated with cemeteries, particularly since the Romantic period, for the good reason that their roots grow straight and deep and don't break into the tombs. Muslim architects favoured the cypress for the same reason: it seeks water at depth and can be planted closely to form a dense evergreen screen.

LARGE WATER CISTERNS

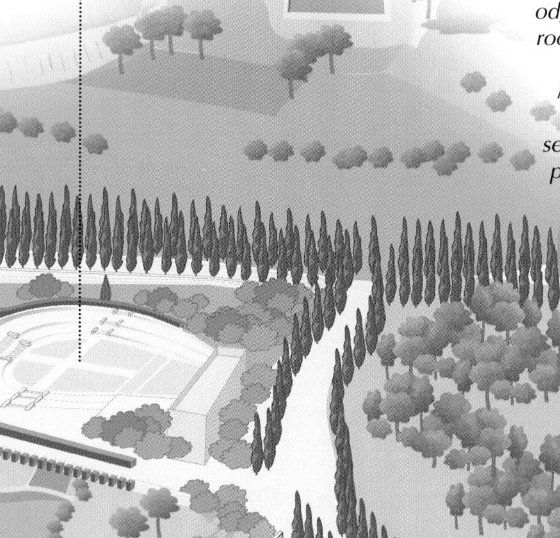

ACCESS TO THE ALHAMBRA

This bridge was constructed quite recently to allow direct access between the Generalife and the Alhambra. In former times the aqueduct alone existed, watched over by the Water Tower.

Entrance

Tickets

The **ground plan** shows what the original shape of the courtyard may have been (in red) towards the beginning of the XIV century, and the elements added either by successive Nasrid rulers or during the Christian era. The north pavilion was lower until another floor was built on top of it. (Adapted from A. Orihuela, Casas y Palacios Nazaríes)

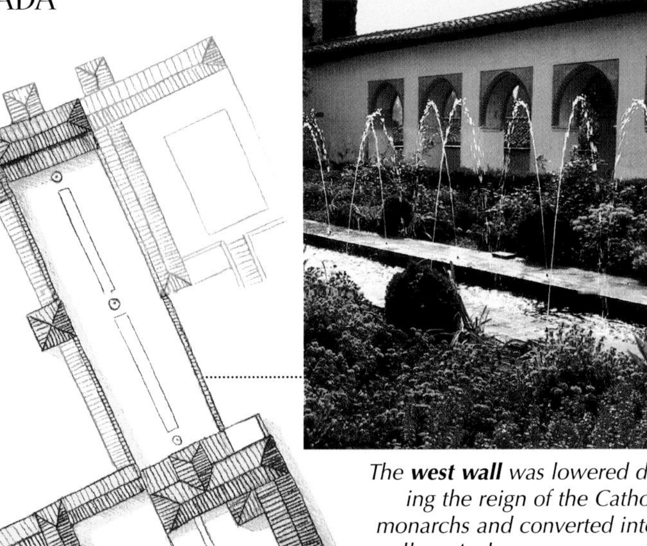

The **west wall** was lowered during the reign of the Catholic monarchs and converted into a gallery. Arches were opened in the wall to allow a view of the countryside around from the courtyard, contrary to the intimate and introspective nature of the Muslim courtyard. Originally the outside could only have been seen from the central mirador (left), the walls of which are decorated in the style of the time of Ismael I, although superimposed on earlier decoration .

The present layout of the buildings can be seen in this elevation by F. Prieto Moreno.

*The **north end**, which appears here in a drawing by Asselineau (1844), is the best preserved of the pavilions. The façade has three round arches supported upon pillars with mocarábe capitals, the arch in the middle being higher than those on either side.*

*A **poem** written on a lapis-lazuli background (below) runs above the arches. It is dedicated to the sultan Abu l-Walid Ismail and the reference to the year of "the great triumph for religion" dates the decorative work to the year 1319.*

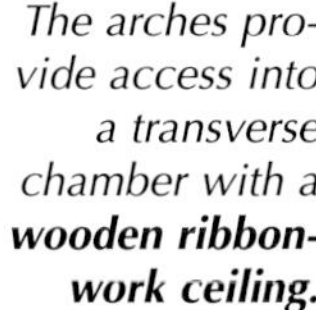

*The arches provide access into a transverse chamber with a **wooden ribbon-work ceiling.***

The position of this room at the far end of the courtyard and the presence of niches for ritual jugs of water (left) suggest that this was the sultan's reception room.

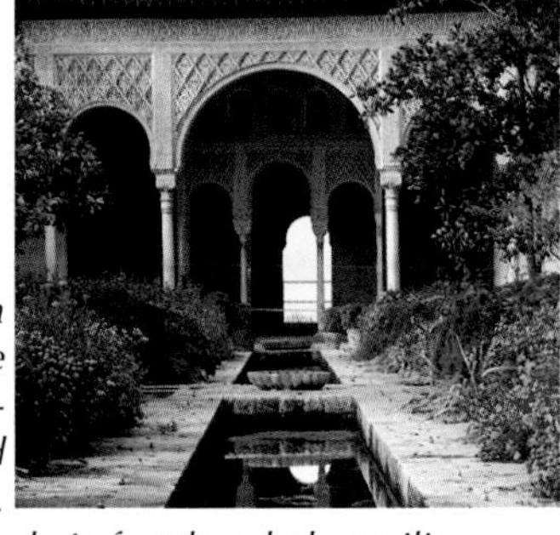

*The chamber finishes in a **mirador** added during the reign of Ismail I (1319), slightly angled to the right compared to the central axis of the pool, as can be seen in the photograph. In fact the whole pavilion is a few degrees out of line with the courtyard.*

It is quite difficult to comprehend how in the hottest months the north mirador always catches a breeze to alleviate the suffocating heat of midday. Doubtless there is a combination of factors to explain this phenomenon, the secrets of which the master builder knew well: the situation, the height, the orientation, so perfect throughout the Alhambra, and here in this mirador, just slightly slanted off-centre to achieve that breath of air which surprises us so much today. It provides an object lesson for architects of the twenty-first century, who are striving to integrate nature into their buildings and create microclimates, even within closed spaces, to relieve the weight of concrete and the visual aggression of cement.

The Generalife was entrusted by the Catholic monarchs into the care of the Knight Commander Fray Juan de la Hinestrosa. After a series of inheritances and marriages the tenancy of the grange passed into the hands of the Granada Venegas family and finally the Marquises of Campotéjar, who were related to the Grimaldi-Palavicinis of Milan

Left, The west gallery of the Courtyard of the Water Garden. Below, the rectangular chamber which precedes the mirador.

After a long legal wrangle in which the Spanish state claimed ownership of the Generalife, the case was settled in favour of the defendants, the private owners. Having won their case they ceded ownership of the Generalife to the Spanish government free of charge in 1921, for which King Alfonso XIII created for the family the Marquissate of the Generalife to reward their generosity.

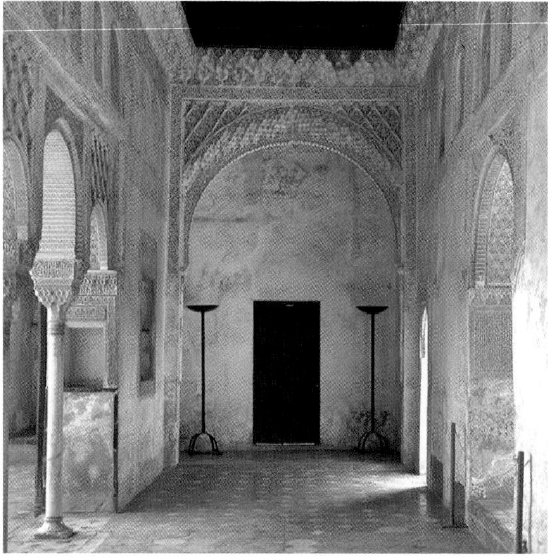

The relentless power of the weather. Anyone comparing this photograph of 1999 with those on pages 156 and 160 will immediately miss the handsome cedars and cypresses to the left, which were uprooted in a storm during the winter of 1998.

Carlos V

The Palace of Charles V

If any one monument can be so controversial and misunderstood, and yet so often referred to as outstanding, it is the Palace of Charles V. Romantic clichés vilified it as an attempt by authoritarian Spanish monarchs to erase the Muslim past but a more dispassionate look at history will reveal the contrary to be true. The Spanish monarchy invested the conquest of Granada, with enormous symbolic value. Their political intention was to reinforce Granada's role as a capital city, which it had enjoyed for so many centuries, by building great new monuments without destroying the old, complementing rather than detracting from the past.

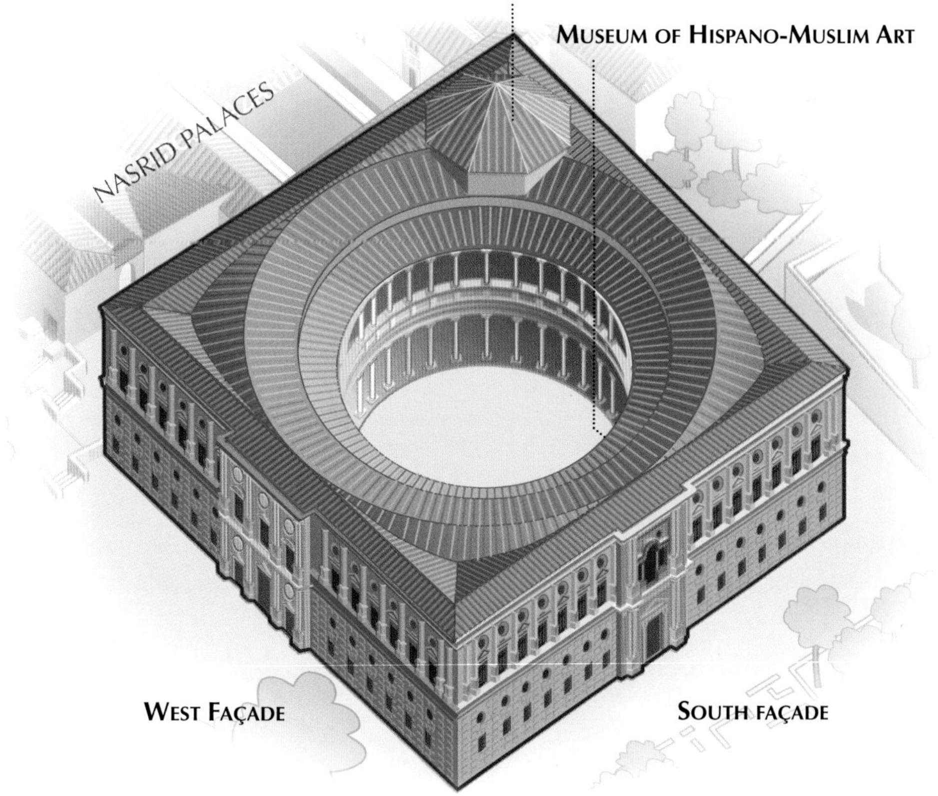

THE PALACE OF CHARLES V

CHAPEL

MUSEUM OF HISPANO-MUSLIM ART

NASRID PALACES

WEST FAÇADE

SOUTH FAÇADE

The palace was built upon an old Christian quarter, a lower annex to the Nasrid city. An error in geometry meant that its design would encroach very slightly upon the Alhambra itself. Within this context, however, it might be worth trying to understand the reasons behind such a new and radical project. It is also probably thanks to the Palace of Charles V that the Alhambra came to be included in the patrimony of the Spanish Royal Palaces instead of being reduced to an archaeological remnant of a defeated culture.

The Catholic monarchs had already built a funerary chapel in Granada, the Royal Chapel. The Emperor Charles V was enthusiastic about ennobling the city and took personal interest in the project. During his state visit to Granada, which coincided with his honeymoon with Isabel of Portugal in 1526, Charles visited the Alhambra and stayed in a suite of rooms which henceforth were known as "the lodgings of Charles V". Proof of his appreciation of the old Nasrid city was his desire to add to it and make it suitable for the needs of a modern court. Thus he entrusted the building of a palace to the Marquis of Mondéjar, governor of the Alhambra. The emperor left no specific orders as to the design or to the way the work should be carried out; he delegated responsibility to men of trust. Thus we cannot really speak about a "Charles V style"; the palace reflected the renaissance style in vogue at the time in Italy. Nevertheless, it will always be the symbol of a reign that began with so much zest for projects which in the end would never be entirely accomplished. It should be remembered for example that the roof over the second floor of this palace is of modern construction. From his seat in Toledo, the Marquis of Mondéjar, scion of the noble family of Mendoza, had contributed towards spreading an appreciation of the new Renaissance art throughout Spain

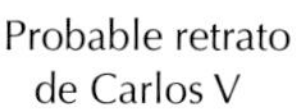

Probable retrato de Carlos V

Roof structure remained uncovered until 1960

Pedro Machuca, who was to be entrusted with the building work, had had a solid apprenticeship in Rome, working with both Michael Angelo and Rafael. Thanks to this training he would have known in theory about the most elaborate creations of the Renaissance. Proof of this lies in his choice of the very singular design of a round courtyard within a square building, which had been the basis of the highest aspirations of ideal design since the days of Alberti.

*Precedents for this palace can probably be found in **San Pietro in Montorio** in Rome (above), which must have been surrounded by a circular courtyard, according to the ground plan published by Serlio (above right), in the round courtyard of the Villa Madama (below) by Rafael and in the drawings of Leonardo da Vinci.*

The interior, is characterised by its completely sober austerity: two floors with Doric and Tuscan lintels and a great stairway which joins the magnificent annular barrel vault over the vestibule.

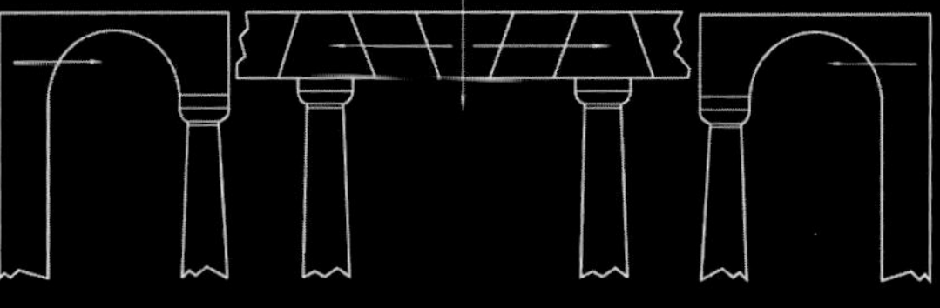

The solution of the architrave is completely original, creating as it does a perfect relationship between force and resistance in the two compositional elements. The annulet is supported in a torus which resists the outward thrust of the stone as though it were a continuous bridge, one foot of which is supported in the annulet and the other in the wall. When the wall is weakened by the presence of a door, as it is in the west wall, the strength of the outer wall is augmented by a depressed vault or with buttresses of some other kind.

BARRIO DE HAZA GRANDE
CARRETERA DE MURCIA
Cruz de Piedra
Camino de San Antonio
Cuesta de los Chinos
Vereda de Enmedio
Camino del Sacromonte
Cuesta del Chapiz
C. San Luis
San Martín
Pcta. Albaida
Veredilla S. Agustín
Pcta. Luque
C. la Vieja
Pino
S. Gregorio Alto
Blanqueo Viejo
Cuestecilla
Pza. de los Castillas
Pza. del Salvador
Carril Tomasas
Carril de S. Agustín
Estrellas
Pza. de Fátima
C. Panaderos
C. Pagés
C. del Agua
Plaza Larga
Cjón. S. Cecilio
S. Nicolás
Atarazana
Cta. Cabras
Callejón Tomasas
Cuesta del Aljibe Trillo
Calle de Guinea
Reyes
Limón
Santísimo
Gloria
Zafra
Grajales
Pcta. Victoria
Cta. Victoria
Gumiel
Valenzuela
Horno del Oro
Toqueros
Candil
Pcta. Almona
Pcta. Olivos
Pcta. Miñas
María la Miel
Pza. de S. Nicolás
Atarazana Vieja
Camino Nuevo de S. Nicolás
C. Aljibe de Trillo
Cjón. Aljibe de Trillo
Pza. Aljibe Trillo
Pcta. S. Bartolomé
Larga de S. Cristóbal
C. Ceniceros
Cuesta Alhacaba
C. Aljibe de la Gitana
C. Pilar Seco
Cjón. Monjas
Sta. Isabel la Real
Calle de la Tina
Pcta. Nevot
Pcta. Carvajales
Pcta. Cruz Verde
Pcta. Sánchez
Carrera del Darro
Oidores
Pl. Cauchiles
S. Miguel Bajo
San José
Pcta. Alminar
Quijada
Cuesta de S. Gregorio
Vereda de S. Cristóbal
Cuesta de S. Antonio
Alpargateros alta
Alpargateros baja
Baja de S. Ildefonso
Barrichuelo
Caracas
Cruz de Arqueros
Carril de la Lona
Calle del Zenete
Cruz de Quirós
Bocanegra
Los Negros
Álamo del Marqués
Cta. Marañas
Correo Viejo
Calderería Nueva
Calderería Vieja
Acera de S. Ildefonso
Pcta. de la Merced
Pza. del Triunfo
Cta. Abarqueros
Cuesta Beteta
Calle Elvira
Capitán Moreno
Cuesta del Hospicio
S. Andrés
Cedrán
Azacayas
Arteaga
Marqués de Falces
Álvaro de Bazán
Los Naranjos
Gobierno Civil
GRAN VÍA DE COLÓN
Capuchinos
Jardines del Triunfo
Natalio Rivas
Nueva del Santísimo
Navarrete
Cardenal Mendoza
Boquerón
Los Santos
Laurel
Santa Paula
Pza. S. Agustín
San Agustín
Cárcel Baja
Cocheras de Sta. Paula
Trabuco
Tendillas Sta. Paula
Candiota
Niños Luchando
C. S. Jerónimo
Horno de Marina
Pza. de la Romanilla
C. S. Juan de Dios
Lavadero de la Cruz
Almona
Mano de Hierro
Arriola
Acera del Triunfo
Almona de S. J. de Dios
Fuente Nueva
C. Santa Bárbara
AVDA. DE LA CONSTITUCIÓN
Acera Canasteros
Ventanilla
Plaza de la Universidad
Colegios
Silencio
Trinidad
Duquesa
Conde Infantes
Laurel de las Tablas
Fábrica Vieja
Angulo
Málaga
PLAZA TRINIDAD
Rector López Argüeta
C. Gran Capitán
Cuenca
Triana
Horno de Haza
PZA. DE LOS LOBOS
Misericordia
Guadalajara
Alonso Cano
Lavadero de las Tablas
C. Tablas
Santa Teresa
2
3
4
6
7
8
9
11
12
14
15
16
17
18
19
21
37
38
39
40
41
42

1. Monasterio de la Cartuja (S. XVI-XVIII)
2. Hospital Real (s. XVI-XVII)
3. Muralla Nazarí (s. XIV-XV)
4. Ermita de S. Miguel Alto
5. Abadía del Sacromonte (s. XVII)
6. Palacio de los Córdova
7. Iglesia del Salvador (antigua Mezquita)
8. Iglesia de S. Nicolás (s. XVI)
9. Casa de Castril. Museo Arqueológico
10. Iglesia de S. Pedro (s. XVI)
11. Convento Sta. Catalina (s. XVI)
12. Baño árabe del Bañuelo (s. XI)
13. Puente del Cadí (s. XIII)
14. Muralla Zirí (s. XI)
15. Puerta de Monaita (s. XI)
16. Palacio de Dar-al-Horra (s. XV)
17. Convento de Sta. Isabel la Real (s. XVI)
18. Iglesia de S. Miguel Bajo (s. XVI)
19. Minarete de S. José (s. X)
20. Iglesia de Sta. Ana (s. XVI)
21. Real Chancillería (s. XVI)
22. Puerta de las Granadas (s. XVI)
23. Torres Bermejas (s. XII-XV)
24. Casa de los Tiros (s. XVI)
25. Casa árabe de los Girones (s.XIII)
26. Iglesia de S. Matías (s. XVI)
27. Iglesia de Sto. Domingo (s. XVII)
28. Iglesia Comendadoras de Santiago
29. Iglesia de S. Cecilio (s. XVI)
30. Carmen de los Mártires (s. XIX)
31. Basílica. de las Angustias (s. XVII)
32. Corral del Carbón (alhóndiga s. XIV)
33. Alcaicería (s. XIV-XIX)
34. Madrasa (escuela coránica) (s. XIV-XVI)
35. Palacio de la Curia
36. Catedral, Capilla Real, Iglesia del Sagrario (s. XVI-XVIII)
37. Iglesia de S. Justo y Pastor (s. XVII)
38. Universidad Vieja (s. XVII), Jardín Botáni
39. Monasterio de S. Jerónimo (s. XVI)
40. Igl. y Hospital S. Juan de Dios (s. XVI-XV
41. Puerta de Elvira (s. XI)
Cuesta de los Chinos
Paseo de los Mártires
Antequeruela Baja
Alhambra Palace
Cam. S. Cecilio
Hoteles de Belén
Callejón del Niño del Royo
Plegadero Alto
Plegadero Bajo
Huerto S. Cecilio
Aire Alta
Cuesta Realejo
Vergeles
Cocheras
CAMPO DEL PRINCIPE
Cuartelillo
Nevot
Belén
CALLE MOLINOS
Calle Santiago
Cruz de Piedra
Alamillos
Azacayuela Alta
Cta. Sta. Catalina
Cta. del Infante
Puerta del Sol
Damasqueros
Plaza del Realejo
Berrocal
Plaza Hospicio
Plaza Fortuny
Moral Alta
Cjón. del Señor
Salvador
Solares
Rodrigo del Campo
Cuchilleros
Sta. Escolástica
Girones
Plaza de Sto. Domingo
Seco de Lucena
Cuesta del Pescado
Colcha
Calle Pavaneras
Pl. Padre Suárez
Jesús y María
Sto. Domingo
Cuarto Real de Sto. Domingo
Cjón. del Tinte
Calle San Matías
Plaza S. J. de la Cruz
Pcta. Cañaveral
Calle Varela
Pcta. de los Campos
Nicuesa
Plaza Lavadero
CALLE REYES CATÓLICOS
PZA. DE ISABEL LA CATÓLICA
Pza. Poeta L. Rosales
Escudo del Carmen
Jazmín
Laurel
A. Castro
Horno de S. Matías
Piedra Santa
Enriqueta Lozano
Concepción
Ancha de la Virgen
Castañeda
Jacinto
Maestro Alonso
Zacatín
Oficios
Lepanto
Ayuntamiento
C. Navas
Sarabia
PZA. DE LA MARIANA
Campillo Bajo
Marisol
San
S. Pedro Mártir
PZA. DEL CARMEN
Gozo
C. GANIVET
PZA. DEL CAMPILLO
Pza. de Bibataubín
CARRERA DEL GENIL
PZA. DE BIB-RAMBLA
Príncipe
Salamanca
Monterería
Boteros
Pcta. Cauchiles
PUERTA REAL
Acera del Casino
ACERA DEL DARRO
Calle Mesones
Hileras
Sierpe Baja
Pcta. Campo Verde
Calle Alhóndiga
Pza. del Lino
Calle
Parraga
Calle San Antón
Pino
C. RECOGIDAS
Calle Puentezuelas
13. Magistrate's Bridge
14. Zirid Walls (XI c)
15. Monaita Gate
16. Dar al-Horra Palace
17. Convent of St. Isabel "la Real"
18. Church of St. Michael
19. Minaret of St. Joseph
20. Church of St. Anne
21. Royal Chancellery
22. Gate of the Pomegranates
23. Crimson Towers
24. House of "los Tiros" (Municipal Archive)
25. House of the Girones
26. Church of St. Mathew
27. Church of St. Dominicus
28. Church of the Sisters of Santiago
29. Church of St. Cecil
30. Carmen of the Martyrs
31. Church of the Virgin of Anguish
32. Corral de Santiago (erstwhile inn)
33. Old Silk Market
34. Arab Madrassa (theologic school)
35. Original Christian Universi
36. Cathedral and Royal Chap
37. Church of St. Just and the Good Shepherd
38. Old University and Botan cal Gardens
39. Monastery of St. Jerome
40. Church of St. John of God
41. Elvira Gate
1. Carthusian Monastery
2. Royal Hospital
3. Nasrid Walls (XIV-XV c.)
4. Hermitage of St. Michael
5. Sacromonte Abbey
6. Palace of the Córdobas
7. Church of Our Saviour (erstwhile mosque)
8. Church of St. Nicholas
9. Archaeological Museum
10. Church of St. Peter
11. Convent of St. Catherine
12. Arab baths

The New Era

All the sovereigns and grandees of this period made elaborate preparations during their lives for their own interment and so, after the conquest of Granada, the Catholic Monarchs decided to build a chapel in the heart of their new domains, just beside the main mosque of the defeated Muslims and the site of the new Christian cathedral. On making this decision they clearly imposed a new spirit and new direction upon the city. The Royal Chapel was intended as a monument to celebrate their success and give thanks to God for bestowing upon them such a triumphant victory. This was the first of many such plans which were to ennoble the city with impressive monumental buildings. New architectural fashions and perspectives were overtaking late-Gothic traditions and Granada offered an ideal *tabula rasa* upon which to execute these new schemes. Two clear artistic tendencies existed side by side: the conservative Gothic, favoured by Queen Isabel and her clergy, lead by Cardinal Cisneros, a man opposed to the pagan novelties of Italian fashion, and the progressive Classic, which was more to the taste of King Ferdinand and the enlightened nobility, who were fond of the neo-Platonic, Roman style, which presumed to make a bridge between classical culture and the Catholic church.

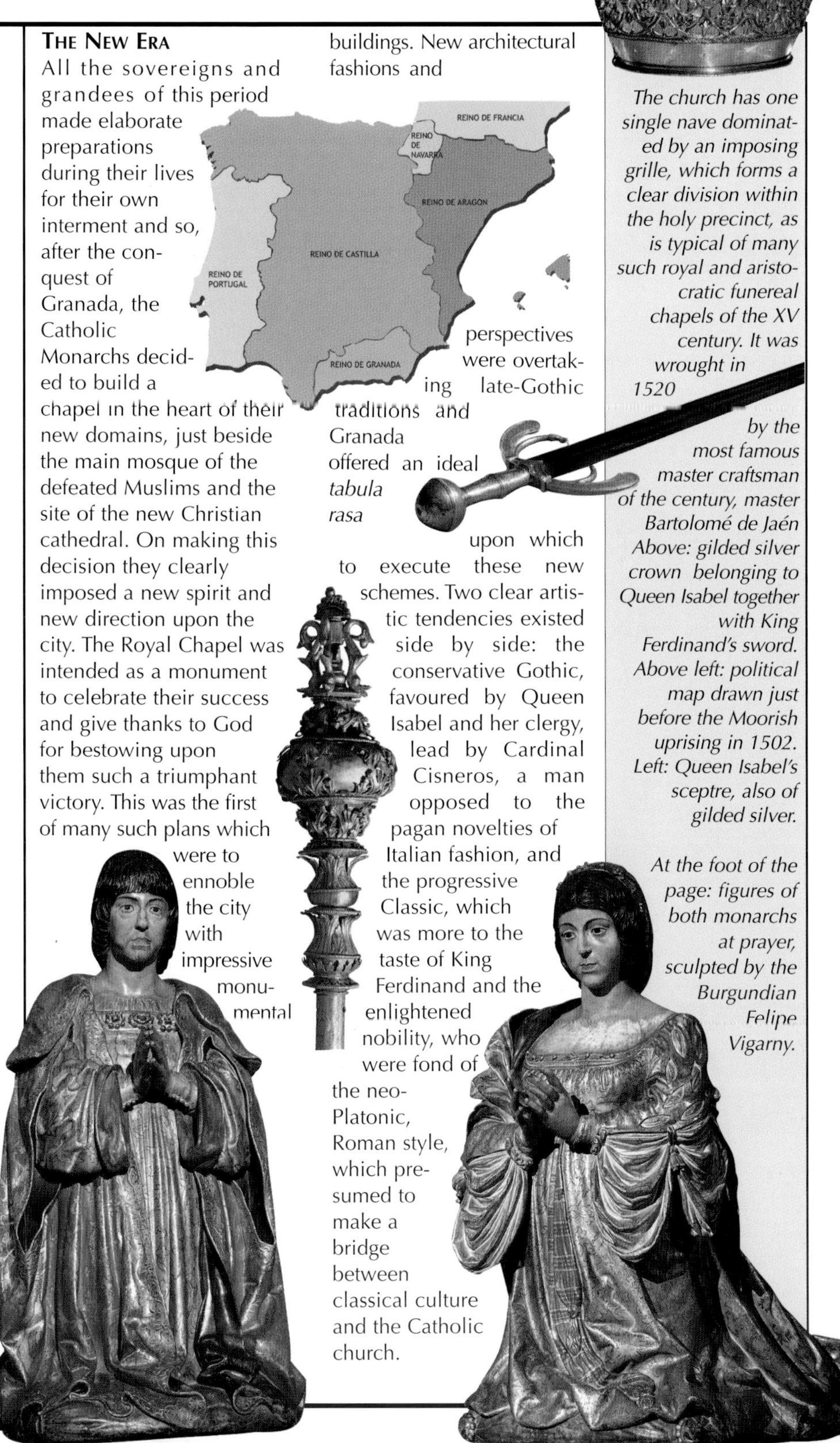

The church has one single nave dominated by an imposing grille, which forms a clear division within the holy precinct, as is typical of many such royal and aristocratic funereal chapels of the XV century. It was wrought in 1520 by the most famous master craftsman of the century, master Bartolomé de Jaén Above: gilded silver crown belonging to Queen Isabel together with King Ferdinand's sword. Above left: political map drawn just before the Moorish uprising in 1502. Left: Queen Isabel's sceptre, also of gilded silver.

At the foot of the page: figures of both monarchs at prayer, sculpted by the Burgundian Felipe Vigarny.

● **THE GRIFFIN** *in ancient times symbolised strength and watchfulness, whilst for Christians it was a negative force representing only cruelty. Nevertheless, here the griffin might be interpreted as representing the triumph of Christianity over paganism. Right, Charles V.*

THE CATAFALQUES

King Ferdinand, whilst being against any over-elaboration in the design of the chapel, did not hesitate to take the Count of Tendilla's advice and choose the Florentine Domenico Alessandro Fancelli to design his cenotaph. Fancelli made it his masterpiece. According to Pita Andrade, "Here we find the epitome of XV century Florentine Renaissance, free-standing funerary sculpture ... it imbues the architecture of the Royal Chapel with a harmonious balance between the purely ornamental (griffins, wreaths and grotesques) and those religious elements which emphasise the transcendental nature of life on earth". The figure of the queen is clothed in a simple tunic and mantle and she wears the Cross of Santiago around her neck. The king is in full armour and clasps a sword to his breast. According to Gómez Moreno, the natural physiognomy of the king could only have been sculpted from life, whereas that of the queen is much less lifelike.

A second sepulchre belongs to the parents of the Emperor Charles V, Philip the Handsome, son of the Emperor Maximillian, and his wife Queen Joan, eldest daughter of the Catholic King and Queen. It was sculpted by Bartolomé Ordoñez, who is accepted as being one of the four great

masters of the Spanish Renaissance style. He also knew and was familiar with the work of Fanacelli, whose style he imitated to a large degree in this mausoleum, possibly following one of his earlier designs, although the sculpture of the figures on this tomb are more lifelike, showing an innate vigour in their forms which betrays much more the influence of Michael Angelo, whom he must have met in Carrara.

The composure of the faces of the king and queen, softened by the texture of the marble, and their bodies, much more richly robed than those of the Catholic Monarchs, contrast with the great vitality which which Ordoñez lent to the rest of the figures, which are sculpted in the purest Italian classical style.

● *Above, the catafalques of the Catholic Monarchs by Domenico Alessandro Fancelli and those of King Phillip the Handsome and Queen Joan by Bartolomé Ordoñez. Above, the gilded, embossed silver casket belonging to Queen Isabet and on the left, the vellum missal of Queen Isabel.*

● **Right: the altar piece of the Royal Chapel**, *by Felipe Vigarny, in which he introduces a first taste of the Renaissance and also portraits of his contemporaries. Queen Isabel's private collection contained works by the most renowned painters of her time, including R. van der Weyden, H. Memling, Dierik Bouts and Boticelli.*

On show in the sacristy there are various personal possessions of considerable historical value, such as the gilded silver crown and sceptre of Queen Isabel and the gold-hilted sword of King Ferdinand, the reliquary of the queen, a collection of liturgical robes and the altar she carried with her on her campaigns against the Moors. Most impressive, however, for their intrinsic value, is Queen Isabel's private collection of Flemish paintings.

THE CATHEDRAL
Plans for the Cathedral were drawn up at the same time as those for the Royal Chapel. It was designed to be the episcopal centre, the symbolic monument to put the seal on the Christian conquest, the hub and point of reference of the new faith.
During his honeymoon and state visit to Granada in 1526 Charles V decided to convert the cathedral into the pantheon for his dynasty, which speeded up the work in hand somewhat, but the real impulse came with the young architect Diego de Siloë, who joined the project in 1528 and immediately made radical changes to the design, offering Renaissance ideas, which affected both its architectural shape and ideological content. It would be rooted in traditional Christianity, the main chapel, intended to be the pantheon of the Habsburgs, being built in the form of a completely independent round tower with an ambulatory reminiscent of the Church of the Holy Sepulchre in Jeru-salem. De Siloës contribution to the architecture of Granada Cathedral was two-fold: his ingenious placing of the columns and the juxtaposition of cubic and cylindrical elements, to which he brought much more daring and original ideas than those of his classicist predecessors. De Siloë's first innovation was to form a solid base from which rose

● **MAIN ARCH** *On the facing page. A view of the inside of the cathedral from the main chapel in which can be seen a gradual slimming of the bulk of the stone within the main arch as it rises upwards towards the keystone in order to maintain the concave, cylindrical shape, despite displacing somewhat the centre of gravity.*
On this page: drawings of the Cathedral.

S·HIERONIMVS

columns embedded into pilasters, topped by Corinthian capitals and entablature up to the recognised height; but then he continued upwards again with a second plinth and pilasters which become the semicircular arches and ribs of the vaults.

The second innovation is the way in which he managed to reconcile the square with the cylindrical. Siloë, proposed a novel solution to the problem by juxtaposing rather than joining both individual elements (a cube and a cylinder fifteen metres higher).

● *Facing page:* **THE MAIN CHAPEL** *drawing of the sanctuary and below: a drawing to scale of the vertical section of the cylinder of the main chapel and its buttresses. The sheer size of these gives some idea of the weight they are supporting.*

● **RIGHT: PLAZA LARGA** *in the Albaicín on the Day of the Cross, and the mirador in front of the church of St. Nicholas. Right: the sacristy of the Carthusian monastery, which lies just outside the borders of this map. Below: façade of the Royal Hospital, built by the Catholic Monarchs, which is nowadays the Chancellory of the University of Granada, together with a view of the Carril de la Lona with the Sierra Nevada in the background.*

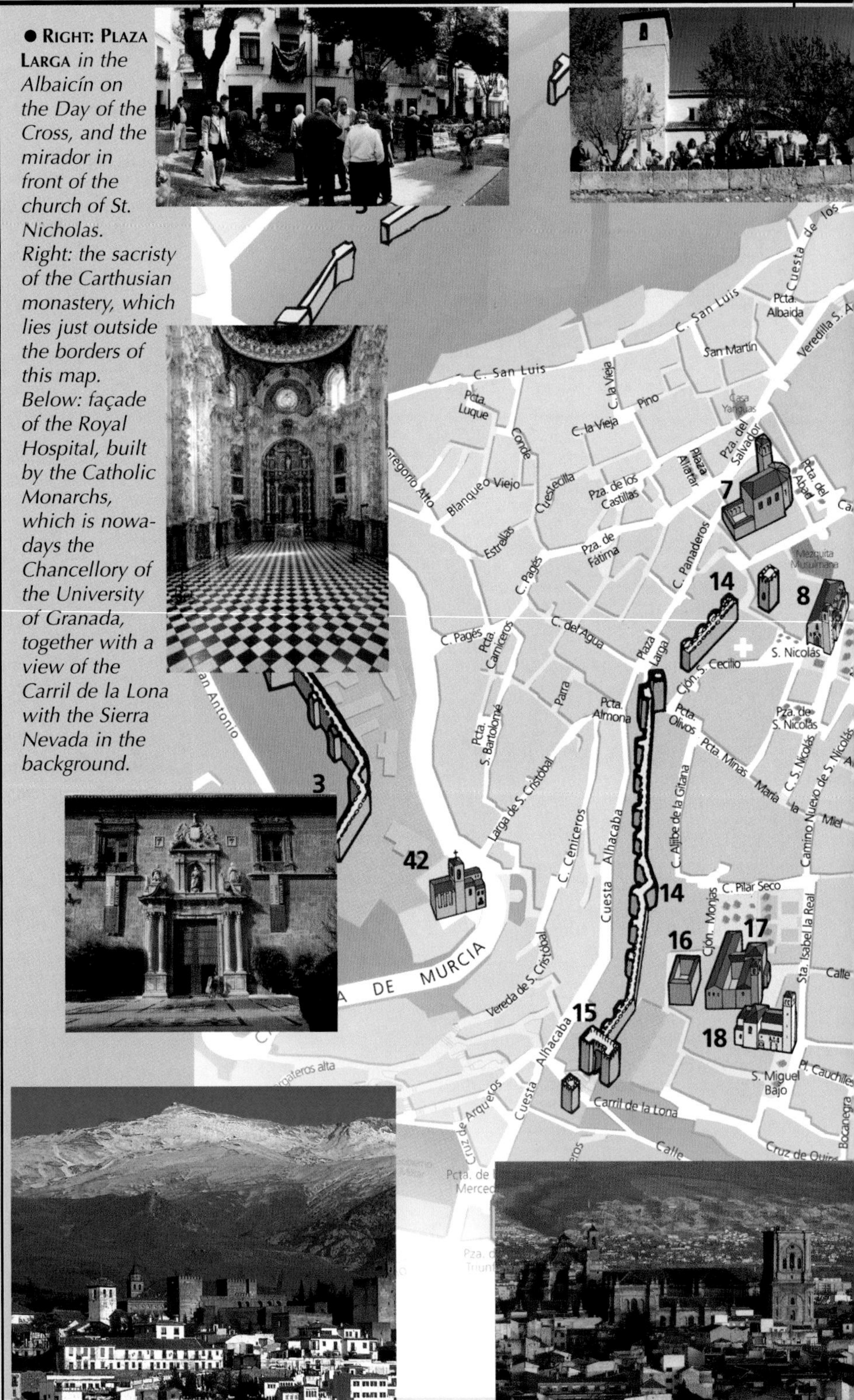

• Far left: (The Magistrate's Bridge), which used to cross the river Darro between the Alhambra and the Albaicín. Left: the Arab baths (Bañuelo) and the Convento de Zafra beside the church of St. Peter. Below: the church of St. Anne, over-looking Plaza Nueva, and the Royal Chancellory. Below: alley-ways in the old silk market (Alcaicería) next to Zacatín street and Bib Rambla square.

Left: courtyard in the Corral del Carbón. Left: façade and north side of the cathedral.

● **The Albaicín quarter,** *dating back to Iberian times, is one of the oldest known continuously inhabited settlements in Europe.*

The Albaicín

The Albaicín is a place of wonder, oozing with the essence of centuries gone by, where history moves indiscernibly. This is as it should be: the inexhaustible legacy of ancient civilisations, the hoary witness who has survived the ravages of time.

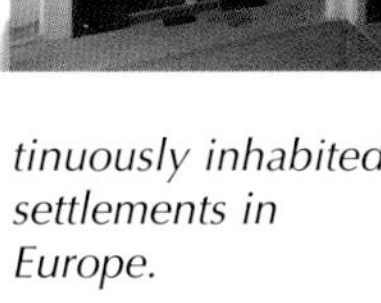

This quarter, the most intriguing and exotic quarter in the whole of Granadas houses jumbled one on top of another like swallows' nests, its inexplicably twisting, narrow streets and alleys, the profusion of flowers and greenery drooping over the walls of its houses and orchards, the sudden, breath-taking views of the Alhambra, the Sierra Nevada and the plain away to the west, the secret corners which suddenly appear and offer themselves to the eyes of the lucky, persistent traveller... There are also vestiges of history that take this quarter back to the earliest cultures and civilisations known in Spain, When at the beginning of the VIII century Asad ibn Abd ar-Rahman al-Saybani ordered the construction of a fortress on what is now the Plaza de San Nicolás, the q'asabat Garnata according to Muslim chroniclers, he could never have imagined the future awaiting it. By the XI century it had become the site of the palatial residence of the first Islamic dynasty to rule these lands, the Zirids. Thus arose the

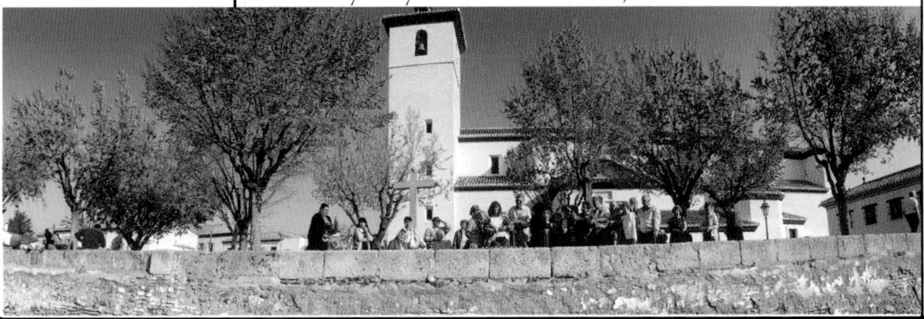

citadel, Alcazaba Cadima, and in the protection of its shadow numerous small districts and quarters until the whole hill was occupied. It continued to prosper, even when in the XIII century Muhammad al-Hamar decided to move his court to the Sabika hill on the other side of the river, which in time would become the imposing city of the Alhambra. The Albaicín, true to its good fortune, continued to grow until it became a veritable city within the city of Granada. In the XIV century it had its own army, civil administration and magistracy; the Nasrid aristocracy built their sumptuous palaces and mansions on its hillsides; it could boast some thirty mosques, including a main mosque more elegant than that in the city of Granada itself. An ingeniously complex network of water mains fed cisterns in every quarter; the constant clacking of looms proclaimed the existence of a busy commerce in high quality cloths and silks; a multitude of wares of all kinds.

This was the Albaicín in its days of glory, admired and to some extent feared, because its population was not only numerous but also fractious and difficult to govern.

● *Above: a small square in the Albaicín. Below: la Cuesta de la Caba, the church of St. Nicholas and the Monaita Gate.*

● **THE MAIN CLOISTER,** *finished in 1519 when the new style of the Renaissance had just arrived in Granada. It has seven chapel doorways, clearly by de Siloé, which bestow a certain classical majesty upon its otherwise monastic simplicity. Below: the cloister after the restoration of its tower.*

THE MONASTERY OF ST. JEROME

This monastery was founded by the Catholic Monarchs as one of the many building projects that they instigated immediately after the conquest in their desire to christianise the city as quickly as possible, a task confided basically to the trust of the three great religious orders of the day: the Franciscans, the Dominicans and the Jeronymites. The monastery was placed in the keeping of this latter order, to which Queen Isabel's personal confessor, Fray Hernando de Talavera, belonged. It quickly became known for being a refuge for Jewish converts. Fray Hernando de Talavera, the first archbishop of Granada, combined humility with wisdom and was also a friend to the defeated Muslims.

The monastery was founded in 1492 but was not begun until 1504 and thus its initial architectural style was Gothic, with a typical convent church in the shape of a Latin cross with only one nave, side chapels and raised choir.

Just one more church among many designed by an anonymous draughtsman, but which had the luck to be touched by the genius of de Siloé, who arrived in Granada in 1526 ostensibly to work on this monastery but obviously attracted by the cathedral project. First to be built was the great Gothic cloister with thirty-six semicircular arches, completed in 1519. The following year the finishing touches were put to the second, smaller cloister, named after the Empress Isabel, who stayed

here during her honeymoon in 1526. The six porches on the first floor of the large cloister, clearly designed by de Siloé, confer a classical majesty upon the monastic simplicity of the earlier construction.The building of the church, which began in 1519, but it was the arrival on the scene of de Siloé two years later that gave a complete new vision to the work and turned the monastery into a first class Renaissance monument, changing the style while work was in progress without creating any lack of harmony, something which can be appreciated immediately by a glance at the large windows, sconces, shields and other decorative details both inside and out. De Siloé was also responsible for constructing the tower, which was destroyed by the French at the beginning of the XIX century and restored in 1916. But where his genius really shines through is in the transept, which was built by el Indaco in close collaboration with de Siloé, covered by an original groined vault in the shape of an octagonal cupola.The twin crossed ribbing allows space within the sculpture to fill the whole with heroic figures, cherubim, satyrs and bearded sages.

● **TRANSEPT AND HIGH ALTAR** *Above Towards the main chapel religious themes are more in evidence: angels with aspects of the Passion, the apostles, the three virtues, the biblical co-existing side by side with the mythical, the whole history of mankind saved by the Passion of Christ, who presides over the altar piece, finally assimilated by Renaissance culture.*

● THE SACRISTY
is considered to be the last great creation of the Spanish Baroque The floor is paved with black and white rhomboids which appear to open outwards, giving an impression of great space and focusing the attention upon the pilasters and the walls, covered in a multitudinous variety of linear shapes in white stucco, thus creating the illusion of airiness and light.

THE CARTHUSIAN MONASTERY

The Carthusian order was founded some nine hundred years ago by St. Bruno Fray Alonso de Ledesma began the initial Gothic structure in 1514. lthough there is no written rule on the subject, all Carthusian monasteries are built in the same shape, which divides the structure of the monastery into a church with a single nave on one side and on the other, two cloisters with their adjoining rooms. Nowadays only the church and the small cloister remain, around which are grouped the refectory, two chapels and the chapter house.The originality of this monastery is to be found above all in two particular areas that make it unique of its kind: the sacristy and the shrine, or sancta sanctorum, where the XVIII century Andalucian Baroque reaches the height of its expressionism. The structure of the church, with its sober exterior, is the cell of Jesus Christ, the first hermit, the monastery's revered guest and its interior decoration must be equal to his splendour. It is also the hub of monasterial life, where the monks may spend up to eight hours a day in prayer. As usual it is composed of three separate sections: at the entrance a choir for laymen, separated by a screen from a second choir devoted to the use of the fathers, and the presbytery, which

here is divided into two sections, the main altar and the shrine. It is in this latter small sanctuary that Hurtado Izquierdo managed to capture in marble and gold the post-tridentine idea of the exaltation of the Eucharist. The central niche, or main shrine, designed to contain the body of Christ, is the source from which all life springs (right).

The adjacent sacristy is considered by many experts on the subject to be the last great creation of the Spanish Baroque. It reminds us of a small church only distinguishable from such by its chests adorned with marquetry inlays of marble, silver, mahogany, rosewood, ebony and tortoiseshell, worked on for thirty-four years by Brother Vásquez, in a labour of prayer and devotion.

● *It used to be possible to cross the Sierra Nevada by the highest road in Europe, rising to nearly 11,000 feet, and from there drive down into the Alpujarras along a beautiful road with views of the Mediterranean and Africa beyond, but this route has recently been closed by the "Ecologists", so if you can't hike a rucksack 20 k uphill, bad luck.*

Sierra Nevada

The Sierra Nevada forms a constant white background to the city, dyed by the sun in a myriad of changing colours as the hours of the day go by, from ice-green to duck-egg blue in the morning to flaming orange and red in the twilight. And that snow is also Granada's secret spring of water during the summer. The mountains cover an area of more than 170,000 hectares, of which half has been made a national nature reserve and is home to a wide array of rare and endemic flora and

The ski resort has seen an enormous rise in both national and international popularity in recent years. It now has 60 kilometres of runs with all the necessary ski lifts and other infrastructure to service them. What is especially attractive about the Sierra Nevada is that because of its latitude the sun shines for more than 240 days a year and because of its height the air is cool enough to make it a good base for mountain walking in summer.

Nevertheless, the Sierra Nevada is a natural paradise during summer and winter and is home to a multitude of rare animals and birds and more than 1,700 plant species of which 50 are endemic

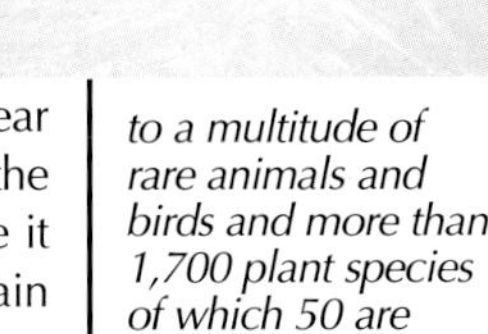

Above: Moclín and one of its streets adorned with potted plants.

Above: Sierra Nevada, below: Montefrío and Salobreña.

GRANADA PROVINCE

The geography and countryside of the Province of Granada is widely varied, ranging from the snows of the high mountains to inland meseta plains and the sub-tropical Mediterranean coast. Amidst such diversity it is possible to ski in the morning and swim in the sea in the afternoon. The province is comprised of seven districts: the Capital City, surrounded by mountains and the fertile plain to the west; Western Granada, with three important towns: Montefrío (above and left), set in impressive rocky countryside interspersed with meadows and the towering Peña de los Gitanos, a stoney scarp containing some interesting prehistoric sites, Loja, known throughout history as "the Gateway to Granada" and Alhama de Granada, with its natural thermal springs and baths. Both these latter towns were important Moorish strongholds before and during the conquest. The third district is that of the Tropical Coast to the south, with seaside towns such as

Above: Negratín reservoir, below: la Peza.

Almuñecar and Salobreña and Motril, where the only sugar cane in Europe is still grown, most of it going to make the superb local rum. On the southern slopes of the Sierra Nevada is the Alpujarra. The Sierra Nevada itself forms the fifth district of the province. Almost all of it is a national park and nature reserve and is home to a large number of endemic species of plants and animals. It also has the southernmost ski resort in Europe. The two remaining districts lie in the north-east of the province and may almost be considered as one, lying as they do on the high Guadix-Baza plain around the dip in the terrain known as the Hoya, which was in recent geological time an inland sea. Archaeologists have discovered here what may be evidence of the first hominids in Europe and the area has certainly been inhabited continuously from earliest prehistoric times. Guadix and Baza were both important Moorish strongholds and the ruins of their fortified Muslim citadels can still be seen today.

Below left: Gorafe
Below: Calahorra Castle

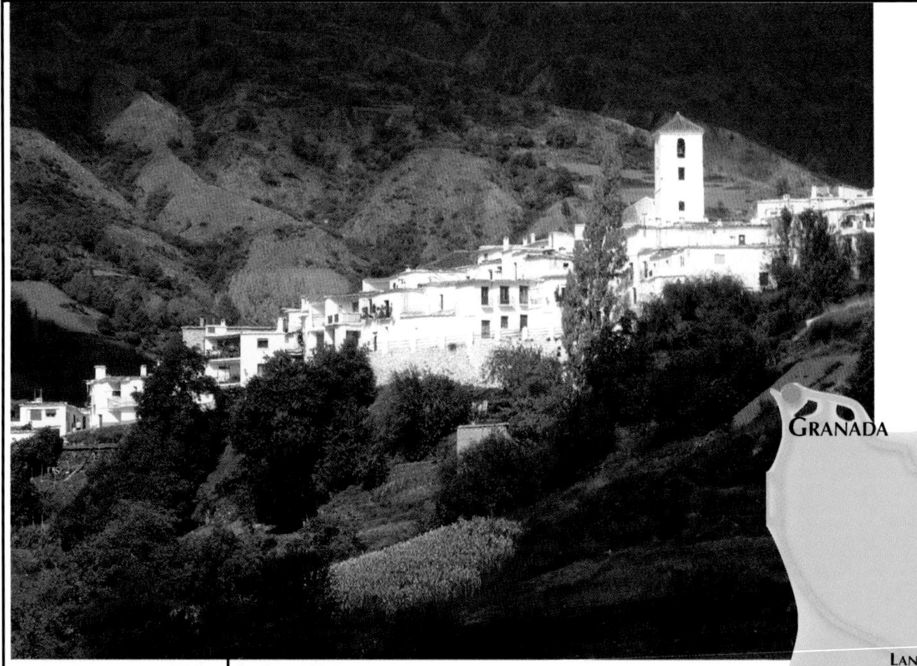

The Alpujarra hillsides have from time immemorial been the refuge of people in search of independence. Above; the village of Bubión and below: typical houses in this region.

THE ALPUJARRA

From the heights of the Sierra Nevada one can see Africa, and just down below there is a scattering of white villages built on the sides of steep green valleys that stretch away towards the Guadalfeo river and thence to the sea. A direct view of the sea is interrupted by the silhouette of the last folds of the Sierra Nevada, the Contraviesa hills and the Sierra de Lújar, as though the mountains were loth to fall too

The Poqueira Gorge: The villages in the Alpujarra cling to the sides of steep river gorges running down towards the River Guadalfeo. The most spectacular of these is the easternmost valley of the river Poqueira, with its three villages, Pampaneira, Bubión and Capileira, as white as the snows just above them. The following valley is that of the river Trevélez (below).

TREVÉLEZ
CAPILEIRA
PAMPANEIRA
BUBIÓN
ÓRGIVA
TRIL

quickly into the Mediterranean. These white villages belong to the Alpujarra, a district which because of its geographical inaccessibility has remained isolated for centuries, following a way of life conditioned by its terrain and its own singular history, making it a relic of the past and a present-day jewel. Few places can offer such scenery and human interest for tourists who are looking for contact with nature and the rural way of life. The Alpujarra has always been a place for peoples who sought isolation or were fleeing from pursuers. The Berbers, who came out worst in the share out of land during the early Arab occupation of Spain, came here to live in the VIII century and turned it into a vast orchard of fruit trees, especially mulberries for the silk trade.

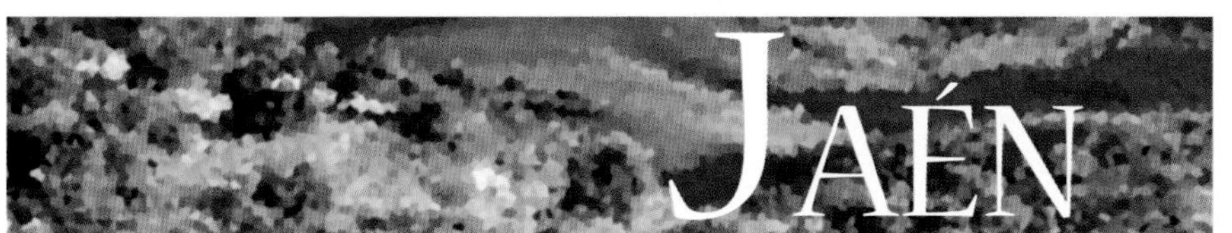

JAÉN

Forming Andalucía's northern frontier with Castilla, Jaén shares something of the character of both. The Guadalquivir, the "Great River" in Arabic, rises in the mountains of Jaén and runs south-westwards through Córdoba and Sevilla until it finally flows into the Atlantic in the Bay of Cádiz. The countryside of Jaén is unmistakable with its light grey hillsides and endless serried ranks of olive trees, whose leaves constantly flirt between green and silver in the breeze. The olive tree, so quintessential to the Mediterranean, occupies almost half the arable land of Jaén. Most of the trees were planted in the XIX century as the basis of a huge, intensive agricultural-estate style of farming. Today the hillsides of Jaén produce more high-quality olive oil than any other region in Spain, and now that olive oil is recognised both for its culinary and health-giving virtues, it represents the mainstay of the province's agricultural economy, along with wheat, barley and rye, grown on the open plains to the west. Apart from agriculture, there are rich deposits of lead, iron, copper and uranium around the towns of Andújar and Linares, which have made them considerably important mining centres.

But what most attracts visitors to the countryside in Jaén are the mountains of Cazorla and Segura, wildlife reserves and remnants of the green wooded landscape that covered much of the Spanish peninsula in Roman times. Down the ages these woodlands of native trees and bushes have survived fire and the axes that felled most of Spain's forests to build ships for the imperial navy. All kinds of autochthonous animals and plant species, some in imminent danger of extinction elsewhere, thrive here free of pollution and safe from human predators.

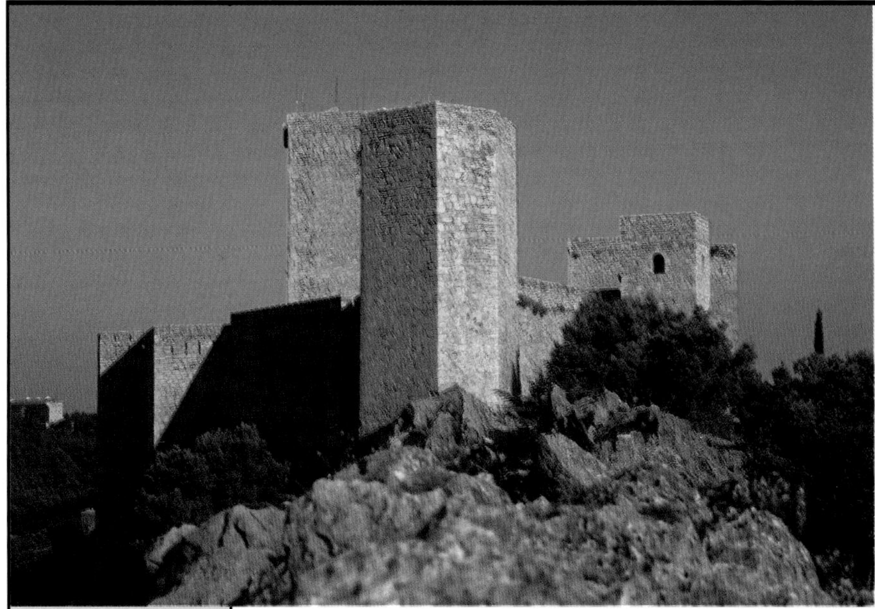

•**JAÉN.** *The history and strategic importance of this town are evident at a glance. The castle of Santa Catalina (above) built on top of a rocky promontory guarded the gateway to the south. This has always been a key fastness, essential for any would-be invader to take and control. It was so during the Christian reconquest and again centuries later when Spaniards fought to repel Napoleon's troops.*

The founder of the last Muslim stronghold in Spain, the kingdom of Granada, Muhammad ibn Nasr al-Ahmar, came from an aristocratic family of the town of Arjona in the province of Jaén. After years of fighting off Christian incursions into his territory he came to an agreement with the Castilian king Fernando III in 1247, whereby he swore vassalage to the Castilian crown in return for leave to rule what today are the provinces of Granada, Málaga and Almería. Thus the Christian forces gained a further crucial foothold in Andalucía to support their recent conquests of Córdoba and Seviila in the west. One of King Fernando's first undertakings was to rebuild the fortress above Jaén (today a state-run hotel, or parador). The whole of the city is laid out beneath this rocky vantage point, where from amongst the houses the huge bulk of the cathedral stands out imposingly (below) with its elegant façade framed by two slim towers (previous facing page).

THE CATHEDRAL

For more than a hundred years after the reconquest the IX century mosque was used as a church until a new structure was built in 1368.

Around the year 1500 plans were drawn up for a cathedral on the same site but the work was not begun until 1536 when it fell to the hand of the master architect Andrés de Vandelvira, to change its design and erect the new cathedral in the Renaissance style. Despite the gradual appearance of the Baroque in

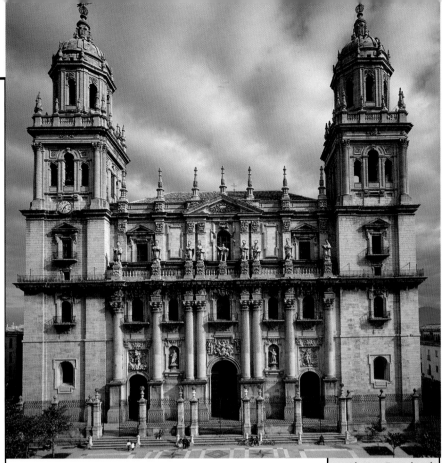

its texture, the cathedral still manages to maintain a classical feeling in its interior design, above all in the Renaissance spirit of the sacristy, where Vandelvira has created one of the great masterpieces of Spanish architecture. It was not until 1688 that the final touches were made to the main façade.

• Above: Façade of Jaén Cathedral. Left: Detail of stone carving of the Holy Face. Below: Interior of the cathedral, where the Renaissance holds its own against the incursion of the Baroque.

• *Above: Square of the Fountain of St. Mary in Baeza. Below: Façade of the Jabalquinto Palace in Baeza.*

BAEZA

The Romans called this town Beatia, from *beatus*, happy or fortunate town; it is the smaller of two towns only nine kilometres apart, Baeza and Úbeda, which for centuries represented the spearhead of the Christian advance upon the kingdom of Granada. Little is left of their Muslim past after years of dominion by a Castilian aristocracy who rebuilt great parts of both towns, leaving a wealth of religious monuments in Baeza and civic buildings in Úbeda. Baeza stands on top of a steep scarp overlooking wide tracts of fertile, arable land, which explains why it was an early target for conquest, falling into Christian hands in 1227, shortly after the decisive battle of Navas de Tolosa in 1212. After the reconquest the mosque was consecrated once more as a Christian church and Baeza became a magnificent exam-

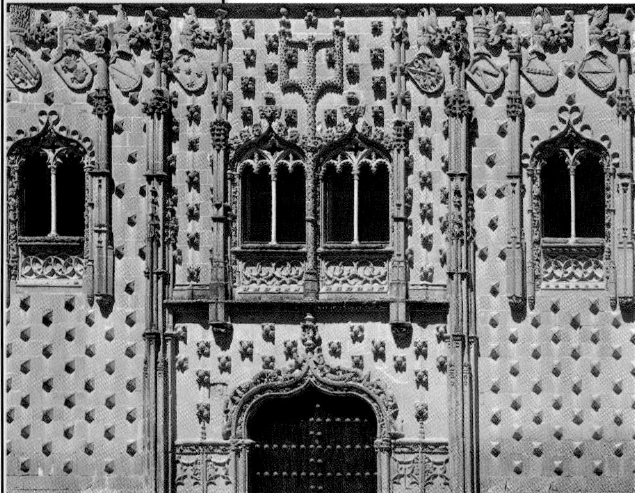

ple of a Castilian town, with open squares such as Santa María (above) and el Pópulo, surrounded by mansions and churches, all of which were designed to be the focus of religious and civic life.
La Plaza de la Fuente de Santa María (The Square of St. Mary's Fount) opens out before the ca-thedral and in its centre stands the eponymous fountain, a highly ornamented, miniature triumphal arch (right).
Strangely it was not until the fall of the kingdom of Gra-nada that Baeza and Úbeda attained their highest splendour and it is for this reason that the cathedral, although containing vestiges of Mus-lim, Mudéjar and Gothic tradition, is above all a XVI century church. It has three aisles with both Renaissance and Gothic vaults (above). On the north side of the square stands the seminary and abutting this the Jabalquinto Palace, with a highly elaborate Façade (below on the facing page) and Renaissance courtyard, which are believed to be the work of Jean Guas.

• Above: Vault of Baeza Cathedral. Left: The fountain of Santa María. Immediately below: Wrought-iron altar screen by

the master crafts-man Bartolomé. Below: Stairway in the Jabalquinto Palace.

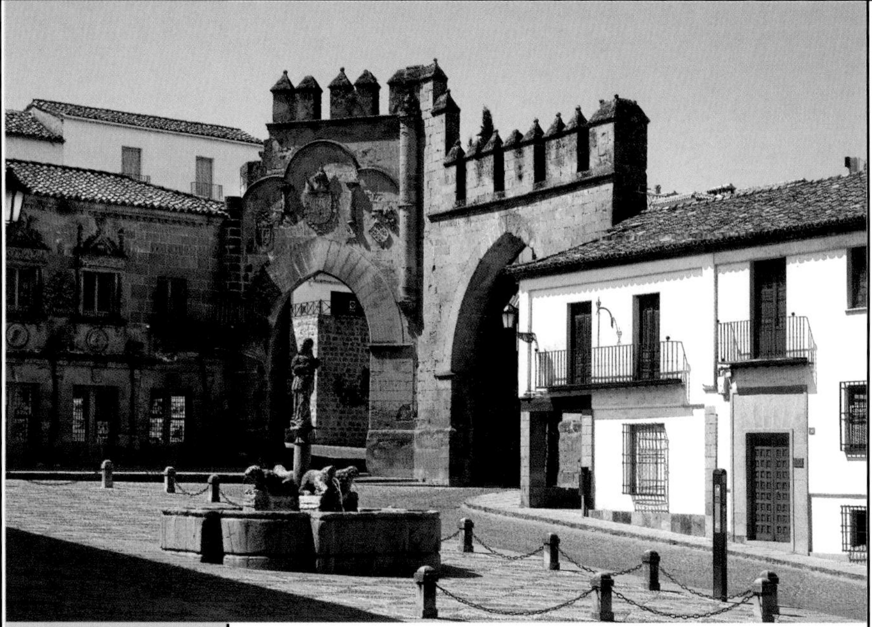

• **PÓPULO SQUARE** *receives its name from the building to the left of the gateway in the picture above, la casa del Pópulo, which in the XVI century housed the chancellery, the law courts and the public notary's office. Below: the XVI century shambles, with the imperial shield on its façade (right), nowadays the municipal museum and archive.*

At the entrance to the city is another spacious square known as La Plaza del Pópulo, a traditional name referring to the Virgin Mary, a statue of whom used to stand on the corner balcony of the principle house in the square, la Casa del Pópulo. This house has seen many public functions during its lifetime, including the law courts, the notary's office and the fraternity of local noblemen. Today it houses the tourist office. In the centre of the square is the Statue of the Lions, which probably dates back to Iberian times. Abutting the Jaén Gate and thus forming the corner of the square is the Villalar Arch, built in1526 to celebrate Charles V victory five years earlier over the comuneros, a serious civil revolt in the cities of Castilla which threatened his very throne. It was in1526 that Charles made a grand state tour of Andalucía with his new bride Isabel of Portugal, reputed to be

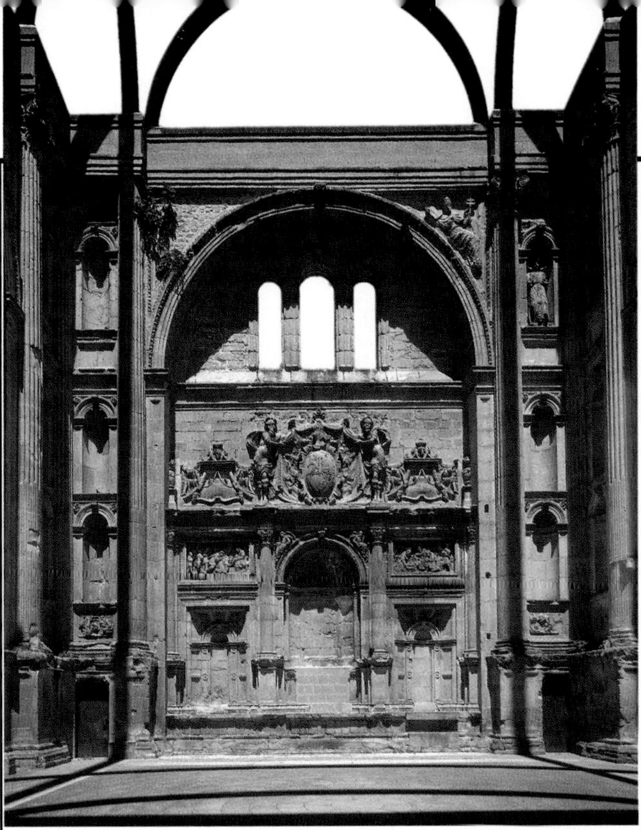

• **Andrés de Vandelvira (1509-1575),** *a disciple of the Renaissance genius Diego de Siloé, was ordered by his illustrious patrons, Francisco de Cobos y Molina, privy secretary to Charles V, and his nephew, Juan Vázquez de Molina, aide to Phillip II, to fill the towns of Baeza and Úbeda with noble Renaissance buildings. These splendid monuments help us to comprehend to some extent the heights of magnificence attained by Spain and her new dominions during this period.*

the most beautiful woman in Europe. The eastern side of the square is occupied by the old shambles (1550), the façade of which would better grace a noble mansion than a slaughter-house and tanning shed. A similar observation might be made about the Town Hall, not far from this square. Built in 1559 its façade is an outstanding example of Renaissance design with numerous touches of the Plateresque in its decoration, although its original use was no grander than that of the town gaol. Below its elegant cornice is a shield of Phillip II (below).

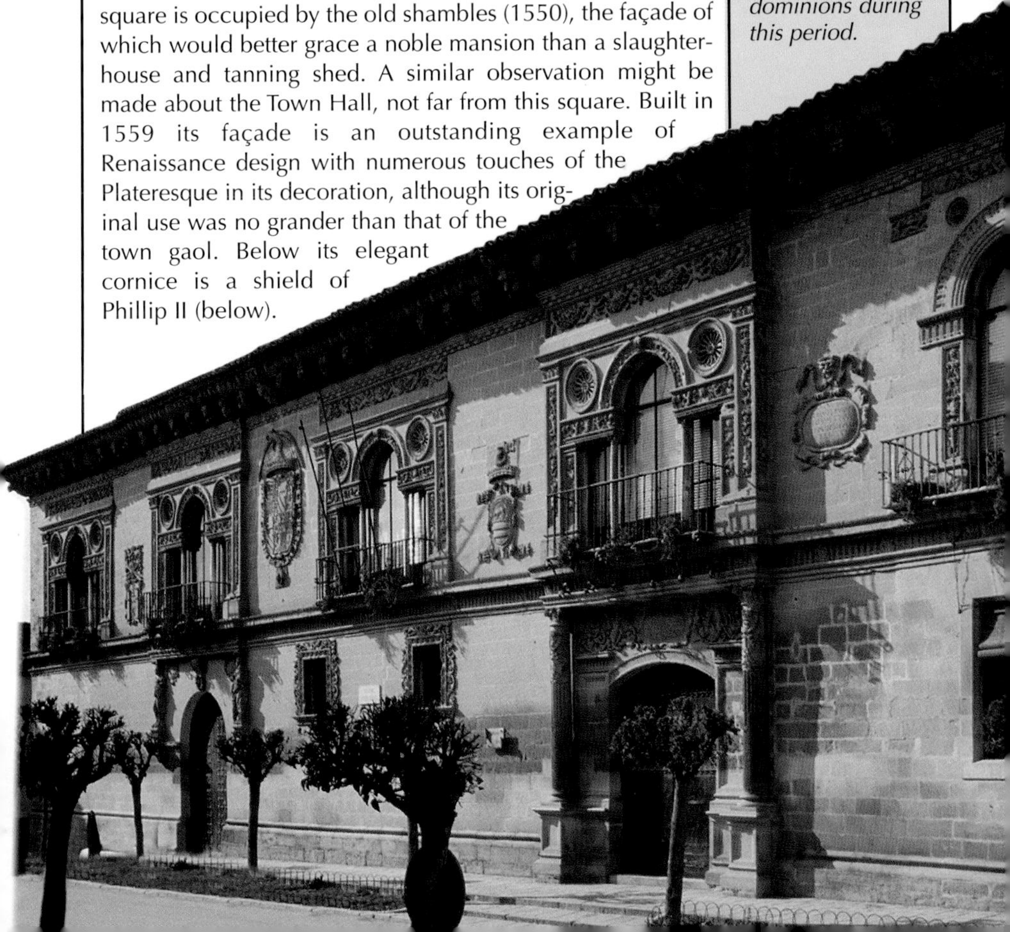

•FAÇADES OF THE CHURCH OF OUR SAVIOUR (ABOVE).

ÚBEDA

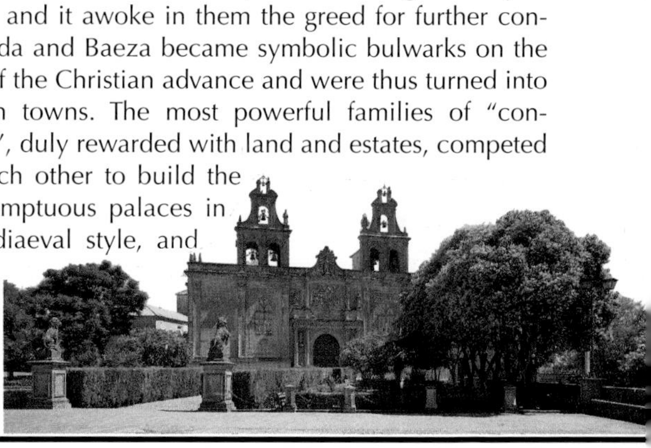

After the battle of Navas de Tolosa just to the north of Jaén in 1212, in which an alliance of Christian forces under King Alfonso VIII of Castilla dealt a crushing blow to the Muslim Almohad army, the fortunes of Andalucía were to change dramatically. The Castilian victors arriving from their inhospitable, high tablelands to the north were astonished at the fertility of the Andalucían countryside and the generosity of its climate, and it awoke in them the greed for further conquest. Úbeda and Baeza became symbolic bulwarks on the front line of the Christian advance and were thus turned into Castilian towns. The most powerful families of "conquerors", duly rewarded with land and estates, competed with each other to build the most sumptuous palaces in the mediaeval style, and turned mosques into Gothic

churches. Strangely, however, the height of their splendour did not arrive until the XVI century, after the fall of the kingdom of Granada, which was when, by decree of Don Francisco Cobos, privy secretary to Charles V, and to all intents and purposes Prime Minister of the Spanish empire, Úbeda became a centre of culture and art. This new nobility was following the Italian model, in which the individual republics were ruled by aristocratic families, except that in Spain this aristocracy governed an empire. The parallels are to be seen quite clearly in their architecture: the Square of Vázquez de Molina in Úbeda is not a city square or public gathering place in the Castillian style, it is a precinct belonging to a single family and thus instead of the usual parochial church it contains the family's private funereal chapel.

• The purity of Renaissance lines

in Úbeda are best expressed in the church of el Salvador (Our Saviour). Its Façade can be seen on the facing page, and on this page above, a detail of the 13 Greek gods in the intrados of the arch and the south door. The sculptor mixed classic iconography with biblical figures to fill the whole with Christian symbolism.
Above: Warriors and ladies support the shields of the founders of the church.
Left: the sacristy.

• INSIDE THE CHURCH OF OUR SAVIOUR *the funereal scheme of the main chapel is repeated: a round chapel beneath a cupola.*
Above: Typical ceramic ware from Úbeda.

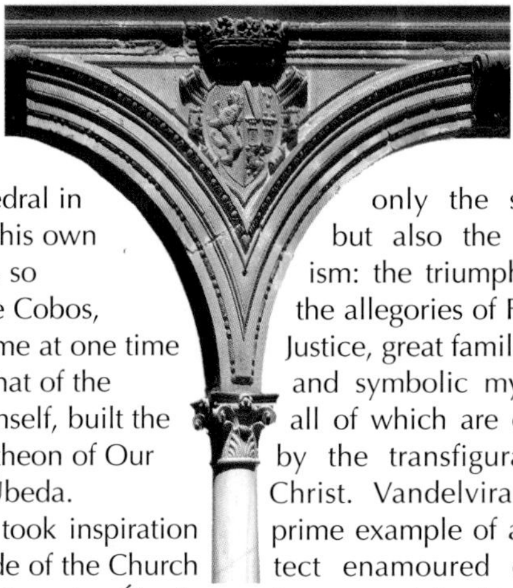

In the same way that Charles V had erected the cathedral in Granada as his own mausoleum, so Francisco de Cobos, whose income at one time exceeded that of the emperor himself, built the Church-Pantheon of Our Saviour in Úbeda.

Vandelvira took inspiration for the façade of the Church of Our Saviour in Úbeda from his master Diego de Siloé's design for the Door of Forgiveress in the Royal Chapel in Granada, copying not only the structure but also the symbolism: the triumphal arch, the allegories of Faith and Justice, great family shields and symbolic mythology, all of which are crowned by the transfiguration of Christ. Vandelvira was a prime example of an architect enamoured of solid forms and in this he was often accompanied by his sculptor and decorator, Jamette, who had worked for

Francis I on his new chateau at Fontainebleau. This might explain to some extent why the sacristy has something of the air of a French ballroom, with hanging vaults, medallions and sculpted figures. Next to the Church of Our Saviour is the palace of the Ortega family, nowadays the Constable Dávalos Parador (a state-run hotel). Vandelvira also lent a touch of Renaissance sobriety to the façade of this mansion, which is almost a foretaste of the Italianate Mannerism of Herrera. After its initial reconquest by the Christians Úbeda also underwent times of upheaval and strife: the Muslim king Muhammad V occupied it and later it was the scene of an internecine struggle for power between Pedro I and his step-brother Enrique, Constable Dávalos, who was eventually hounded to his death. In 1517 the town also confronted the Spanish regent Cardinal Cisneros and sided with the comuneros of Castilla, amongst other vicissitudes in its history. The Church of San Pablo (St. Paul) was originally a mosque. Some of its capitals are Romanesque but the south façade is a beautiful example of the late Gothic and the Plateresque tower is very reminiscent of many others standing out upon the Castilian plains. Much the same might be said of the churches of San Pedro, San Isidoro, San Lorenzo, Santo Domingo and Trinidad, which fill Úbeda with an astounding array of masterpieces of Spanish Renaissance architecture.

• Above: Façade of the Palace of Chains, built for Juan Vázquez de Molina, privy secretary to Phillip II. Its courtyard (below) belongs very much to the style of those of noble Renaissance Spain. It is now Úbeda's town hall.

• VIEW OF THE TOWN OF CAZORLA *(above), with its castle (Castillo de la Yedra) standing above it. The castle controlled the gateway to the Cazorla mountains and their valuable timber resources, one of the reasons why the town became an important bulwark of the Christian advance upon the Muslim south.*
Below: The town of Segura de la Sierra, where imperial eagles still build their eyries, overlooking the course of the young Guadalquivir river.

The countryside of Jaén is a sea of olive trees, "silver Jaén" as it has often been called by poets. But we must not forget that the province also has four very different types of nature reserve, among which is the Cazorla, Segura-Las Villas national park, the foremost in Spain. Apart from Cazorla the mountainous areas of Despeñaperros (facing page), Andújar and Mágina have all been designated protected areas, making some 300,000 hectares in all. It also has two wildlife reserves, one at Laguna del Chinche (Bug Lake) and another at Laguna Honda (Deep Lake), close to Alcaudete, and other areas of natural beauty such as the headwaters of the river Guadalquivir.

These different landscapes and ecosystems harbouring such a wide variety of flora and fauna may not be far away in terms of kilometres but are nevertheless remote and wild enough to satisfy the keenest lover of natural solitude. An eagle flying high above will see the Guadalquivir as the central artery of the province. It rises in the south-east, flows north for some 30 kilometres and then heads west-south-west, curling through the valleys beneath the hillsides of Jaén's undulating countryside. Between its headwaters here in

Cazórla at 1,600 metres above seal level and its estuary in the Bay of Cádiz, the valley of the River Guadalquivir contains half the plant species known in Europe and most of those native to North Africa. On the northern edge of the fertile valley the Morena mountains can just be made out, home to industrial cities such as Linares, Bailén and Andújar. To the south the Mágina and Cazorla-Segura chains whose hillsides are also tapestried with the olive trees that produce the best *picual* olives and hence the finest of oils. In the province of Jaén there are some fifty million olive trees and the municipal district of Martos (near Baena) can justly claim to be the worlds largest producer of olives and olive oil. Above: two views of Cazorla and its castles, la Yedra and la Iruela. On the facing page: Segura de la Sierra (left) and Alcalá la Real (right).

• The poet Machado wrote, "Campo, campo, campo, Y entre los olivos, Los cortijos blancos...". (Acres and acres and acres of olive groves, and amongst them, white farmhouses.) Immediately above: Despeñaperros and below: la Guardia.

MARIA DE MAR
3 AM 2 2101

Almería

Almería is the easternmost, sunniest and consequently driest province of Andalucía. Its capital is a maritime city lying on the plain between the Gador mountain range and the equally mountainous Cabo de Gata (Cape Cat). It is an ancient port with a long history of commerce with other civilisations throughout the Mediterranean world. The Romans knew it as Portus Magnus, the Great Port, whilst to the Arabs it was al-Mariyah, the Mirror of the Sea. But the history of the province goes back much farther. Just 25 kilometres inland is Los Millares, one of the most extensive and important copper-age settlements in Europe. For more than a thousand years thick defensive walls protected a well-organised village, where copper tools, ornaments and weapons were moulded. The site was abandoned at the beginning of the bronze age when even more sophisticated societies grew up at nearby towns such as El Agar and El Oficio, where the first remains are found of the bell-beaker pottery that was to become widespread throughout most of central Europe.

Abd ar-Rahman III, the first Muslim caliph in Spain, considered al-Mariyah to be his commercial gateway to the Maghrib countries in North Africa and the eastern Mediterranean and the Red Sea. He built a shipyard here and in 995 started work on a huge fortress complex to defend the area. It was also a highly strategic naval port and from here the fleets of successive Islamic rulers defended their Spanish possessions. Early mediaeval seafarers' charts and maps bear witness to the intimate knowledge that sailors of the day had of the whole Mediterranean coast and it was their knowledge of boatbuilding that led to the development of ships such as the caravel, which, after the Christian reconquest, were to enable Columbus to cross the Atlantic in search of the New World.

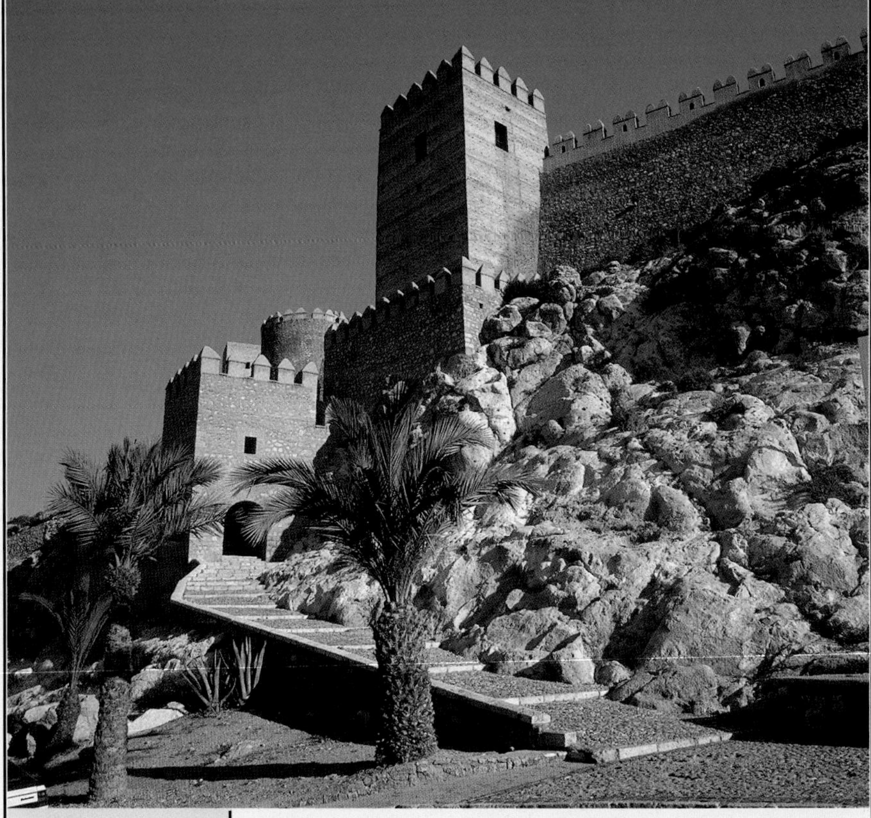

Almería's most impressive monument is its fortress citadel (Alcazaba), the walls of which hug the contours of the hillside for more than half a kilometre. Today visitors can see the ruins of one of the largest military fortifications in Muslim Spain and at the same time enjoy magnificent views across the modern city and the bay of Almería.

When the caliphate fell at the beginning of the XI century Almería continued to prosper as the capital of a *taifa* kingdom until in 1147 it was overrun by an alliance of Spanish and Genoan Christian forces. From then on it was a lively, cosmopolitan port used by Spaniards, Italians and Arabs alike until its final subjugation by Ferdinand and Isabel in 1489 and its general decline as the balance of international interest shifted towards Andalucía's Atlantic ports and America. But the decadence of the town was irreversible, so much so that in 1658 after an earthquake a census revealed that only 500 living inhabitants remained in the town. And thus were its fortunes to remain until its miraculous revival during the latter half of the XX century.

For centuries Almería languished in relative poverty until in the 1960's its dry, inhospitable deserts and badlands attracted the attention of American film makers, who found that the landscape and climate was particularly suited to their needs, especially as far as westerns were concerned. But the real turnaround in its fortune has been the realisation on the part of the local landowners that they can profit from the almost constant sunshine of this part of Spain to turn it into the market garden of Europe. Most of the flat plains between the coast and the mountains are now covered in greenhouses, which produce a wide range of fruit and vegetables such as beans, tomatoes, peppers, cucumbers, melons and water melons when they are out of season anywhere else. Almería's climate has also prompted scientific research in the area into efficient ways of generating solar power and desalinating sea water. This in turn has prompted engineering works to find and store water for irrigation and domestic use, making this part of Andalucía one of the wealthiest in the region. Today the province can be fairly evenly divided into two quite different environments: to the east the Cabo de Gata - Níjar nature reserve, a desert of palm trees, cacti and scrub; a place of wonder for naturalists and geologists alike, with its fossilised Miocene coral reefs from the last time the earth underwent "global warming" and a place of tranquil beauty for those who enjoy swimming in solitary coves hidden along a mountainous shoreline; and to the west of the city larger, busier towns, but still retaining the charm of the fishing villages they were just a generation ago.

The port of Almería was under constant danger of attack by Berber pirates and incursions by disaffected Moors which is why the Gothic-Renaissance cathedral has the appearance more of a fortress than a church.

Top left: the village of Ohanes in the Almerían Alpujarra hills, between the mountains and the irrigated plains. Top right: the castle at Tabernas with the snowy peaks of the Sierra Nevada on the horizon and the desert immediately beneath. Left: Gérjal, a village on the edge of the cereal-growing belt and the desert. Below: salt pans at

ADRA

Cabo de Gata, part of the 26,000 hectares of marine and land wildlife reserve, which includes the municipalities of Nijar, Carboneras and Almería and their shorelines. The reserve is home to more than 1,000 animal and plant species. Above: desert landscape at Tabernas with bare, arid *ramblas,* watercourses subject to flash flooding in storms. Right: the astronomical observatory at Calar Alto. Below: rugged coastline

• **HOUSE IN CARBONERAS**
Below: Cabo de Gata.

• *Right:* **Castle at Vélez Blanco.** *Nearly a hundred years ago the Renaissance courtyard of this castle was dismantled stone by stone and transported to the New York Metropolitan Museum, where it is considered to be one of the most remarkable examples of its genre.*
Below: Mojácar, hidden in the mountains.
Facing page: plateau among the hills, the site of the mini-Hollywood, centre of the dream factory which Almería became in the 1960's at the height of the vogue for spaghetti westerns.

• **KURT HIELSCHER** *was one of the last romantic travellers, who journeyed the length and breadth of Spain at the beginning of the XX century. Camera ever at the ready, he portrayed the face of Spain in much the same way as Roberts or Owen had drawn and engraved it, and like them he particularly fell in love with Andalucía. What most impressed him, were the women of Mojácar with their faces covered in Muslim style. (On his return home he confused Mojácar with Vélez de la Frontera but the photographs show the truth of the matter.) He was entranced by the exotic quality of the village, with its sign at the entrance saying "Mojácar, Kingdom of Granada", as though the last 400 years had never been.*
Above right: a photograph of Mojácar taken by Hielscher almost 100 years ago. Right: a woman from Mojácar with her face covered.

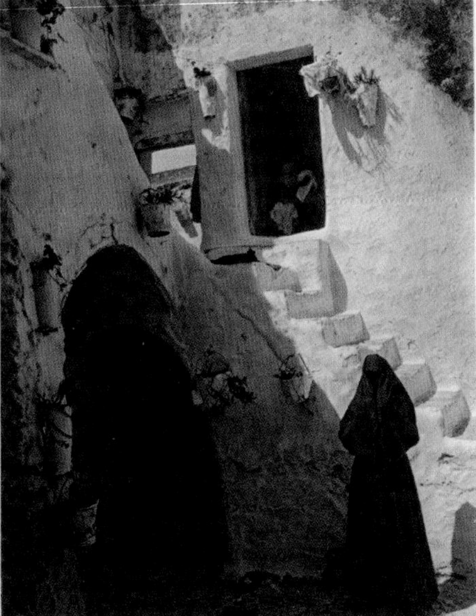

Only a few years ago the people of Almería had to work in the north or abroad to make a living but now the shoe is on the other foot and many immigrants are arriving here to find work in the greenhouses.

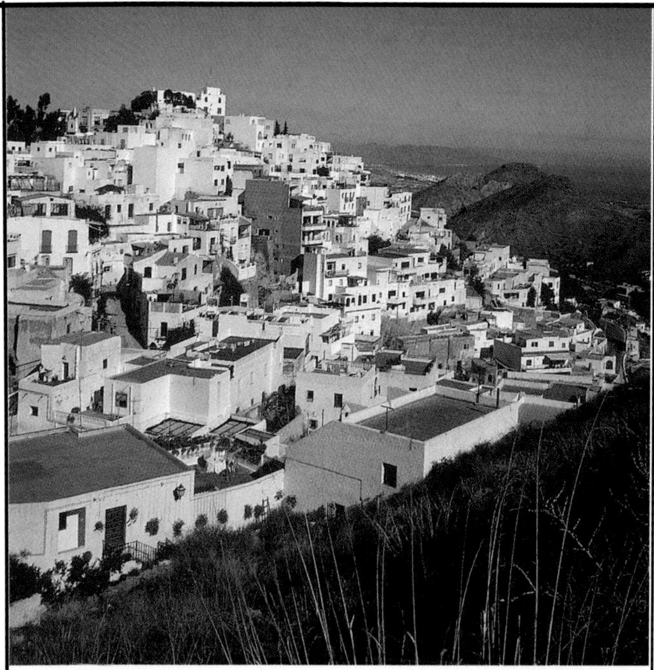

Such an abrupt social change cannot occur without some friction but no one doubts that the province's ancient, cosmopolitan, maritime tradition will help it to face up to its new role as provider rather than seeker of wealth.

Almería has without doubt evolved economically and socially more than any other Spanish province during recent decades, moving from a subsistence economy to spectacular development and putting itself at the head of intensive agricultural production. Nowadays it is the garden of Europe.

Left: picture of a modern tourist housing development on the coast at Roquetas, and above: telescope at Calar Alto, both examples of the way in which Almería is following a sustainable course of development into the XXI century.

BIBLIOGRAFÍA

Obras generales

AA. VV.: *Los andaluces.* Istmo, Madrid, 1980.

Acosta Sánchez, José: *Historia y cultura del pueblo andaluz.* Barcelona, 1979.

Aguilar Piñal, F.: *La Sevilla de Olavide.* Sevilla, 1966.

Albornoz, Nicolás: *Historia de la ciudad de Cabra.* Madrid, 1909.

Arjona Castro, A.: *Historia de la villa de Luque.* Córdoba, 1977.

Conejo, R.: *Historia de Archidona.* Córdoba, 1973.

Cortés Alonso, Vicenta: "Panorama de las fuentes documentales de Andalucia", en *Actas del Primer Congreso de Historia de Andalucia,* tomo 1.

Criado Hoyo, Manuel: *Apuntes para la historia de la ciudad de Montoro.* Ceuta, 1932.

Cuenca Toribio, José Manuel: *Andalucía. Una introducción histórica.* Córdoba,1979.

Domínguez Ortiz, Antonio: "El reino de Sevilla a fines del siglo XVIII". Archivo Hispalense núms. 7-8.

Fortea, José I: *Córdoba en el siglo XVI.* Córdoba, 1981.

Gan Giménez, Pedro: "Problemas andaluces de fines del siglo XVII", en *Primer Coloquio de Historia de Andalucía Moderna.* Córdoba, 1980.

García Figueras, Tomás: *Un siglo de historia e historiadores de Jerez de la Frontera. Jerez,* 1974.

Garzón Pareja, Manuel: *Historia de Granada.* Granada, 1981. 2 vols.

Góngora, A. de: *Materiales para la historia de Jerez. Reedición v adiciones por Manuel Ruiz Lagos.* Jerez, 1976.

Guillén Robles: *Historia de Málaga y su provincia.* Málaga, 1974.

Historia de Sevilla, editada por la Universidad hispalense. Los colaboradores de la Sevilla moderna son F. Morales Padrón, A. Domínguez Ortiz y F. Aguilar Piñal.

Losada Campos, A.: *Historia de Puente Genil.* Madrid, 1971.

Martínez Delgado, F.: *Historia de la ciudad de Medina Sidonia.* Cádiz, 1875.

Moreno Alonso, Manuel: *Historia General de Andalucía.* Sevilla, 1981.

Huelva. *Introducción. Geohistoria.* Huelva, 1975.

Moreno Olmedo, María Angustias: *Heráldica y Genealogía granadinas.* Granada 1976.

Morales Álvarez, Manuel: *Historia de Utrera.* Utrera, 1969, 3 vols.

Moretti, Juan José: *Historia de Ronda.* Málaga, 1867.

Morillo Crespo, A.: *Véjer de la Frontera y su comarca.* Cádiz, 1974.

Muro, Antonio: *Panorámica de la villa de Puerto Real en el siglo XVIII.* Cádiz, 1975.

Ocaña Prados, Juan: *Historia de Villanueva de Córdoba.* Madrid, 1911.

Pasquau, Juan: *Biografía de Úbeda.* Úbeda, 1958.

Peláez del Rosal, M., y Rivas Carmona, J.: *Priego de Córdoba.* Salamanca, 1979.

Redondo Guillén, F: *Pozoblanco, capital de Los Pedroches.* Córdoba, 1980.

Retegui y Bensusan, M.: *Cádiz en el siglo XVIII.* Cádiz, 1951.

Romero Muñoz, Vicente: *Alcalá de Guadaira.* Alcalá, 1575.

Ruiz Lagos, M.: *Ensayo de historia de Jerez. Jerez,* 1961.

Rubio-Argüelles, Ángeles: *Pequeña historia de Málaga en el siglo XVIII.* Madrid, 1951.

Sánchez del Arco, E.: *Monografía de Alcalá de los Gazules.* Cádiz, 1893.

Sancho, Hipólito: *Historia de Jerez,* tomo, III. El siglo XVII (editado póstumo, con la colaboración de don Juan de la Lastra). Jerez, 1965.

Sanz Sampelayo, Juan: Granada en el siglo XVIII. Granada, 1980.

Sureda Blanes, Francisco: *Abyla herculeana. Introducción al estudio de la etnología berberisca y al de la historia de Ceuta.* 1925.

Tapia, J. A.: Vélez Blanco: *La villa señorial de los Fajardo.* Almería, 1959.

Varela Escobar, N.: *Bosquejo histórico de la ciudad de Écija.* Sevilla, 1898.

Valverde Perales, Francisco: *Historia de la villa de Baena.* Toledo, 1903.

Historia política

Domínguez Ortiz, Antonio: *Alteraciones andaluzas.* Madrid, 1974.

-:"*La conspiración del duque de Medina Sidonia y el marqués de Ayamonte*". (incluido en el volumen misceláneo *Crisis y decadencia de la España de los Austrias*).

-:"La incorporación a la Corona de Sanlúcar de Barrameda"., AH, núm. 147.

-:"Un embajador marroquí en Sevilla" (incluido en el volumen *Sociedad y mentalidad en la Sevilla del Antiguo Régimen*).

Gamboa y Eraso, Luis de: *Verdad de lo sucedido en ocasión de la venida de la armada inglesa sobre Cádiz.* Cádiz, 1626.

Lourido Díaz, Ramón: *El sultanato de Sidi Muhamed ben Abdallah (1757-1790).* Granada, 1970.

De Bernardo, José Manuel: *Los juicios de residencia como fuente para la histora urbana,* CAM.

Blanco White: *Autobiografía.* Sevilla, 1975.

Contreras, Jaime y Dedieu, Jean Pierre: "*Geografia de la Inquisición española*".Hispania, núm. 144.

Suberbiola, Jesús: Real Patronato de Granada y Absolutismo, tesis doctoral, 1975.

SUPERVISIÓN FINAL Y BIBLIOGRAFÍA: LUIS RECIO MATEO